Prentice Hall
Algebra 1

Student Companion

PEARSON

Boston, Massachusetts • Chandler, Arizona • Glenview, Illinois • Upper Saddle River, New Jersey

Acknowledgements **Illustration: Kevin Banks:** 161; **Christopher Wilson:** 264, 368; **XNR Productions:** 340 **Photo:** All photographs not listed are the property of Pearson Education **Back Cover:** © Gary Bell/zefa/Corbis; **Page 81,** Shubroto Chattopadhyay/Corbis; **228 t,** brt PHOTO/Alamy; **228 b,** Paulo Fridman/Corbis; **268,** Jxpfeer/Dreamstime.com.

PEARSON

ISBN-13: 978-0-13368892-4
ISBN-10: 0-13-368892-5

2 3 4 5 6 7 8 9 10   VO16   13 12 11 10 09

Contents

Contents

Welcome to **Algebra 1!**

Your Prentice Hall Algebra 1 program is designed to help you achieve mastery of Algebra 1 topics. Your *Prentice Hall Algebra 1 Student Companion* is written to support you as you study. Your Student Companion is designed to work with your Student Edition textbook and PowerAlgebra.com by providing a place to practice the concepts, skills, and vocabulary you'll learn in each lesson.

Using the Algebra 1 Student Companion

Your Student Companion provides daily support for each lesson by targeting the following areas:

- **Vocabulary** Building your math vocabulary is an important part of success this year. You'll use your Student Companion to learn and understand the vocabulary words you need for Algebra 1.

- **Got It?** You'll use your Student Companion to check your understanding of example problems from your Student Edition.

- **Lesson Check** You'll use your Student Companion to make sure you're ready to tackle your homework.

Together, these sections will help you prepare to master the topics covered in your Student Edition — and lead to a successful year in Algebra 1.

Using PowerAlgebra.com

All your Student Companion pages are available for downloading and printing from PowerAlgebra.com.

Variables and Expressions

Vocabulary

● Review

What mathematical *operation* is shown in each equation? Write *addition, subtraction, multiplication,* or *division.*

1. $6 \cdot 2 = 12$ **2.** $14 - 4 = 10$ **3.** $27 \div 3 = 9$ **4.** $13 + 7 = 20$

_____   _____   _____   _____

● Vocabulary Builder

> a, x, and m are often used as **variables**.
> 100, $\frac{1}{a}$, and $3m$ are *not* variables.

variable (noun) VEHR ee uh bul

Related Words: vary (verb), varied (adjective), various (adjective)

Definition: A **variable** is a symbol, usually a letter, that represents one or more values of a quantity that changes.

Main Idea: The value given to a **variable** can change or vary. A quantity that changes, or varies, is called a *variable quantity*.

Example: The letter y is the **variable** in the algebraic expression $4 + y$. You can replace y with different numbers to find values for the expression.

● Use Your Vocabulary

5. Circle the *variable(s)* in each algebraic expression.

$8 + 4x$ $y + 12$ $9z + y$ $\frac{8}{w} + 4w$

An **algebraic expression** is a mathematical phrase that includes one or more variables. A **numerical expression** is a mathematical phrase involving numbers and operation symbols, but no variables.

6. Write **N** next to each *numerical expression.* Write **A** next to each *algebraic expression.*

_____ $6x$ _____ $\frac{5}{r} - 4$ _____ $11 + 5$ _____ $30 + 14k$

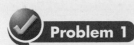 **Problem 1** **Writing Expressions With Addition and Subtraction**

Got It? What is an algebraic expression for 18 more than a number n?

7. Complete the table with *add* or *subtract*.

Phrase	Math Operation
more than a number	
less a number	
sum of two numbers	
fewer than a number	

8. Circle the expression you could use to find 18 more than 6.

6×18 $\qquad$ $6 + 18$ $\qquad$ $18 - 6$ $\qquad$ $18 + 18 + 18 + 18 + 18 + 18$

9. Now write an algebraic expression for 18 more than a number n.

n $\quad$ 18

 Problem 2 **Writing Expressions With Multiplication and Division**

Got It? What is an algebraic expression for the following word phrase?

6 times a number n

10. Complete each sentence with *add, subtract, multiply,* or *divide.* One word is used more than once.

The phrase "8 less than a number" tells you to __?__ 8.

The phrase "the product of a number x and 4" tells you to __?__ x and 4.

The phrase "the quotient of 6 and a number" tells you to __?__ 6 by x.

The phrase "n times 12" tells you to __?__ n and 12.

The phrase "the sum of a number n and 59" tells you to __?__ n and 59.

11. Now write an algebraic expression for 6 times a number n.

6 $\quad$ n

Lesson 1-1

Problem 3 Writing Expressions With Two Operations

Got It? What is an algebraic expression for the following word phrase?
8 less than the product of a number x and 4

12. Write an algebraic expression for the product of a number x and 4.

13. Underline the correct phrase to complete the sentence.

The phrase "8 less than a certain number" tells you to

subtract 8 from a number / subtract a number from 8 .

14. Cross out the expressions that do NOT represent the word phrase "8 less than the product of a number x and 4."

$4x - 8$ $4x + 8$ $x - 8$ $8x - 4$

 Problem 4 Using Words for an Expression

Got It? What word phrase can you use to represent each algebraic expression?

$x + 8.1$ $10x + 9$ $\frac{n}{3}$ $5x - 1$

15. Complete the word phrase for each expression.

the ⎯?⎯ of a number x and 8.1

the ⎯?⎯ of 10 ⎯?⎯ a number x and 9

the quotient of ⎯?⎯ and 3

1 ⎯?⎯ the product of ⎯?⎯

 Problem 5 Writing a Rule to Describe a Pattern

Got It? Suppose you draw a segment from any one vertex of a regular polygon to the other vertices. A sample for a regular hexagon is shown at the right. Use the table to find a pattern. What is a rule for the number of nonoverlapping triangles formed? Give the rule in words and as an algebraic expression.

Triangles in Polygons

Number of Sides of Polygon	Number of Triangles
4	4 − 2
5	5 − 2
6	6 − 2
n	■

16. Use the table. Find the number of nonoverlapping triangles in each figure.

a polygon with 4 sides   a polygon with 5 sides

17. Underline the correct word or words to complete the sentence.

The value of the expression in the table for a 6-sided figure is / is not the same as the number of triangles in the drawing of the hexagon.

18. Give a rule in words to find the number of nonoverlapping triangles in a polygon.

_____

_____

19. Write an algebraic expression for the number of nonoverlapping triangles in a polygon that has *n* sides.

Lesson Check • Do you UNDERSTAND?

Reasoning Use the table to decide whether $49n + 0.75$ or $49 + 0.75n$ represents the total cost to rent a truck that you drive *n* miles.

Truck Rental Fees

Number of Miles	Cost
1	$49 + ($.75 × 1)
2	$49 + ($.75 × 2)
3	$49 + ($.75 × 3)
n	■

20. Write a rule in words for the pattern shown in the table.

_____

_____

21. Now write an algebraic expression to represent the total cost of renting a truck.

Math Success

Check off the vocabulary words that you understand.

☐ variable   ☐ algebraic expression   ☐ numerical expression

Rate how well you can *write algebraic expressions*.

| Need to review | 0   2   4   6   8   10 | Now I get it! |

Vocabulary

● Review

To *simplify* a numerical expression means to replace it with its single numerical value. Circle the *simplified form* of each expression.

1. 2 · 3 · 4

| 4 · 3 · 2 | 6 · 4 | 9 | 24 |

2. $\frac{1}{2}$ · 36

| $36 \cdot \frac{1}{2}$ | 12 | 18 | $36\frac{1}{2}$ |

3. 16 − 4 + 7

| 16 − 7 + 4 | 5 | 10 | 19 |

● Vocabulary Builder

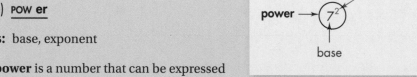

power (noun) POW er

Related Words: base, exponent

Definition: A **power** is a number that can be expressed using a base and an exponent.

Main Idea: **Powers** provide a shorthand way for showing repeated multiplication.

Example: The diagram above shows a **power**, its *base*, and its *exponent*. You can read the expression as, "seven to the second power."

● Use Your Vocabulary

Draw a line from each expression in Column A to the word in Column B that describes the red letter(s).

Column A	Column B
4. 4^x	base
5. m^7	power
6. w^z	exponent

Problem 1 Simplifying Powers

Got It? What is the simplified form of 3^4?

7. Follow the steps to find the simplified form of the expression.

1 Identify the base and the exponent in the expression 3^4.

base: ☐   exponent: ☐

⬇

2 Expand the expression to show the repeated multiplication indicated by the exponent.

$3^4 =$ ☐ · ☐ · ☐ · ☐

⬇

3 Write the simplified form of the expression 3^4.

$3^4 =$ ☐

take note

Key Concept   Order of Operations

1. Perform any operation(s) inside grouping symbols, such as parentheses ( ) and brackets [ ]. A fraction bar also acts as a grouping symbol.

2. Simplify powers.

3. Multiply and divide in order from left to right.

4. Add and subtract in order from left to right.

 Problem 2 Simplifying a Numerical Expression

Got It? What is the simplified form of $5 \cdot 7 - 4^2 \div 2$?

8. Circle the part of the expression that you should simplify first.

$5 \cdot 7 - 4^2 \div 2$

9. Without simplifying the expression, explain how you know that subtraction will be the last operation.

_____

_____

10. Simplify $5 \cdot 7 - 4^2 \div 2$. Show and justify each step.

Lesson 1-2

 **Problem 3** **Evaluating Algebraic Expressions**

Got It? What is the value of $3b - a^2$ when $a = 3$ and $b = 4$?

11. Complete for $a = 3$ and $b = 4$.

$a = $ [ ] and $a^2 = $ [ ] $b = $ [ ] and $3b = $ [ ]

12. Replace each variable with the given values. Then use the Order of Operations to simplify.

$$3b - a^2 = 3 \cdot \boxed{} - \boxed{}$$
$$= \boxed{} - \boxed{}$$
$$= \boxed{}$$

13. So, when $a = 3$ and $b = 4$, $3b - a^2 = $ [ ].

 Problem 4 **Evaluating a Real-World Expression**

Got It? The shipping cost for an order at an online store is $\frac{1}{10}$ the cost of the items you order. What is an expression for the total cost of a given order? What are the total costs for orders of $43, $79, $95, and $103?

14. Complete the model.

Relate   total cost of an order   is   the cost of the items   plus   the shipping costs: $\frac{1}{10} \cdot$ the cost of the items

Define   Let $c = $ the cost of the items.

Write   total cost $= \boxed{} + $

15. Use the model to complete the table for each value of c.

Cost of Items	Shipping Cost	Total Cost of Order
$43	$\frac{1}{10} \cdot \$43 = \$4.30$	$\$43 + \$4.30 = \$$ [ ]
$79	$\frac{1}{10} \cdot \$79 = \$$ [ ]	$\$79 + \$7.90 = \$$ [ ]
$95	$\frac{1}{10} \cdot \$95 = \$$ [ ]	$\$95 + \$$ [ ] $= \$104.50$
$103	$\frac{1}{10} \cdot \$103 = \$$ [ ]	$\$103 + \$$ [ ] $= \$$ [ ]

Lesson Check • Do you UNDERSTAND?

Error Analysis A student simplifies an expression as shown below. Find the error and simplify the expression correctly.

$$23 - 8 \cdot 2 + 3^2 = 23 - 8 \cdot 2 + 9$$
$$= 15 \cdot 2 + 9$$
$$= 30 + 9$$
$$= 39$$

16. What operation did the student do first? Is this correct? Explain.

_____

_____

_____

17. What operation did the student do next? Is this correct? Explain.

_____

_____

18. Now simplify the expression $23 - 8 \cdot 2 + 3^2$ correctly.

Math Success

Check off the vocabulary words that you understand.

☐ power ☐ exponent ☐ base ☐ simplify ☐ evaluate

Rate how well you can *evaluate expressions using the Order of Operations.*

Need to review   0   2   4   6   8   10   Now I get it!

1-3 Real Numbers and the Number Line

Vocabulary

Review

1. Circle the numbers that are *perfect squares*.

| 1 | 12 | 16 | 20 |
| 100 | 121 | 200 | 289 |

Vocabulary Builder

square root (noun) <u>skwer root</u>

Definition: The **square root** of a number is a number that when multiplied by itself is equal to the given number.

Using Symbols: $\sqrt{16} = 4$

Using Words: The **square root** of 16 is 4. It means, "I multiply 4 by itself to get 16."

square root
$\downarrow$
$\sqrt{16} = 4$
because
$4^2 = 16$

Use Your Vocabulary

2. Use what you know about *perfect squares* and *square roots* to complete the table.

Number	Number Squared
1	1
2	4
3	
4	
5	
	36

Number	Number Squared
7	49
	64
	81
11	

 **Problem 1** Simplifying Square Root Expressions

Got It? What is the simplified form of $\sqrt{64}$?

3. Circle the equation that uses the positive square root of 64.

$16 \cdot 4 = 64$ $\qquad$ $32 \cdot 2 = 64$ $\qquad$ $8 \cdot 8 = 64$

4. The simplified form of $\sqrt{64}$ is ___ .

 Problem 2 Estimating a Square Root

Got It? What is the value of $\sqrt{34}$ to the nearest integer?

5. Use the number lines below to find the perfect squares closest to 34.

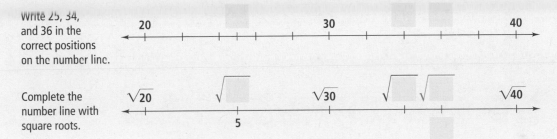

Write 25, 34, and 36 in the correct positions on the number line.

Complete the number line with square roots.

6. Since 34 is closer to ___ than to ___ ,

$\sqrt{34}$ is closer to ___ than to ___ .

So, the value of $\sqrt{34}$ to the nearest integer is ___ .

You can classify numbers using *sets*. A **set** is a well-defined collection of objects. Each object in the set is called an **element** of the set. A **subset** of a set consists of elements from the given set. You can list the elements of a set within braces { }.

7. Complete the *sets* of numbers.

Natural numbers

$\left\{ 1, , 3, ... \right\}$

Whole numbers

$\left\{ , 1, , 3, ... \right\}$

Integers

$\left\{ ..., -2, , 0, 1, , 3, ... \right\}$

A **rational number** is any number that you can write in the form $\frac{a}{b}$, where a and b are integers and $b \neq 0$. A rational number in decimal form is either a terminating decimal such as 5.45 or a repeating decimal such as 0.333..., which you can write as $0.\overline{3}$.

8. Cross out the numbers that are NOT *rational numbers*.

π $\qquad$ $-\frac{7}{4}$ $\qquad$ $\sqrt{5}$ $\qquad$ $0.\overline{9}$ $\qquad$ 7.35

An **irrational number** cannot be represented as the quotient of two integers. In decimal form, irrational numbers do not terminate or repeat. Irrational numbers include π and $\sqrt{2}$.

Lesson 1-3

Problem 3 Classifying Real Numbers

Got It? To which subsets of the real numbers does each number belong?

$\sqrt{9}$ $\frac{3}{10}$ -0.45 $\sqrt{12}$

9. Is each number an element of the set? Place a ✔ if it is. Place an ✗ if it is not.

Number	Whole Numbers	Integers	Rational Numbers	Irrational Numbers
$\sqrt{9}$	✔	✔	✔	✗
$\frac{3}{10}$	☐	☐	☐	☐
-0.45	☐	☐	☐	☐
$\sqrt{12}$	☐	☐	☐	☐

take note

Concept Summary   Real Numbers

10. Write each of the numbers -7, -5.43, 0, $\frac{3}{7}$, π, and $\sqrt{7}$ in a box below. The number 5 has been placed for you.

Real Numbers

Rational numbers

Integers

Whole numbers

Natural numbers

5

Irrational numbers

Problem 4 Comparing Real Numbers

Got It? What is an inequality that compares the numbers $\sqrt{129}$ and 11.52?

11. What is the approximate value of $\sqrt{129}$ to the nearest hundredth?

12. Use $<$, $>$, or $=$ to complete the statement.

$\sqrt{129}$ ☐ 11.52

Problem 5 Graphing and Ordering Real Numbers

Got It? Graph 3.5, −2.1, $\sqrt{9}$, $-\frac{7}{2}$, and $\sqrt{5}$ on a number line. What is the order of the numbers from least to greatest?

13. Simplify the radicals and convert the fraction to a mixed number.

$$\sqrt{9} = \boxed{} \qquad\qquad -\frac{7}{2} = \boxed{} \qquad\qquad \sqrt{5} \approx \boxed{}$$

14. Now use the number line to graph the five original numbers. Be sure to label each point with the correct number.

15. Now list the five original numbers from *least* to *greatest*.

$$\boxed{}, \boxed{}, \boxed{}, \boxed{},$$

Lesson Check • Do you UNDERSTAND?

Reasoning Tell whether $\sqrt{100}$ and $\sqrt{0.29}$ are *rational* or *irrational*. Explain.

16. First try to simplify the expression. If it does not simplify, put an ✗ in the box.

$$\sqrt{100} = \boxed{} \qquad\qquad \sqrt{0.29} = \boxed{}$$

17. Tell whether each square root is *rational* or *irrational*. Explain your reasoning.

_____

_____

_____

Math Success

Check off the vocabulary words that you understand.

☐ square root   ☐ rational numbers   ☐ irrational numbers   ☐ real numbers

Rate how well you can *classify and order real numbers*.

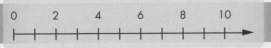

Lesson 1-3

1-4 Properties of Real Numbers

Vocabulary

● Review

1. Write two examples of *numerical expressions* and *algebraic expressions*.

Numerical Expressions	Algebraic Expressions

2. **Reasoning** Lan has three pens and some pencils. Why does she need an algebraic expression to represent the number of writing tools she has? Explain.

● Vocabulary Builder

counterexample (noun) KOWN tur eg ZAM pul

> You need only one **counterexample** to prove that a statement is false.

Definition: A **counterexample** is an example that shows that a statement is not always true.

Related Words: counteract (verb), counterargument (noun), counterclockwise (adjective)

Example: For all real numbers, $a + b = a \cdot b$ is a *false* statement. You can show the statement is false by using a **counterexample** like the one below.

$$5 + 3 = 8 \text{ is } not \text{ equal to } 5 \cdot 3 = 15.$$

● Use Your Vocabulary

Draw a line from each statement to a *counterexample* that shows it to be false.

Statement	Counterexample
3. If you live in Miami, you live in Florida.	Mexico is in North America.
4. If you live near an ocean, you live near the Atlantic Ocean.	People in California live near the Pacific Ocean.
5. If you live in North America, you live in the United States.	Miami is a city in Ohio.

Draw a line from each property in Column A to the equation that illustrates it in Column B.

Column A	Column B
6. Associative Property of Addition	$15y + 0 = 15y$
7. Associative Property of Multiplication	$7b \cdot 2 = 2 \cdot 7b$
8. Commutative Property of Addition	$(c \cdot 3) \cdot 5 = c \cdot (3 \cdot 5)$
9. Commutative Property of Multiplication	$6x + 5y = 5y + 6x$
10. Identity Property of Addition	$a \cdot 1 = a$
11. Identity Property of Multiplication	$(g + 11h) + 9h = g + (11h + 9h)$
12. Multiplication Property of −1	$7\lambda \cdot 0 = 0$
13. Zero Property of Multiplication	$15m \cdot (-1) = -15m$

✓ Problem 1   Identifying Properties

Got It? What property is illustrated by $4x \cdot 1 = 4x$?

14. For each question, determine if the stated characteristic is or is not being illustrated by $4x \cdot 1 = 4x$.

Is the same number being added to both sides of the equation?	Yes / No
Are groupings being changed in the equation?	Yes / No
Is 0 or 1 part of the equation?	Yes / No

15. Think of the operation symbol that will make the equation $4x \; ■ \; 1 = 4x$ true. What property is illustrated by $4x \cdot 1 = 4x$?

_____

✓ Problem 2   Using Properties for Mental Calculations

Got It? A can holds 3 tennis balls. A box holds 4 cans. A case holds 6 boxes. How many tennis balls are in 10 cases? Use mental math.

16. Complete the boxes below to write an expression for the number of tennis balls in 10 cases.

Relate	number of cases of tennis balls	times	number of boxes per case	times	number of cans per box	times	number of tennis balls per can
Write	☐	·	☐	·	☐	·	☐

17. Mental Math Circle the simplified expression.

| 24 | 60 | 120 | 720 |

18. What is one of the properties you used to simplify the expression? Explain how you used the property.

Problem 3 Writing Equivalent Expressions

Got It? Simplify each expression.

$2.1(4.5x)$ $6 + (4h + 3)$ $\dfrac{8m}{12mn}$

In Exercises 19–20, each expression is simplified. Justify each step.

19. $2.1(4.5x) = (2.1 \cdot 4.5)x$

$= 9.45x$

20. $6 + (4h + 3) = (4h + 3) + 6$

$= 4h + (3 + 6)$

$= 4h + 9$

21. Complete each step of the simplification.

$$\dfrac{8m}{12mn} = \dfrac{2 \cdot \boxed{} \cdot \boxed{} \cdot 1}{3 \cdot 4 \cdot m \cdot n}$$

$$= \dfrac{2}{3} \cdot \dfrac{\boxed{}}{\boxed{}} \cdot \dfrac{\boxed{}}{\boxed{}} \cdot \dfrac{1}{n} = \dfrac{2}{3} \cdot \boxed{} \cdot \boxed{} \cdot \dfrac{1}{n} = \dfrac{2}{3} \cdot \boxed{} = \boxed{}$$

Problem 4 Using Deductive Reasoning and Counterexamples

Got It? **Reasoning** Is the statement *true* or *false*? If it is false, give a counterexample. If true, use properties of real numbers to show the expressions are equivalent.

For all real numbers j and k, $j \cdot k = (k + 0) \cdot j$.

22. Simplify the right side of the equation above and state the property that you used.

$(k + 0) \cdot j = \boxed{} \cdot j$

23. Complete: The simplified expression is equal to $j \cdot k$ by the __?__ Property of Multiplication.

24. So, the statement $j \cdot k = (k + 0) \cdot j$ is __?__.

True / False

Got It? **Reasoning** Is the statement *true* or *false*? If it is false, give a counterexample. If true, use properties of real numbers to show the expressions are equivalent.

For all real numbers m and n, $m(n + 1) = mn + 1$.

Evaluate each expression for $m = 4$ and $n = 5$.

25. $m(n + 1) = $ [ ] $\cdot ($ [ ] $+ 1)$ 26. $mn + 1$

        $= $ [ ] $\cdot$ [ ]

        $= $ [ ]

27. Is the value of the expression in Exercise 25 equal to the value of the expression in Exercise 26?   Yes / No

28. Is the original statement *true* or *false*? If it is false, give a counterexample. If true, use properties of real numbers to show the expressions are equivalent.

_____

_____

Lesson Check • Do you UNDERSTAND?

Justify each step to show that $3 \cdot (10 \cdot 12) = 360$.

29. The left side of the expression is simplified below. Write a reason for each step.

$3 \cdot (10 \cdot 12) = 3 \cdot (12 \cdot 10)$ _____

           $= (3 \cdot 12) \cdot 10$ _____

           $= 36 \cdot 10$ _____

           $= 360$ _____

Math Success

Check off the vocabulary words that you understand.

☐ Commutative Properties   ☐ Associative Properties   ☐ Identity Properties

     ☐ equivalent expressions   ☐ deductive reasoning   ☐ counterexample

Rate how well you can *use the properties of addition and multiplication.*

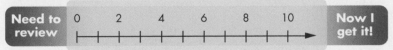

Need to review   0   2   4   6   8   10   Now I get it!

Lesson 1-4

Vocabulary

● Review

1. Cross out the expressions that do NOT show a *difference*.

| 15 + 6 | 14 − 3 | 4 · 8 | 48 ÷ 12 |

2. Circle the expression that shows a *sum*.

| 45 − 26 | 12 ÷ 3 | 42 + 3 | 22 − 9 |

3. Find the *difference* of 20 and 15.　　　　**4.** Find the *sum* of 38 and 19.

● Vocabulary Builder

inverse (noun) **in** VUHRS

Related Word: invert (verb)

Definition: An **inverse** is the opposite, or reverse, of something.

Example: −5 and 5 are additive **inverses,** or *opposites*. They are the same distance from zero on a number line.

What It Means: Additive **inverses** have a sum of 0.

> **additive inverses**
> $-5 + 5 = 0$
> $5 + (-5) = 0$

● Use Your Vocabulary

5. Write the additive *inverse* of each number.

7　　　　　−3　　　　　−11　　　　　9

The **absolute value** of a number is its distance from 0 on a number line. The **absolute value** of −7, written $|-7|$, is equal to 7, because −7 is 7 units from 0 on a number line.

Compare. Write <, >, or =.

6. $|3|$ ☐ $|-3|$　**7.** $|-3|$ ☐ 3　**8.** −3 ☐ $|-3|$　**9.** $|3|$ ☐ −3

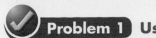 **Problem 1** **Using Number Line Models**

Got It? What is −8 + 4? Use a number line.

10. Use the number line to help you find the sum.

−10 −9 −8 −7 −6 −5 −4 −3 −2 −1 0 1

Start at 0.

Move 8 units left. Graph a point at −8 on the number line.

Then move 4 units right. Graph a point at −4 on the number line.

11. Underline the correct word to complete each sentence.

The number −8 tells you to start at 0 and move 8 units to the left / right .

The number 4 tells you to then move 4 units to the left / right .

12. Complete: −8 + 4 = ☐

take note

Key Concept **Adding Real Numbers**

To add two numbers with the **same sign**, add their absolute values. The sum has the same sign as the addends.

To add two numbers with **different signs,** subtract their absolute values. The sum has the same sign as the addend with the greater absolute value.

 Problem 2 **Adding Real Numbers**

Got It? What is the sum −16 + (−8)?

13. The addends −16 and −8 have different signs / the same sign .

14. When −16 and −8 are added, the answer will be positive / negative .

15. Complete: −16 + (−8) = ☐

Got It? What is the sum −11 + 9?

16. The addends −11 and 9 have different signs / the same sign .

17. When −11 and 9 are added, the answer will be positive / negative .

18. Complete: −11 + 9 = ☐

Got It? What is the sum 9 + (−11)?

19. The addends of this exercise and those of Exercise 18 are the same / different .

20. Complete: 9 + (−11) = ☐

Got It? What is the sum −6 + (−2)?

21. Complete: −6 + (−2) = ☐

Lesson 1-5

Vocabulary

● Review

1. How is a *product* different from a *quotient*?

_____

_____

2. Circle the *product* of 12 and 4. Underline the *quotient* of 12 and 4.

| 3 | 8 | 16 | 48 |

● Vocabulary Builder

reciprocal (noun) **rih** SIP **ruh kul**

Related Term: multiplicative inverse

Definition: Two numbers are **reciprocals** if their product is 1.

Main Idea: To write the **reciprocal** of a fraction, switch the numerator and denominator of the fraction.

Examples: $\frac{4}{5}$ and $\frac{5}{4}$, $-\frac{7}{8}$ and $-\frac{8}{7}$, 5 and $\frac{1}{5}$, $1\frac{1}{2}$ and $\frac{2}{3}$

> **reciprocals**
> $\frac{a}{b}$ and $\frac{b}{a}$, where
> $a \neq 0$ and $b \neq 0$

● Use Your Vocabulary

3. Draw a line from each expression in Column A to its *reciprocal* in Column B.

Column A	Column B
$\frac{3}{4}$	2
$\frac{1}{2}$	$-\frac{3}{5}$
-2	$-\frac{1}{2}$
$1\frac{3}{4}$	$\frac{4}{3}$
$-\frac{5}{3}$	$\frac{4}{7}$

Key Concept Multiplying and Dividing Real Numbers

The product or quotient of two real numbers with different signs is negative.

The product or quotient of two real numbers with the same sign is positive.

The quotient of 0 and any nonzero real number is 0.

The quotient of any real number and 0 is undefined.

4. Write *negative, positive, undefined,* or *zero* for each result.

$5(-9)$

$-8(-2)$

$0 \div 9$

$9 \div 0$

_____ _____ _____ _____

5. Write 4 or (-4) to make each equation true.

$6 \cdot \boxed{} = 24$ $6 \cdot \boxed{} = -24$ $24 \div \boxed{} = -6$ $24 \div \boxed{} = 6$

Problem 1 **Multiplying Real Numbers**

Got It? What is each product?

$6(-15)$ $12(0.2)$ $-\dfrac{7}{10}\left(\dfrac{3}{5}\right)$ $(-4)^2$

6. In $6(-15)$ and $-\dfrac{7}{10}\left(\dfrac{3}{5}\right)$, the signs of the numbers are the same / different .

So, the product of 6 and (-15) and the product of $-\dfrac{7}{10}$ and $\dfrac{3}{5}$ will be positive / negative .

7. Multiply.

$6(-15) = \boxed{}$ $-\dfrac{7}{10}\left(\dfrac{3}{5}\right) = \boxed{}$

8. In $12(0.2)$ and $(-4)(-4)$, the signs of the numbers are the same / different .

9. Multiply.

$12(0.2) = \boxed{}$ $(-4)^2 = (-4)(-4) = \boxed{}$

Problem 2 **Simplifying Square Root Expressions**

Got It? What is the simplified form of $\sqrt{100}$?

10. Circle the equation that uses the positive square root of 100.

$2 \cdot 50 = 100$ $4 \cdot 25 = 100$ $10 \cdot 10 = 100$

11. Will the simplified form of $\sqrt{100}$ be *positive* or *negative*? Explain.

_____

_____

12. The simplified form of $\sqrt{100}$ is $\boxed{}$.

Lesson 1-6

Problem 3   Dividing Real Numbers

Got It? You make five withdrawals of equal amounts from your bank account. The total amount you withdraw is $360. What is the change in your account balance each time you make a withdrawal?

13. Complete the model.

Relate | total amount withdrawn | divided by | number of withdrawals | is | change in account balance each time |

Write   [   ]   ÷   5   =   [   ]

14. The change in the account balance per withdrawal is −$[   ].

 take note

Property   Inverse Property of Multiplication

For every nonzero real number a, there is a **multiplicative inverse** $\frac{1}{a}$ such that $a\left(\frac{1}{a}\right) = 1$.

The reciprocal of a nonzero number of the form $\frac{a}{b}$ is $\frac{b}{a}$. The product of a number and its reciprocal is 1, so the reciprocal of a number is its multiplicative inverse.

Dividing by a fraction is equivalent to multiplying by the reciprocal of the fraction. In general, $\frac{a}{b} \div \frac{c}{d} = \frac{a}{b} \cdot \frac{d}{c}$ for b, c, and $d \neq 0$.

Problem 4   Dividing Fractions

Got It? What is the value of $\frac{3}{4} \div \left(-\frac{5}{2}\right)$?

Underline the correct word to complete each sentence.

15. The expression shows multiplication / division .

16. To divide fractions, multiply the first / second fraction by the reciprocal of the first / second fraction.

17. Simplify the expression below.

$$\frac{3}{4} \div \left(-\frac{5}{2}\right) = \frac{3}{4} \cdot \left(-\frac{}{}\right) \qquad \text{Multiply by the reciprocal of } -\frac{5}{2}.$$

$$= -\frac{}{20} \qquad \text{Multiply.}$$

$$= \qquad \text{Simplify.}$$

Got It? Reasoning Is $\frac{3}{4} \div \left(-\frac{5}{2}\right)$ equivalent to $-\left(\frac{3}{4} \div \frac{5}{2}\right)$? Explain.

18. Dividing a number by $\frac{5}{2}$ is equivalent to multiplying the number by [   ].

19. Simplify $-\left(\dfrac{3}{4} \div \dfrac{5}{2}\right)$.

20. Is $\dfrac{3}{4} \div \left(-\dfrac{5}{2}\right)$ equivalent to $-\left(\dfrac{3}{4} \div \dfrac{5}{2}\right)$? Explain.

_____

_____

Lesson Check • Do you UNDERSTAND?

Reasoning Use a number line to explain why $-15 \div 3 = -5$.

21. In words, $-15 \div 3$ means dividing -15 into ▭ equal groups.

22. To model $-15 \div 3$ on a number line, start at -15. Then use arrows to show three equal groups. The first equal group is shown.

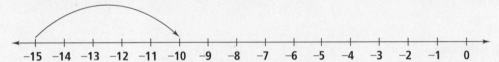

23. What do the three arrows showing the equal groups represent?

_____

_____

24. Divide: $-15 \div 3 = $ ▭ .

Math Success

Check off the vocabulary words that you understand.

☐ Inverse Property of Multiplication ☐ multiplicative inverse ☐ reciprocal

Rate how well you can *multiply and divide real numbers.*

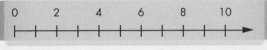

Lesson 1-6

1-7 · The Distributive Property

Vocabulary

● Review

1. Circle the *property* of addition illustrated by $7 + 0 = 7$.

| Associative Property | Commutative Property | Identity Property | Zero Property |

2. Circle the *property* of multiplication illustrated by $4 \cdot 0 = 0$.

| Associative Property | Commutative Property | Identity Property | Zero Property |

3. Circle the *property* of addition that is illustrated by $(63 + 9) + 1 = 63 + (9 + 1)$.

| Associative Property | Commutative Property | Identity Property |

4. Circle the *property* of multiplication that is illustrated by $52 \cdot (-1) = -52$.

| Identity Property | Zero Property | Property of -1 |

● Vocabulary Builder

distribute (verb) **dih STRIB yoot**

Other Word Forms: distributive (adjective), distribution (noun)

Definition: To **distribute** means to give out or hand out.

$$7(3 + 6) = 7 \cdot 3 + 7 \cdot 6$$
The factor 7 is **distributed** to the 3 and the 6.

● Use Your Vocabulary

Complete each sentence with *distribute*, *distribution*, or *distributed*.

5. The teacher __?__ a marked test to each student in the class.

6. The __?__ of tests grades shows that there are 12 A's, 10 B's, and 8 C's.

7. After reviewing the test scores, the teacher will __?__ tonight's homework.

Property Distributive Property

8. Complete the table.

Algebra Let a, b, and c be real numbers.	Example
$a(b + c) = ab + ac$	$3(10 + 4) = 3 \cdot \boxed{} + 3 \cdot \boxed{}$
$(b + c)a = ba + ca$	$(5 + 3)7 = 5 \cdot \boxed{} + 3 \cdot \boxed{}$
$a(b - c) = ab - ac$	$9(8 - 2) = 9 \cdot \boxed{} - 9 \cdot \boxed{}$
$(b - c)a = ba - ca$	$(28 - 6)4 = 28 \cdot \boxed{} - 6 \cdot \boxed{}$

Problem 1 Simplifying Expressions

Got It? What is the simplified form of $5(x + 7)$?

9. Circle how you read the expression $5(x + 7)$.

   5 times x plus 7   5 times the quantity x plus 7

10. To simplify $5(x + 7)$, which number do you distribute? How do you know?

_____

_____

11. Finish simplifying the expression.

   $5(x + 7) = 5 \cdot \boxed{} + \boxed{} \cdot 7$

   $= \boxed{}$

Got It? What is the simplified form of $12(3 - \frac{1}{6}t)$?

12. Complete the steps to simplify the expression.

   $12(3 - \frac{1}{6}t) = \boxed{} \cdot 3 - \boxed{} \cdot \frac{1}{6}t$

   $= \boxed{} - \dfrac{\boxed{}}{6} \cdot t$

   $= \boxed{} - \boxed{} \cdot t$

Lesson 1-7

Problem 2 **Rewriting Fraction Expressions**

Got It? What sum or difference is equivalent to $\frac{4x - 16}{3}$?

13. Recall that a fraction $\frac{a}{b}$ can be written as $\frac{1}{b} \cdot a$.

So, $\frac{4x}{3}$ can be written as $\dfrac{\boxed{}}{\boxed{}} \cdot 4x$.

14. Now complete the steps to find an expression equivalent to $\frac{4x - 16}{3}$.

$\frac{4x - 16}{3} = \boxed{} \cdot (4x - 16)$ Write the division as multiplication.

$= \boxed{} \cdot (4x) - \boxed{} \cdot (16)$ Use the Distributive Property.

$= \boxed{} \, x - \boxed{}$ Simplify.

The Multiplication Property of -1 states that $-1 \cdot x = -x$. To simplify an expression such as $-(x + 6)$, you can rewrite the expression as $-1(x + 6)$.

Problem 3 **Using the Multiplication Property of -1**

Got It? What is the simplified form of $-(a + 5)$?

15. Underline the correct word to complete the sentence.

A negative sign in front of the parentheses means that the entire expression inside the parentheses is the same / opposite .

16. Simplify $-(a + 5)$ by completing each step.

$-(a + 5) = -\boxed{} \cdot (a + 5)$ Multiplication Property of -1

$= (\boxed{})(a) + (\boxed{})(5)$ Distributive Property

$= \boxed{}$ Simplify.

Problem 4 **Using the Distributive Property for Mental Math**

Got It? Julia commutes to work on the train 4 times each week. A round-trip ticket costs $7.25. What is her weekly cost for tickets? Use mental math.

17. The expression $4 \cdot 7.25$ is simplified below using steps that could be used to do the problem mentally. Complete the missing parts.

$4(7.25) = 4(7 + \boxed{})$ Write 7.25 as $7 + 0.25$.

$= \boxed{} \cdot 7 + \boxed{} \cdot 0.25$ Distributive Property

$= \boxed{} + \boxed{}$ Multiply.

$= \boxed{}$ Add.

18. The weekly cost for her tickets is $\boxed{}$.

A *term* is a number, a variable, or the product of a number and one or more variables. *Like terms* have the same variable factors.

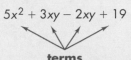

terms

$3xy$ and $2xy$ are *like terms* because they both have the variable factor xy.

Circle the variable factors in each expression. Then circle *Yes* if they are *like terms* or *No* if they are not.

19. $3x^2 + 5x^2$

Yes / No

20. $z^2w - zw^2$

Yes / No

Problem 5 Combining Like Terms

Got It? What is the simplified form of $3y - y$?

21. Are the terms $3y$ and $-y$ *like terms*?   Yes / No

22. Use the Distributive Property to write $3y - y$ as a product. Then simplify.

$3y - y = y(\quad - \quad)$

$= y(\quad)$

Lesson Check • Do you UNDERSTAND?

Reasoning Is each expression in simplified form? Justify your answer.

$4xy^3 + 5x^3y$ $-(y - 1)$ $5x^2 + 12xy - 3yx$

23. Does $4xy^3 + 5x^3y$ have any like terms?

Yes / No

Is the expression simplified?

Yes / No

24. Can the -1 in front of $-(y - 1)$ be distributed?

Yes / No

Simplify the expression.

25. Can the last term of $5x^2 + 12xy - 3yx$ be written as $3xy$?

Yes / No

Simplify the expression.

Math Success

Check off the vocabulary words that you understand.

☐ Distributive Property   ☐ term   ☐ like terms

Rate how well you can *use the Distributive Property*.

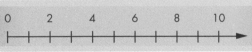

Need to review   0   2   4   6   8   10   Now I get it!

Lesson 1-7

Vocabulary

● Review

1. Circle each pair of *opposites*.

$\frac{1}{5}$ and 5 -17 and 17   0 and 1 $\frac{3}{20}$ and $-\frac{3}{20}$

2. An *equation* is a mathematical sentence that uses an equal sign (=). Circle each equation below.

$y - 3 = 12$ $7 = \frac{w}{7}$ $5x - 7 + 2$ $43 = 43$

Use mental math to solve each *equation*.

3. $10 + \boxed{} = 13$ **4.** $17 = 8 + \boxed{}$ **5.** $43 + \boxed{} = 99$

● Vocabulary Builder

solution (noun) **suh LOO shun**

Related Word: solve (verb)

Definition: A **solution** is any value or values that make an equation true.

Example: The **solution** of the equation $x + 4 = 12$ is 8.

Nonexample: 6 is NOT a **solution** of the equation $x - 4 = 10$.

> 7 is a **solution** of $x + 2 = 9$ because $7 + 2 = 9$.

● Use Your Vocabulary

6. Cross out the equation for which 24 is NOT the *solution*.

$x + 4 = 28$ $y - 2 = 22$ $3w = 24$ $\frac{48}{2} = z$

7. Circle the equation for which 20 is the *solution*.

$10 + m = 20$ $25 = n - 5$ $5x + 5 = 95$ $\frac{y}{5} = 4$

8. Circle the *solution* of $7 - x = 9$.

-16 -2 2 16

An equation is *true* if the expressions on either side of the equal sign are equal. An equation is *false* if the expressions on either side of the equal sign are not equal. An equation that contains one or more variables is called an **open sentence**.

 Problem 1 Classifying Equations

Got It? Is the equation $3y + 6 = 5y - 8$ *true, false,* or *open*? Explain.

9. Does the equation contain one or more variables? Yes / No

10. Is the equation *true, false,* or *open*? Explain.

_____

Got It? Is the equation $16 - 7 = 4 + 5$ *true, false,* or *open*? Explain.

11. $16 - 7 = $ ▢   **12.** $4 + 5 = $ ▢

13. Does $16 - 7 = 4 + 5$? Yes / No

14. Is the equation *true, false,* or *open*? Explain.

_____

Got It? Is the equation $32 \div 8 = 2 \cdot 3$ *true, false,* or *open*? Explain.

15. $32 \div 8 = $ ▢   **16.** $2 \cdot 3 = $ ▢

17. Does $32 \div 8 = 2 \cdot 3$? Yes / No

18. Is the equation *true, false,* or *open*? Explain.

_____

 Problem 2 Identifying Solutions of an Equation

Got It? Is $m = \frac{1}{2}$ a solution of the equation $6m - 8 = -5$?

19. Complete the reasoning model below.

Think	Write
I can substitute ▢ for *m*.	$6 \cdot$ ▢ $- 8 \overset{?}{=} -5$
Now I can simplify.	▢ $- 8 \overset{?}{=} -5$ ▢ $= -5$
Finally, I can write a sentence to answer the question.	$\frac{1}{2}$ is / is not a solution of $6m - 8 = -5$.

Lesson 1-8

Problem 3 Writing an Equation

Got It? The length of the ball court at La Venta is 14 times the height of its walls. Write an equation that can be used to find the height of a model of the court that has a length of 49 cm.

20. Complete the model below.

Relate   the length of the model court   is   fourteen   times   the height of its walls

Define   Let $h = $ _?_ . Circle your choice below.

   area of wall   height of wall   width of wall

Write   ☐   =   14   ·   ☐

21. Now write an equation that you can use to find the height of the model.

 Problem 4 Using Mental Math to Find Solutions

Got It? What is the solution of $12 - y = 3$? Use mental math.

22. Think: "What number added to / subtracted from 12 is equal to 3?"

23. Circle the solution.   **24.** Check your work.

   15   12   9   6

Problem 5 Using a Table to Find a Solution

Got It? What is the solution of $25 - 3p = 55$? Use a table.

25. Complete the table for each value of p.

p	$25 - 3p$	Value of $25 - 3p$
0	$25 - 3 \cdot$ ☐	☐
10	$25 - 3 \cdot$ ☐	☐
−5	$25 - 3 \cdot$ ☐	☐
−10	$25 - 3 \cdot$ ☐	☐

26. Complete each sentence.

When $p = $ ☐ , the value of $25 - 3p$ is 55.

So, the solution of $25 - 3p = 55$ is ☐ .

Problem 6 Estimating a Solution

Got It? What is the solution of $3x + 3 = -22$? Use a table.

27. Use the table at the right to help you estimate and find the integer values of x between which the solution must lie.

28. The solution lies

between ☐ and ☐ .

x	3x + 3	Value of 3x + 3
−2	3 · ☐ + 3	☐
−7	3 · ☐ + 3	☐
−8	3 · ☐ + 3	☐
−9	3 · ☐ + 3	☐

Lesson Check • Do you UNDERSTAND?

Compare and Contrast Use two different methods to find the solution of the equation $x + 4 = 13$. Which method do you prefer? Explain.

29. Solve the problem using mental math.

30. Solve the problem using a table.

x	x + 4	Value of x + 4
☐	☐	☐
☐	☐	☐
☐	☐	☐

31. Explain which method you prefer.

_____

Math Success

Check off the vocabulary words that you understand.

☐ equation ☐ open sentence ☐ solution of an equation

Rate how well you can *solve an equation.*

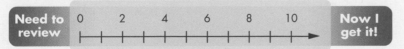

Lesson 1-8

Vocabulary

● Review

1. Draw a line from each pair of numbers in Column A to its description in Column B.

Column A	Column B
$\frac{5}{6}$ and $-\frac{5}{6}$	opposites (additive inverses)
$\frac{3}{4}$ and $\frac{4}{3}$	reciprocals (multiplicative inverses)
-2 and $-\frac{1}{2}$	

● Vocabulary Builder

inductive reasoning (noun) in DUK tiv REE zun ing

Definition: **Inductive reasoning** is the process of reaching a conclusion based on an observed pattern.

Main Idea: You can use **inductive reasoning** to go from a set of particular observations to a general rule.

Example: Each piece of ice in this bucket is cold. I conclude, by **inductive reasoning,** that all ice is cold.

● Use Your Vocabulary

Use the table at the right for Exercises 2–4. Complete each statement with one of the words or phrases below.

  add   inductive reasoning   multiply   pattern   subtract

Item Number	Value
1	1
2	4
3	9
4	16
5	■

2. To find the value of Item 5, you can look for a ? .

3. To obtain the value for an item, you can ? the item number by itself.

4. You can use ? to predict the value of Item 5.

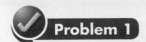

Problem 1 **Identifying Solutions of a Two-Variable Equation**

Got It? Is the ordered pair (5, 20) a solution of the equation $y = 4x$?

5. Complete the reasoning model below.

Think	Write
In (5, 20), I need to identify the x-coordinate and the y-coordinate.	x-coordinate: ☐ ; y-coordinate: ☐
Now I can substitute 5 for x and 20 for y.	$y = 4x$ ☐ $= 4 \cdot$ ☐
Then I can simplify the equation.	☐ $=$ ☐

6. Is (5, 20) a solution of $y = 4x$?　　　　Yes / No

Problem 2 **Using a Table, an Equation, and a Graph**

Got It? Will runs 6 laps before Megan joins him at the track. They then run together at the same pace. How can you represent the relationship between the number of laps Will runs and the number of laps Megan runs in different ways? Use a table, an equation, and a graph.

Exercises 7 and 8 help you use a table to represent the relationship.

7. Complete the table.

Number of laps Megan runs	0	1	☐	☐	☐	☐	☐	☐
Number of laps Will runs	6	☐	☐	☐	☐	☐	☐	☐

8. Circle the relationship that is represented in the table.

| Will runs 13 more laps than Megan. | Megan runs 6 times as many laps as Will. | Will runs 7 more laps than Megan. | Will runs 6 more laps than Megan. |

Exercises 9–11 help you write an equation to represent the relationship.

9. Let $x =$ the number of laps Megan runs.

Then let $y =$ _____.

10. Underline the correct words to complete the sentence.

In the relationship, y will always be greater than / less than x.

11. Now write an equation to represent the relationship.

_____

Lesson 1-9

Exercises 12–14 help you graph the relationship.

12. The ordered pair that corresponds to Megan arriving at the track is (, 6).

13. Use the table in Exercise 7. Write three more
ordered pairs.

(2,)　　(, 10)　　(,)

14. Graph the ordered pairs you wrote in Exercises 12
and 13 on the coordinate plane at the right.
Then connect the points with a line.
Be sure to label the axes.

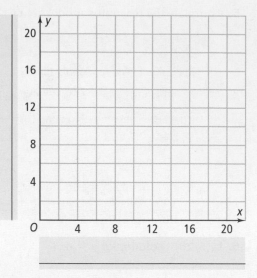

 Problem 3 **Extending a Pattern**

Got It? Use the figure below. Make a table showing the number of orange tiles and
the total number of tiles in each figure. How many tiles in all will be in a figure with
24 orange tiles?

15. Complete the table.

Figure	Number of Orange Tiles	Total Number of Tiles
1	4	
2		
3		

16. **Multiple Choice** For each new figure, how does the total number of tiles change as
the number of orange tiles increases by 4?

Ⓐ it doubles　　　Ⓑ it triples　　　Ⓒ it increases by 4　　　Ⓓ it increases by 9

17. A figure with 24 orange tiles will have total tiles.

Got It? Make a table showing the number of blue tiles and the number of yellow
tiles in each figure. How many yellow tiles will be in a figure with 24 blue tiles?

18. Complete the table.

Figure	Number of Blue Tiles	Number Yellow of Tiles
1	1	2
2		
3		

19. Circle the correct description of the relationship between the figure number and the number of blue tiles.

They are the same.	The number of blue tiles is double the figure number.	The number of blue tiles is triple the figure number.

20. Circle the correct description of the relationship between the number of blue tiles and the number of yellow tiles.

They are the same.	The number of yellow tiles is double the number of blue tiles.	The number of yellow tiles is triple the number of blue tiles.

21. A figure with 24 blue tiles will have ____ yellow tiles.

Lesson Check • Do you UNDERSTAND?

Reasoning Which of (3, 5), (4, 6), (5, 7), and (6, 8) are solutions of $y = x + 2$? What is the pattern in the solutions of $y = x + 2$?

22. Check each ordered pair in the equation $y = x + 2$. Circle the solutions.

(3, 5) (4, 6) (5, 7) (6, 8)

23. In Exercise 22, each value of y is greater than / less than each value of x.

24. Describe the pattern in the solutions of $y = x + 2$.

_____

Math Success

Check off the vocabulary words that you understand.

☐ solution of an equation   ☐ inductive reasoning

Rate how well you can *identify solutions of a two-variable equation.*

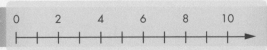

Need to review 0 2 4 6 8 10 Now I get it!

2-1 Solving One-Step Equations

Vocabulary

● Review

1. Circle the *multiplicative inverse* of $\frac{1}{2}$. Underline the *additive inverse* of $\frac{1}{2}$.

| 2 | 1 | $\frac{1}{2}$ | $-\frac{1}{2}$ | -2 |

2. Circle the *multiplicative inverse* of -3. Underline the *additive inverse* of -3.

| 3 | 1 | $\frac{1}{3}$ | $-\frac{1}{3}$ | -3 |

● Vocabulary Builder

isolate (verb) EYE suh layt

Main Idea: To **isolate** a variable in an equation means you get the variable with a coefficient of 1 alone on one side of the equation.

Other Word Forms: isolation (noun), isolated (adjective)

variable *isolated*
$x = 12$

variable NOT
isolated
$5x = 60$

● Use Your Vocabulary

3. Choose the correct form of the word *isolate* to complete each statement.

isolate   isolation   isolated

A very ill patient was placed in __?__, away from the other patients.

In order to __?__ a variable, you may need to perform mathematical operations.

A person living on a small island felt __?__ from the rest of the world.

4. Circle the equations that show the variable *isolated*.

| $4x + 1 = 13$ | $x = 12 - 7$ | $\frac{x}{3} = 10$ | $\frac{2}{5} = x$ |

Property   Addition and Subtraction Properties of Equality

5. Complete the table.

Property	Algebra	Example
Addition Property of Equality	For any real numbers a, b, and c, if $a = b$, then $a + c = b + $ ___ .	$n - 7 = 12$ $n - 7 + 7 = 12 + $ ___
Subtraction Property of Equality	For any real numbers a, b, and c, if $a = b$, then $a - c = b - $ ___ .	$n + 8 = 9$ $n + 8 - $ ___ $= 9 - $ ___

Problem 1   Solving an Equation Using Subtraction

Got It? What is the solution of $y + 2 = -6$? Check your answer.

6. Underline the correct word to complete each sentence.

The equation $y + 2 = -6$ shows addition / subtraction .

The inverse of that operation is addition / subtraction .

7. Use the justifications to solve the equation.

$y + 2 = -6$ Write the original equation.

$y + 2 - $ ___ $= $ ___ $- $ ___   Subtract 2 from each side.

$y = $ ___   Simplify.

8. Check your answer by substituting it in the original equation for y. Then simplify.

Does ___ $+ 2 = -6$?   Yes / No

Property   Multiplication and Division Properties of Equality

9. Complete the table.

Property	Algebra	Example
Multiplication Property of Equality	For any real numbers a, b, and c, if $a = b$, then $a \cdot c = b \cdot$ ___ .	$\dfrac{x}{5} = 10$ $\dfrac{x}{5} \cdot 5 = 10 \cdot$ ___
Division Property of Equality	For any real numbers a, b, and c, such that $c \neq 0$, if $a = b$, then $\dfrac{a}{c} = \dfrac{b}{\text{___}}$.	$6x = 30$ $\dfrac{6x}{6} = \dfrac{30}{\text{___}}$

Problem 3 **Solving an Equation Using Division**

Got It? What is the solution of $10 = 15x$? Check your answer.

10. The equation is solved below. Write a justification for each step.

$10 = 15x$ _____

$\dfrac{10}{15} = \dfrac{15x}{15}$ _____

$\dfrac{2}{3} = x$ _____

11. Check your answer.

$10 \stackrel{?}{=} 15 \cdot$ ☐

$10 =$ ☐

 Problem 4 **Solving an Equation Using Multiplication**

Got It? What is the solution of $19 = \dfrac{r}{3}$?

12. Underline the correct word or number to complete the sentence.

To isolate the variable, you should multiply / divide each side of the equation by 3 / 19 .

13. When you isolate the variable, you obtain $r =$ ☐.

 Problem 5 **Solving an Equation Using Reciprocals**

Got It? What is the solution of $12 = \dfrac{3}{4}x$? Check your answer.

14. To solve the equation, divide / multiply both sides of the equation by the reciprocal of $\dfrac{3}{4}$.

15. Multiple Choice Choose the reciprocal of $\dfrac{3}{4}$.

Ⓐ $\dfrac{3}{4}$ Ⓑ $\dfrac{1}{4}$ Ⓒ $\dfrac{4}{3}$ Ⓓ 4

16. Use the reciprocal of $\dfrac{3}{4}$ to solve $12 = \dfrac{3}{4}x$ for x.

17. Now check your answer. Does $12 = \dfrac{3}{4} \cdot$ ☐ ? Yes / No

Problem 6 **Using a One-Step Equation as a Model**

Got It? An online DVD rental company offers gift certificates that you can use to purchase rental plans. You have a gift certificate for $30. The plan you select costs $5 per month. How many months can you purchase with the gift certificate?

18. Complete the model to solve the problem.

Relate | cost per month | times | number of months | is | amount of the gift certificate

Define   Let m = _____.

Write $\$\square$ $\cdot$ $\square$ $=$ $\$\square$

19. Solve the equation to find the number of months you can purchase.

 ## Lesson Check • Do you UNDERSTAND?

Vocabulary Which property of equality would you use to solve $3 + x = -34$? Why?

20. What operation does the equation $3 + x = -34$ show?

   addition   division   multiplication   subtraction

21. Which property of equality would you use to solve $3 + x = -34$? Explain.

Math Success

Check off the vocabulary words that you understand.

☐ equivalent equations   ☐ isolate   ☐ inverse operations   ☐ Addition Property

     ☐ Subtraction Property   ☐ Multiplication Property   ☐ Division Property

Rate how well you can *use the properties of equality*.

Need to review   0   2   4   6   8   10   Now I get it!

Lesson 2-1

Solving Two-Step Equations

Vocabulary

Review

1. Circle the equation(s) in which the variable is *isolated*.

$6y = 36$ $\qquad$ $\frac{x}{2} + 7 = 19$ $\qquad$ $8 + 4 = w$ $\qquad$ $y = 3 - \frac{1}{2}$

Draw a line from each equation in Column A to its *solution* in Column B.

Column A	Column B
2. $x = 16$	$x = -6$
3. $x = 17$	$x = 4$
4. -2	$x = 12$

Vocabulary Builder

> **deduce** (noun) **dee DOOS**
>
> **Other Word Forms:** deducible (adjective), deduction (noun)
>
> **Definition:** When you **deduce** something, you reach a logical conclusion through reasoning.
>
> **Example:** You find that when $a = 2$, $0a = 0$; when $a = \frac{1}{3}$, $0a = 0$; and when $a = -7$, $0a = 0$. You **deduce** that for any value of a, $0a$ will equal 0.

Use Your Vocabulary

Place a ✓ in the box if the statement is a logical *deduction*. Place an ✗ if it is NOT a logical *deduction*.

5. A multiple of 5 always ends in 0 or 5. So, 240 is a multiple of 5.

6. If a number is a whole number, it is also a rational number. So, all rational numbers must be whole numbers.

7. Consider $a + b = 100$ for values of a and b. When a increases, b decreases. So, when b increases, a decreases.

A two-step equation involves two operations. To solve $2 \cdot x + 3 = 15$, undo the operations in the *reverse order* of the order of operations.

Order of Operations   First multiply.   Then add.

$$2 \cdot x + 3 = 15$$

Operations Used to Solve Equations   Undo multiplication with division after you undo addition.   First, undo addition with subtraction.

Circle the first operation you would undo in solving each equation. Then write the inverse operation you would use to undo the circled operation.

8. $3 \cdot r + 16 = 31$

9. $\frac{1}{2} \cdot d - 7 = 10$

10. $12 = -5y + 2$

Problem 1 **Solving a Two-Step Equation**

Got It? What is the solution of $5 = \frac{t}{2} - 3$?

11. Circle the first operation you will undo.

addition   subtraction   multiplication   division

12. Circle the second operation you will undo.

addition   subtraction   multiplication   division

13. Which two operations, in order, will you use to solve the equation?

_____ then _____

14. Now solve the equation.

Problem 2 Using an Equation as a Model

Got It? You are making a bulletin board to advertise community service opportunities in your town. You plan to use one quarter of a sheet of construction paper for each ad and four full sheets for the title banner. You have 18 sheets of construction paper. How many ads can you make?

15. Use the model to complete the equation.

Relate | number of sheets for the ads | plus | number of sheets for the title | is | total number of sheets

Define Let a = the number of ads that you can make.

Write $\frac{1}{4}a$ +   [ ]   =   [ ]

16. Circle the operation you can use to undo multiplication by a fraction.

addition of the opposite   division by the reciprocal   multiplication by the reciprocal

17. Now solve the equation.

18. The number of ads that you can make is [ ].

Problem 3 Solving With Two Terms in the Numerator

Got It? What is the solution of $6 = \frac{x - 2}{4}$?

19. The equation has two operations: subtraction and   ? .

To isolate x, use addition and   ? .

20. Use the justifications at the right to solve the equation.

$6 = \frac{x - 2}{4}$ Write the original equation.

$6 \cdot \boxed{} = \frac{x - 2}{4} \cdot \boxed{}$ Multiply each side by 4.

$\boxed{} = x - \boxed{}$ Simplify.

$\boxed{} + \boxed{} = x - \boxed{} + \boxed{}$ Add 2 to each side.

$\boxed{} = x$ Simplify.

Problem 4 Using Deductive Reasoning

Got It? What is the solution of $\frac{x}{3} - 5 = 4$? Justify each step.

21. The equation $\frac{x}{3} - 5 = 4$ is solved below. Use one of the reasons from the box to justify each step.

$\frac{x}{3} - 5 = 4$	Write the original equation.
$\frac{x}{3} - 5 + 5 = 4 + 5$	_____
$\frac{x}{3} = 9$	_____
$3 \cdot \frac{x}{3} = 3 \cdot 9$	_____
$x = 27$	_____

> Multiply each side by 3.
> Simplify.
> Add 5 to each side.

Lesson Check • **Do you UNDERSTAND?**

What properties of equality would you use to solve $-8 = \frac{s}{4} + 3$? What operation would you perform first? Explain.

22. Circle the operations you will undo when you solve $-8 = \frac{s}{4} + 3$.

addition	subtraction	multiplication	division

23. Which properties of equality would you use to undo these operations?

_____

_____

24. What operation would you perform first? Explain.

_____

_____

_____

Math Success

Check off the vocabulary words that you understand.

☐ isolated   ☐ solution   ☐ equation

Rate how well you can solve a *two-step equation*.

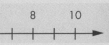

Need to review   0   2   4   6   8   10   Now I get it!

2-3 Solving Multi-Step Equations

Vocabulary

● **Review**

1. Circle the *variable* or *variables* in each equation below.

   $x - 11 = 35$ $-2y + 6 + y = 6$ $2t + 14 = t$ $19 = 3 + 4b$

2. Find the *solution* of $19 = 3 + 4b$.

● **Vocabulary Builder**

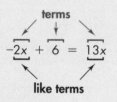

term (noun) **turm**

Definition: A **term** is a number, a variable, or the product of a number and one or more variables. *Like terms* have exactly the same variable factors.

Main Idea: Combining *like terms* helps you solve equations.

● **Use Your Vocabulary**

3. Write the number of *terms* in each equation.

   $14 = x + 6$ $2z + z - 5 = 10$ $9 = 6 + 2m - 7m$

4. The variables in each expression are shown in red. Write **Y** if the terms of each expression are *like terms*. Write **N** if they are NOT *like terms*.

   $5x + (-2x)$ _____ $6w - 6z$ _____ $\frac{m}{2} + \frac{m}{3}$ _____

Write T for *true* or F for *false*.

_____ **5.** Expressions with only numbers are always *like terms*.

_____ **6.** The expressions xy and yx are *like terms*.

Problem 1 Combining Like Terms

Got It? What is the solution of $11m - 8 - 6m = 22$?

7. Circle the like terms in the expression. $\quad 11m - 8 - 6m$

8. Underline the correct word to complete the sentence.

I can rewrite the equation as $11m - 6m - 8 = 22$ using the

Associative / Commutative Property of Addition.

9. Now solve the equation.

Problem 2 Solving a Multi-Step Equation

Got It? Noah and Kate are shopping for new guitar strings in a music store. Noah buys 2 packs of strings. Kate buys 2 packs of strings and a music book. The book costs $16. Their total cost is $72. How much is one pack of strings?

10. Complete the model to write the equation.

Relate	amount Noah spent on strings	plus	amount Kate spent on strings and a music book	is	total amount spent by Noah and Kate

Define Let $c =$ _____ .

Write $\quad 2 \cdot \boxed{} \qquad + \qquad 2 \cdot \boxed{} + \boxed{} \qquad = \qquad \boxed{}$

11. Combine like terms to solve the equation.

12. The cost of one pack of strings is $ ____ .

Lesson 2-3

Problem 3 Solving an Equation Using the Distributive Property

Got It? What is the solution of $18 = 3(2x - 6)$? Check your answer.

13. Use the justifications at the right to solve the equation.

$18 = 3(2x - 6)$ Write the original equation.

$18 = \boxed{} \cdot (2x) - \boxed{} \cdot (6)$ Use the Distributive Property.

$18 = \boxed{} \cdot (x) - 18$ Multiply.

$18 + \boxed{} = \boxed{} - 18 + \boxed{}$ Use the Addition Property of Equality.

$\boxed{} = 6x$ Add.

$\dfrac{\boxed{}}{6} = \dfrac{6x}{\boxed{}}$ Use the Division Property of Equality.

$\boxed{} = x$ Simplify.

14. Check your answer. $18 = 3(2x - 6)$

$18 \stackrel{?}{=} 3(2 \cdot \boxed{} - 6)$

$18 \stackrel{?}{=} 3 \cdot (\boxed{})$

 Problem 4 Solving an Equation That Contains Fractions

Got It? What is the solution of $\dfrac{2b}{5} + \dfrac{3b}{4} = 3$? Why did you choose the method you used?

15. Circle the first step you could use to solve the equation. Then underline the second step you could use.

| Combine like terms. | Divide each side by 5. | Multiply each side by 4. | Multiply each side by 20. |

16. Suppose you began by writing the fractions with a common denominator. What would your second step be?

_____

17. Now use one of the methods from Exercise 15 or Exercise 16 to solve the equation.

 Problem 5 Solving an Equation That Contains Decimals

Got It? What is the solution of $0.5x - 2.325 = 3.95$? Check your answer.

18. Because the equation contains thousandths, multiply each side by $10^{\boxed{}}$, or $\boxed{}$.

19. Rewrite the equation without decimals.

$$\boxed{} - 2325 = \boxed{}$$

20. Now solve the equation.

21. Check your answer.

Does $0.5 \cdot \boxed{} - 2.325 = 3.95$? Yes / No

Lesson Check • Do you UNDERSTAND?

Reasoning Ben solves the equation $-24 = 5(g + 3)$ by first dividing each side by 5. Amelia solves the equation by using the Distributive Property. Whose method do you prefer? Explain.

22. Complete Ben's solution and Amelia's solution.

Ben's Solution

$$-24 = 5(g + 3)$$

$$\frac{-24}{5} = \frac{5(g + 3)}{5}$$

$$\frac{-24}{5} - \boxed{} = g + 3 - \boxed{}$$

$$\boxed{} = g$$

Amelia's Solution

$$-24 = 5(g + 3)$$

$$-24 = 5g + 15$$

$$\frac{-39}{\boxed{}} = \frac{5g}{\boxed{}}$$

$$\boxed{} = g$$

23. Whose method do you prefer? Explain.

_____

_____

Math Success

Check off the vocabulary words that you understand.

☐ one-step equation   ☐ multi-step equation

Rate how well you can *solve a multi-step equation*.

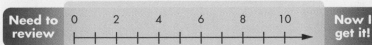

Vocabulary

Review

Write the *like terms* in each expression or equation.

1. $5x + 2x + 6$

2. $1.5y - 1.2 + 1.2z + y$

3. $\frac{1}{2}x + \frac{1}{2} = 3x$

Vocabulary Builder

> $m = m$
> is an **identity**.
>
> $m = 15$
> is NOT
> an **identity**.

identity (noun) **eye** DEN **tuh tee**

Main Idea: Any equation that is always true is an **identity**.

Examples: The equation $39 = 39$ is an **identity** because it is always true.
The equation $y + 3 = y + 3$ is an **identity** because it is true for all values of y.

Nonexample: The equation $x + 5 = 8$ is *not* an **identity** because it is *not* always true. It is true only when $x = 3$.

Use Your Vocabulary

Write a number or expression to make each equation an *identity*.

4. $25 + \boxed{} = 25$

5. $27 \cdot \boxed{} = 27$

6. $-5x + 3 = \boxed{} + 3$

7. Multiple Choice Which equation is NOT an *identity*?

Ⓐ $0 + 7 = 7$ Ⓑ $1 \cdot 9 = 9$ Ⓒ $x + 3 = 3 + x$ Ⓓ $x + 1 = x$

8. Draw a line from each equation in Column A to its description in Column B.

Column A	Column B
$x = x - 1$	always true
$x + x = 2x$	sometimes true
$5x = 15$	never true

Problem 1 Solving an Equation With Variables on Both Sides

Got It? What is the solution of $7k + 2 = 4k - 10$?

9. There is a variable on each side of the equation. Are they like terms? **Yes / No**

10. Use one of the reasons from the box to justify each step. You may use a reason more than once.

| Division Property of Equality |
| Simplify. |
| Subtraction Property of Equality |
| Subtract. |

$$7k + 2 = 4k - 10$$ Write the original equation.

$$7k + 2 - 4k = 4k - 10 - 4k$$ _____

$$3k + 2 = -10$$ _____

$$3k + 2 - 2 = -10 - 2$$ _____

$$3k = -12$$ _____

$$\frac{3k}{3} = -\frac{12}{3}$$ _____

$$k = -4$$ _____

Problem 2 Using an Equation With Variables on Both Sides

Got It? An office manager spent $650 on a new energy-saving copier that will reduce the monthly electric bill for the office from $112 to $88. In how many months will the copier pay for itself?

11. Complete the model below.

Relate

| cost of the copier | plus | new monthly cost | times | number of months | is | old monthly cost | times | number of months |

Define Let $m = \underline{?}$. Circle the correct answer.

| Cost of the copier | Number of months | Amount of savings |

Write

| $650 | + | $88 | · | ☐ | = | $ ☐ | · | ☐ |

12. Now write and solve the equation.

13. The copier will pay for itself in about ☐ months.

Problem 3 Solving an Equation With Grouping Symbols

Got It? What is the solution of $4(2y + 1) = 2(y - 13)$?

14. Use the justifications at the right to solve the equation.

$$4(2y + 1) = 2(y - 13)$$ Write the original equation.

$4 \cdot (2y) + \boxed{} \cdot (1) = \boxed{} \cdot (y) - \boxed{} \cdot (13)$ Distributive Property

$\boxed{} \cdot (y) + \boxed{} = \boxed{} \cdot (y) - \boxed{}$ Multiply.

$\boxed{} \cdot (y) + \boxed{} - 4 = \boxed{} \cdot (y) - \boxed{} - 4$ Subtraction Property of Equality

$\boxed{} \cdot (y) = \boxed{} \cdot (y) - \boxed{}$ Subtract.

$\boxed{} \cdot (y) - \boxed{} \cdot (y) = \boxed{} \cdot (y) - \boxed{} - \boxed{} \cdot (y)$ Subtraction Property of Equality

$\boxed{} \cdot (y) = \boxed{}$ Subtract.

$\dfrac{\boxed{}}{\boxed{}} = \dfrac{\boxed{}}{\boxed{}}$ Division Property of Equality

$y = \boxed{}$ Simplify.

15. Check your answer by substituting it for y in the original equation.

Problem 4 Identities and Equations With No Solution

Got It? What is the solution of $3(4b - 2) = -6 + 12b$?

16. Circle the first step you would take to isolate the variable. Underline the second step you would take.

| Multiply each side by 3. | Distribute the 3. | Subtract 12b from each side. |

17. Solve the equation.

18. Because $-6 = -6$ is always true, the original equation has

no solution / infinitely many solutions .

Concept Summary   Solving Equations

Remember to follow these steps when solving equations.

STEP 1   Use the Distributive Property to remove any grouping symbols.
Use properties of equality to clear decimals and fractions.

STEP 2   Combine like terms on each side of the equation.

STEP 3   Use the properties of equality to get the variable terms on one side
of the equation and the constants on the other.

STEP 4   Use the properties of equality to solve for the variable.

STEP 5   Check your solution in the original equation.

Lesson Check • Do you UNDERSTAND?

Vocabulary Tell whether each equation has *infinitely many solutions, one solution,*
or *no solution.*

$$3y - 5 = y + 2y - 9 \qquad 2y + 4 = 2(y + 2) \qquad 2y - 4 = 3y - 5$$

Write the steps to isolate the variable in each equation.

19. $3y - 5 = y + 2y - 9$

20. $2y + 4 = 2(y + 2)$

21. $2y - 4 = 3y - 5$

22. Tell whether each equation has *infinitely many solutions, one solution,* or *no solution.*

$$3y - 5 = y + 2y - 9 \qquad 2y + 4 = 2(y + 2) \qquad 2y - 4 = 3y$$

Math Success

Check off the vocabulary words that you understand.

☐ like terms   ☐ identity

Rate how well you can *solve equations with variables on both sides.*

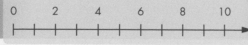

Literal Equations and Formulas

Vocabulary

● Review

Write the letter of each *formula* next to its description.

A. $C = 2\pi r$ B. $P = 2\ell + 2w$ C. $A = \frac{1}{2}bh$ D. $C = \frac{5}{9}(F - 32)$

_____ **1.** perimeter (P) of a rectangle with length (ℓ) and width (w)

_____ **2.** area (A) of a triangle with base (b) and height (h)

_____ **3.** circumference (C) of a circle with radius (r)

_____ **4.** temperature in degrees Celsius (C) given the same temperature in degrees Fahrenheit (F)

● Vocabulary Builder

literal (adjective) **LIT ur ul**

Related Words: letter (noun), literature (noun), literary (adjective)

Definition: When something is **literal**, it uses the exact, or primary, meaning of a word or words. It is also something that uses or is expressed by letters.

Math Usage: A **literal** equation is an equation that involves two or more letters (variables).

Example: The formula in the box is a **literal** equation with three variables. You can solve for any of the three variables in terms of the other two.

Nonexample: $2x + 5 = 12$ is *not* a **literal** equation because it does *not* contain two or more variables.

> These **literal** equations relate distance (d), rate (speed, r), and time (t).
> $$d = r \cdot t$$
> $$\frac{d}{r} = t$$
> $$\frac{d}{t} = r$$

Use Your Vocabulary

Complete each statement with the appropriate word from the list.

letter   literature   literary   literal equation

5. The word *Boston* begins with the __?__ B.

6. A novel is an example of a __?__ work.

7. The equation $2x + 5 = 12$ is *not* an example of a __?__ because it has only one variable.

8. You study classic __?__ in English class.

Problem 1 Rewriting a Literal Equation

Got It? Solve the equation $4 = 2m - 5n$ for m. What are the values of m when $n = -2, 0,$ and 2?

Simplify.

Divide each side by 2.

Add 5n to both sides.

9. The equation is solved below. Choose a justification from the box for each step.

$4 = 2m - 5n$ Write the original equation.

$4 + 5n = 2m - 5n + 5n$

$4 + 5n = 2m$

$\dfrac{4 + 5n}{2} = \dfrac{2m}{2}$

$2 + \dfrac{5}{2}n = m$

10. Complete the table to find the value of m for each given value of n.

n	Substitute the value of n into the equation.	m
−2	$\boxed{} + \dfrac{5}{2} \cdot \boxed{} = m$ $\boxed{} = m$	$\boxed{}$
0	$\boxed{} + \dfrac{5}{2} \cdot \boxed{} = m$ $\boxed{} = m$	$\boxed{}$
2	$\boxed{} + \dfrac{5}{2} \cdot \boxed{} = m$ $\boxed{} = m$	$\boxed{}$

Lesson 2-5

Problem 2 Rewriting a Literal Equation With Only Variables

Got It? What equation do you get when you solve $-t = r + px$ for x?

11. Use the justifications at the right to solve the equation.

$-t = r + px$	Write the original equation.
$-t - \boxed{} = r + px - \boxed{}$	Subtract the same amount from each side.
$-t - \boxed{} = px$	Simplify.
$\dfrac{-t - r}{\boxed{}} = \dfrac{px}{p}$	Divide each side by the same amount.
$-\dfrac{t}{p} - \dfrac{\boxed{}}{\boxed{}} = x$	Simplify.

 Problem 3 Rewriting a Geometric Formula

Got It? What is the height of a triangle that has an area of 24 in.^{2} and a base with a length of 8 in.?

12. Circle the formula for the area of a triangle.

$A = \pi r^2$	$A = \frac{1}{2}bh$	$d = rt$	$A = \ell w$

13. Circle the rewritten formula you will use to find the height of the triangle.

$\ell = \dfrac{P - 2w}{2}$	$r = \sqrt{\dfrac{A}{\pi}}$	$t = \dfrac{d}{r}$	$h = \dfrac{2A}{b}$

14. Now find the height of a triangle with an area of 24 in.^{2} and a base of 8 in.

Problem 4 Rewriting a Formula

Got It? Pacific gray whales migrate annually from the waters near Alaska to the waters near Baja California, Mexico, and back. The whales travel a distance of about 5000 mi each way at an average rate of 91 mi per day. About how many days does it take the whales to migrate one way?

15. Write the formula that relates distance, rate, and time.

$$\boxed{} = \boxed{} \cdot \boxed{}$$

16. Circle what you are asked to find in the problem.

distance	rate	time

17. Complete the reasoning model below.

Think	Write
To isolate *t*, I divide each side of the formula by *r*.	$\dfrac{d}{\boxed{}} = \dfrac{rt}{\boxed{}}$
Then I simplify.	$\boxed{}$
Now I substitute 5000 for *d* and 91 for *r*.	$\boxed{}$

18. Simplify. The whales take about $\boxed{}$ days to migrate one way.

Lesson Check • Do you UNDERSTAND?

Compare and Contrast How is the process of rewriting literal equations similar to the process of solving equations in one variable? How is it different?

19. When you rewrite a literal equation, you are solving it for one of the variables. How is this process similar to solving an equation in one variable?

_____

_____

20. Describe one difference between rewriting a literal equation and solving an equation in one variable.

_____

_____

Math Success

Check off the vocabulary words that you understand.

☐ literal equation   ☐ formula

Rate how well you can *rewrite literal equations*.

Need to review | 0 2 4 6 8 10 | Now I get it!

Vocabulary

● Review

1. Write a fraction with a *numerator* of 12 and a *denominator* of 13.

2. Circle the fractions that are in simplest form.

$$\frac{15}{30} \qquad\qquad \frac{5}{18} \qquad\qquad \frac{17}{42} \qquad\qquad \frac{22}{33}$$

3. Circle the *greatest common divisor* of the *numerator* and the *denominator* of a fraction that is in simplest form.

0	1	2	3

● Vocabulary Builder

> You read the **rate**
> **45 mi/h**
> as
> **"45 miles per hour."**

rate (noun) **rayt**

Definition: A **rate** is a ratio that compares quantities measured in *different* units.

Examples: miles per gallon, cost per ounce, words per minute

Using Symbols: $\dfrac{23\text{ mi}}{1\text{ gal}}$, $\dfrac{\$1.32}{8\text{ oz}}$, $\dfrac{302\text{ words}}{5\text{ minutes}}$

● Use Your Vocabulary

Write a *rate* for each situation.

4. Chandler bicycles 20 miles per hour.

5. Ann makes 80 bagels every 3 days.

6. So far, you have read 35 pages out of a 50-page assignment. Explain why the ratio 35 pages out of 50 pages is NOT a *rate*.

_____

_____

Problem 1 Comparing Unit Rates

Got It? The prices for one shirt at three different stores are shown in the box at the right. If Store B lowers its price to $42 for four shirts, which store offers the best deal for one shirt? Explain.

Price for 1 Shirt
Store A: $12.50
Store B: $11.25
Store C: $10

7. Circle the store that offered the best deal before Store B lowered its price.

Store A   Store B   Store C

8. Find Store B's new unit rate based on $42 for 4 shirts.

$$\frac{\text{cost of shirts}}{\text{number of shirts}} = \frac{\boxed{}}{\boxed{}} = \frac{\boxed{}}{1 \text{ shirt}}$$

9. Circle the store that offers the best deal now.

Store A   Store B   Store C

10. Why does this store have the best deal?

_____

_____

A *conversion factor* is a ratio of two equivalent measures in different units. A conversion factor is always equal to 1.

11. Complete each conversion factor.

$$\frac{1 \text{ ft}}{\boxed{} \text{ in.}} \qquad \frac{\boxed{} \text{ mi}}{5280 \text{ ft}} \qquad \frac{1 \text{ m}}{\boxed{} \text{ cm}} \qquad \frac{\boxed{} \text{ h}}{60 \text{ min}}$$

Problem 2 Converting Units

Got It? What is 1250 cm converted to meters?

12. There are ☐ centimeters in one meter.

Underline the correct word to complete each sentence.

13. When you convert from centimeters to meters, the number of meters will be

greater than / less than the number of centimeters.

14. When you convert from centimeters to meters, the appropriate conversion factor

will allow you to multiply / divide out the common units.

15. Multiple Choice Choose the conversion factor for converting centimeters to meters.

Ⓐ $\frac{1 \text{ m}}{100 \text{ cm}}$ Ⓑ $\frac{1 \text{ m}}{1000 \text{ cm}}$ Ⓒ $\frac{100 \text{ cm}}{1 \text{ m}}$ Ⓓ $\frac{1000 \text{ cm}}{1 \text{ m}}$

16. Complete the conversion.

$$1250 \text{ cm} \cdot \frac{\boxed{}}{\boxed{}} = \boxed{} \text{ m}$$

Lesson 2-6

Problem 3 **Converting Units Between Systems**

Got It? The Sears Tower in Chicago, Illinois, is 1450 ft tall. How many meters tall is the tower? Use the fact that 1 m ≈ 3.28 ft.

17. Follow the steps to find how many meters tall the Sears Tower is.

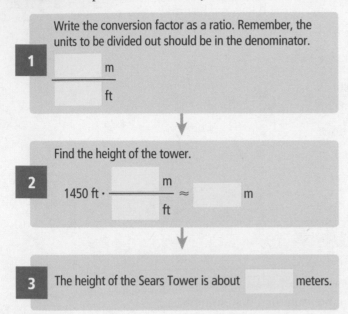

1 Write the conversion factor as a ratio. Remember, the units to be divided out should be in the denominator.

$$\frac{\boxed{}\ \text{m}}{\boxed{}\ \text{ft}}$$

2 Find the height of the tower.

$$1450\ \text{ft} \cdot \frac{\boxed{}\ \text{m}}{\boxed{}\ \text{ft}} \approx \boxed{}\ \text{m}$$

3 The height of the Sears Tower is about $\boxed{}$ meters.

You can also convert rates. Because rates compare measures in two different units, you must multiply by two conversion factors to change both of the units.

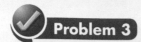 **Problem 4** **Converting Rates**

Got It? An athlete ran a sprint of 100 ft in 3.1 s. At what speed was the athlete running in miles per hour? Round to the nearest mile per hour.

18. Circle what you know. Underline what you want to find out.

speed of the athlete in feet per second   speed of the athlete in miles per hour

19. Underline the correct word to complete the sentence.

When writing a conversion factor, if the unit to be converted is in the numerator, then

that unit should be in the numerator / denominator of the conversion factor.

20. You will need to perform two conversions to solve the problem. Circle the conversion factor you will use to convert to miles per second. Underline the conversion factor you will use to convert to miles per hour.

$$\frac{1\ \text{mi}}{5280\ \text{ft}} \qquad \frac{5280\ \text{ft}}{1\ \text{mi}} \qquad \frac{3600\ \text{s}}{1\ \text{h}} \qquad \frac{1\ \text{h}}{3600\ \text{s}}$$

21. Use the conversion factors to solve the problem.

Lesson Check • Do you UNDERSTAND?

Reasoning Does multiplying by a conversion factor change the amount of what is being measured? How do you know?

22. Circle the equations that are true.

$$39 \cdot 1 = 39 \qquad 1 \cdot x = x \qquad x \cdot 1 = x + 1 \qquad \frac{5}{5} \cdot x = x$$

23. A conversion factor is always equal to ____ .

24. Underline the correct word, words, or number to complete the sentence.

Multiplying by a conversion factor changes / does not change what is being

measured because you are multiplying by 0 / 1 .

Lesson Check • Do you UNDERSTAND?

Reasoning If you convert pounds to ounces, will the number of ounces be *greater* or *less* than the number of pounds? Explain.

25. There are ____ ounces in 1 pound.

26. Convert 2 pounds to ounces.

$$2 \text{ lb} \cdot \frac{}{} = \boxed{} \text{ oz}$$

27. Convert 48 ounces to pounds.

$$48 \text{ oz} \cdot \frac{}{} = \boxed{} \text{ lb}$$

28. Underline the correct word to complete the sentence.
If you convert pounds to ounces, the number of ounces will be greater / le
than the number of pounds.

29. Explain your answer to Exercise 28.

_____

_____

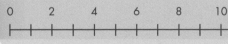

Math Success

Check off the vocabulary words that you understand.

☐ ratio ☐ rate ☐ unit rate ☐ conversion factor ☐ unit analysis

Rate how well you can *compare and convert ratios and rates.*

Need to review 0 2 4 6 8 10 Now I get it!

Lesson 2-6

Vocabulary

● **Review**

Write each *unit rate* in words.

1. 65 mi/h

sixty-five _____ per _____

2. 7 ft/day

seven _____ per _____

3. $3.99/lb

three dollars ninety-nine _____ per _____

4. 11 km/s

eleven _____ per _____

● **Vocabulary Builder**

proportion (noun) **pruh PAWR shun**

Definition: A **proportion** is an equation that states that two ratios are equal.

What It Means: Any equation of the form $\frac{a}{b} = \frac{c}{d}$, where $b \neq 0$ and $d \neq 0$, is a **proportion**. You read a proportion "*a* is to *b* as *c* is to *d*."

Related Word: proportional (adjective)

> A **proportion** always has an **equal sign**.
>
> $\frac{1}{5} = \frac{6}{30}$

● **Use Your Vocabulary**

Complete each statement with the correct word from the list below.

proportion   ratios   proportional

5. A scaled map of the roads in a city is __?__ to the actual roads.

_____

6. When making fruit punch, you have to be sure that the amount of ginger ale is in __?__ to the amount of fruit juice.

_____

7. Because $\frac{5}{8}$ is not equal to $\frac{15}{20}$, the __?__ $\frac{5}{8}$ and $\frac{15}{20}$ do not form a proportion.

_____

Problem 1 Solving a Proportion Using the Multiplication Property

Got It? What is the solution of the proportion $\frac{x}{7} = \frac{4}{5}$?

8. Use the justifications at the right to solve the proportion.

$$\frac{x}{7} = \frac{4}{5}$$ Write the original equation.

$$\boxed{} \cdot \frac{x}{7} = \boxed{} \cdot \frac{4}{5}$$ Multiply each side by $\boxed{}$.

$$\boxed{} = \frac{28}{5}$$ Simplify.

$$x = \boxed{}$$ Divide.

In the proportion $\frac{a}{b} = \frac{c}{d}$, the products *ad* and *bc* are called *cross products*. You can use the following property of cross products to solve proportions.

take note

Property   Cross Products Property of a Proportion

9. Complete the table.

Words	The cross products of a proportion are equal.
Algebra	If $\frac{a}{b} = \frac{c}{d}$, where $b \neq 0$ and $d \neq 0$, then $ad = \boxed{}$.
Example	$\frac{2}{3} = \frac{8}{12}$, so $2 \cdot \boxed{} = 3 \cdot \boxed{}$, or $24 = \boxed{}$.

 Problem 2 Solving a Proportion Using the Cross Products Property

Got It? What is the solution of the proportion $\frac{y}{3} = \frac{3}{5}$?

10. Use the model to help you find the cross products.

$$5 \cdot \boxed{} \longrightarrow \underset{\underset{3 \; = \; 5}{}}{(y) \times (3)} \longleftarrow 3 \cdot \boxed{}$$

11. Solve the proportion $\frac{y}{3} = \frac{3}{5}$.

Lesson 2-7

Got It? What is the solution of the proportion $\frac{n}{5} = \frac{2n + 4}{6}$?

12. Complete the reasoning model below.

Think	Write
First I write the original proportion.	
Next I use the Cross Products Property.	( )n = 5( )
Then I use the Distributive Property.	· n = 10 · +
I subtract 10n from each side.	$6n -$ = $10n +$ −
I simplify both sides.	· n =
Now I divide each side by −4.	$\dfrac{}{-4} = \dfrac{}{-4}$
Finally, I simplify.	n =

When you model a real-world situation with a proportion, you must write the proportion carefully. Be sure that the order of what is compared in each ratio is the same.

Correct: $\dfrac{100 \text{ mi}}{2 \text{ h}} = \dfrac{x \text{ mi}}{5 \text{ h}}$ **Incorrect:** $\dfrac{100 \text{ mi}}{2 \text{ h}} = \dfrac{5 \text{ h}}{x \text{ mi}}$

13. Suppose you can buy 3 pounds of meat for $12. Cross out the proportion below that will NOT help you find the cost of 5 pounds of meat.

$\dfrac{12 \text{ dollars}}{3 \text{ lb}} = \dfrac{x \text{ dollars}}{5 \text{ lb}}$ $\dfrac{12 \text{ dollars}}{3 \text{ lb}} = \dfrac{5 \text{ lb}}{x \text{ dollars}}$ $\dfrac{3 \text{ lb}}{12 \text{ dollars}} = \dfrac{5 \text{ lb}}{x \text{ dollars}}$

14. Suppose you need 9 pieces of wood to build 4 birdhouses. Cross out the proportion below that will NOT help you find the number of pieces of wood you will need to build 15 birdhouses.

$\dfrac{15 \text{ birdhouses}}{x \text{ pieces}} = \dfrac{4 \text{ birdhouses}}{9 \text{ pieces}}$ $\dfrac{9 \text{ pieces}}{4 \text{ birdhouses}} = \dfrac{x \text{ pieces}}{15 \text{ birdhouses}}$ $\dfrac{9 \text{ pieces}}{15 \text{ birdhouses}} = \dfrac{x \text{ pieces}}{4 \text{ birdhouses}}$

15. Suppose you can knit 3 scarves from 5 packages of yarn. Let x = the number of scarves you can knit from 12 packages of yarn. Complete the proportion.

$\dfrac{5 \text{ packages}}{3 \text{ scarves}} = \dfrac{}{}$

Problem 4 Using a Proportion to Solve a Problem

Got It? An 8-oz can of orange juice contains about 97 mg of vitamin C. About how many milligrams of vitamin C are there in a 12-oz can of orange juice?

16. Let $c = $ _____ .

17. Circle the proportion you will use to solve this problem.

$$\frac{8\text{ oz}}{12\text{ oz}} = \frac{c\text{ mg}}{97\text{ mg}} \qquad \frac{12\text{ oz}}{8\text{ oz}} = \frac{c\text{ mg}}{97\text{ mg}} \qquad \frac{8\text{ oz}}{97\text{ mg}} = \frac{12\text{ oz}}{c\text{ mg}} \qquad \frac{12\text{ oz}}{8\text{ oz}} = \frac{97\text{ mg}}{c\text{ mg}}$$

18. Solve the problem using the proportion you chose.

19. There are about _____ mg of vitamin C in a 12-oz can of orange juice.

 Lesson Check • **Do you UNDERSTAND?**

Reasoning When solving $\frac{x}{5} = \frac{3}{4}$, Lisa's first step was to write $4x = 5(3)$. Jen's first step was to write $20\left(\frac{x}{5}\right) = 20\left(\frac{3}{4}\right)$. Will both methods work? Explain.

20. Circle the property that Lisa used. Underline the property that Jen used.

Multiplication Property   Cross Products Property

21. Solve: $4x = 5(3)$.

22. Solve: $20\left(\frac{x}{5}\right) = 20\left(\frac{3}{4}\right)$.

23. Will both methods work? Explain.

Math Success

Check off the vocabulary words that you understand.

☐ proportion   ☐ cross products   ☐ Cross Products Property

Rate how well you can *solve proportions*.

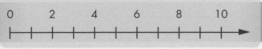

Lesson 2-7

Proportions and Similar Figures

Vocabulary

● Review

Do the ratios in each pair form a *proportion*? Explain.

1. $\frac{2}{5}$ and $\frac{10}{25}$

2. $\frac{1}{3}$ and $\frac{30}{100}$

● Vocabulary Builder

similar (adjective) <u>SIM</u> uh lur

Related Word: similarly (adverb)

Definition: Objects are **similar** if they are alike, but not necessarily identical.

Main Idea: In mathematics, **similar** figures have the same shape, but not necessarily the same size.

> **similar figures**
>
> same shape   different size

● Use Your Vocabulary

3. Explain how a lion and a giraffe are *similar*.

How is a lion like a giraffe?

How is a lion different from a giraffe?

4. Consider each pair of figures. Circle the figures that are *similar*.

The symbol ~ means "is similar to." In Problem 1 below, △ABC ~ △DEF.

In similar figures, the measures of corresponding angles are equal, and corresponding side lengths are in proportion. In Problem 1, the pairs of corresponding sides are $\overline{AB}$ and $\overline{DE}$, $\overline{AC}$ and $\overline{DF}$, and $\overline{BC}$ and $\overline{EF}$.

Problem 1 Finding the Length of a Side

Got It? In the diagram, △ABC ~ △DEF. What is AC?

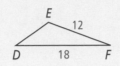

5. Underline the correct word or words to complete the sentence.

   Because the triangles are similar, the ratios of the corresponding sides are

   equal / not equal .

6. Use the diagram above. Circle the ratio that forms a proportion with $\frac{BC}{EF}$.

   $\frac{AC}{DE}$ $\frac{AC}{EF}$ $\frac{AC}{DF}$ $\frac{AC}{AB}$

7. Use the ratios from Exercise 6 to write a proportion. Solve your proportion for AC.

Problem 2 Applying Similarity

Got It? A man who is 6 ft tall is standing next to a flagpole. The shadow of the man is 3.5 ft and the shadow of the flagpole is 17.5 ft. What is the height of the flagpole?

8. Label the diagram. Let $h =$ the height of the flagpole.

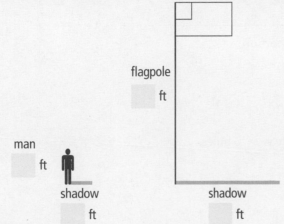

Lesson 2-8

9. Complete the reasoning model below.

Think	Write
First I write a proportion to find the height, h, of the flagpole.	$\dfrac{6}{\boxed{}} = \dfrac{h}{\boxed{}}$
Then I use the Cross Products Property.	$\boxed{} \cdot h = 6 \cdot \boxed{}$
Then I simplify.	$3.5h = \boxed{}$
Now I divide each side by 3.5.	$\dfrac{3.5h}{\boxed{}} = \dfrac{\boxed{}}{\boxed{}}$
And now I simplify.	$h = \boxed{}$
Finally I write a sentence to answer the question.	The height of the flagpole is $\boxed{}$ ft.

 Problem 3 **Interpreting Scale Drawings**

Got It? On a map the scale is 1 in. : 110 mi. The distance from Jacksonville to Gainesville on the map is about 0.6 in. What is the actual distance from Jacksonville to Gainesville?

10. Let $x = $ _____ .

11. Use the given information to write and solve a proportion.

12. The actual distance from Jacksonville to Gainesville is $\boxed{}$ miles.

Problem 4 **Using Scale Models**

Got It? A scale model of a building is 6 in. tall. The scale of the model is 1 in. : 50 ft. How tall is the actual building?

13. Complete the equation in the model.

Relate   [scale of model]   equals

Define   Let x = the actual height of the building.

Write $\square$ $=$ $\dfrac{\square}{\square}$

14. Now write and solve a proportion.

15. The actual building is [ ] ft tall.

Lesson Check • Do you UNDERSTAND?

Reasoning Suppose $\triangle ABC \sim \triangle TUV$. Determine whether each pair of measures is equal.

the measures of $\angle A$ and $\angle T$ the perimeters of the two triangles   the ratios of the sides $\dfrac{BC}{UV}$ and $\dfrac{\ }{V}$

Underline the correct word to complete each sentence.

16. In similar triangles, corresponding sides always have the same length / ratio .

17. In similar triangles, corresponding angles always have equal / unequal measures.

Use the triangles at the right. Write T for *true* or F for *false*.

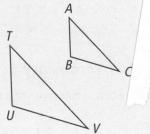

___ **18.** The measures of $\angle A$ and $\angle T$ are equal.

___ **19.** The perimeters of the two triangles are equal.

___ **20.** The ratios $\dfrac{BC}{UV}$ and $\dfrac{AC}{TV}$ are equal.

Math Success

Check off the vocabulary words that you understand.

☐ similar figures   ☐ scale   ☐ scale drawing   ☐ scale model

Rate how well you can *use proportions to solve similar-figure problems*.

Need to review   0   2   4   6   8   10   Now I get it!

Percents

Vocabulary

● Review

1. Circle each *rational* number.

$$\sqrt{5} \qquad \frac{19}{100} \qquad \sqrt{64} \qquad -3.89$$

Write an *equivalent fraction* with a denominator of 100.

2. $\frac{4}{5}$ **3.** $\frac{7}{25}$ **4.** $\frac{8}{50}$

● Vocabulary Builder

percent (noun) pur SENT

Related Words: cents (noun), century (noun), centimeter (noun)

Definition: A **percent** is a ratio that compares a number to 100.

Word Origin: **per** means "for every"; **-cent** means "hundred." So, 39 **percent** means "39 for every hundred."

> The symbol for **percent** is %.

● Use Your Vocabulary

Complete each statement with the correct word from the list below.

> percent   cents   century   centimeters

5. One dollar has the same value as 100 __?__ .

6. There are 100 years in a __?__ .

7. There are 100 __?__ in 1 meter.

8. One part out of 100 is 1 __?__ .

13. Complete the equation in the model.

Relate   scale of model   equals $\dfrac{\text{model height}}{\text{actual height}}$

Define   Let $x =$ the actual height of the building.

Write $\boxed{} = \dfrac{\boxed{}}{\boxed{}}$

14. Now write and solve a proportion.

15. The actual building is $\boxed{}$ ft tall.

Lesson Check   •   Do you UNDERSTAND?

Reasoning Suppose $\triangle ABC \sim \triangle TUV$. Determine whether each pair of measures is equal.

the measures of $\angle A$ and $\angle T$ the perimeters of the two triangles   the ratios of the sides $\dfrac{BC}{UV}$ and $\dfrac{AC}{TV}$

Underline the correct word to complete each sentence.

16. In similar triangles, corresponding sides always have the same length / ratio .

17. In similar triangles, corresponding angles always have equal / unequal measures.

Use the triangles at the right. Write T for *true* or F for *false*.

_____ **18.** The measures of $\angle A$ and $\angle T$ are equal.

_____ **19.** The perimeters of the two triangles are equal.

_____ **20.** The ratios $\dfrac{BC}{UV}$ and $\dfrac{AC}{TV}$ are equal.

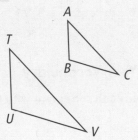

Math Success

Check off the vocabulary words that you understand.

☐ similar figures   ☐ scale   ☐ scale drawing   ☐ scale model

Rate how well you can *use proportions to solve similar-figure problems.*

| Need to review | 0 | 2 | 4 | 6 | 8 | 10 | Now I get it! |

Lesson 2-8

2-9 Percents

Vocabulary

● Review

1. Circle each *rational* number.

$\sqrt{5}$ $\qquad$ $\frac{19}{100}$ $\qquad$ $\sqrt{64}$ $\qquad$ -3.89

Write an *equivalent fraction* with a denominator of 100.

2. $\frac{4}{5}$ $\qquad$ **3.** $\frac{7}{25}$ $\qquad$ **4.** $\frac{8}{50}$

● Vocabulary Builder

> **percent** (noun) **pur SENT**
>
> **Related Words:** cents (noun), century (noun), centimeter (noun)
>
> **Definition:** A **percent** is a ratio that compares a number to 100.
>
> **Word Origin:** **per** means "for every"; **-cent** means "hundred."
> So, 39 **percent** means "39 for every hundred."

> The symbol for
> **percent**
> is
> %.

● Use Your Vocabulary

Complete each statement with the correct word from the list below.

percent   cents   century   centimeters

5. One dollar has the same value as 100 __?__ .

6. There are 100 years in a __?__ .

7. There are 100 __?__ in 1 meter.

8. One part out of 100 is 1 __?__ .

Chapter 2

70

Key Concept   The Percent Proportion and Percent Equation

You can represent "*a* is *p* percent of *b*" using either the percent proportion or the percent equation. In each case, *b* is the *base* and *a* is a *part* of *base b*.

The Percent Proportion

$$\frac{a}{b} = \frac{p}{100}$$

where base $b \neq 0$

The Percent Equation

$$a = p\% \cdot b$$

9. Complete the percent proportion and the percent equation by placing *part, whole,* and *p* in the correct places.

$$\frac{\boxed{}}{\text{whole}} = \frac{\boxed{}}{100}$$

$$\text{part} = \boxed{}\% \cdot \boxed{}$$

Problem 2 Finding a Percent Using the Percent Equation

Got It?   Reasoning What percent of 84 is 63? Use the percent equation to solve. Then use the percent proportion. Compare your answers.

10. Solve the *percent equation* for *p*.

$$\text{part} = p\% \cdot \text{whole}$$

$$63 = p\% \cdot \boxed{}$$

$$\frac{63}{\boxed{}} = p\%$$

$$\boxed{} = p\%$$

$$(\boxed{} \cdot 100)\% = p\%$$

$$\boxed{} = p$$

11. Solve the *percent proportion* for *p*.

$$\frac{\text{part}}{\text{whole}} = \frac{p}{100}$$

$$\frac{\boxed{}}{84} = \frac{p}{\boxed{}}$$

$$\boxed{} \cdot 100 = \boxed{} \cdot p$$

$$\boxed{} = 84p$$

$$\boxed{} = p$$

12. Compare your answers.

_____

_____

Problem 3 Finding a Part

Got It? A family sells a car to a dealership for 60% less than they paid for it. They paid $9000 for the car. For what price did they sell the car?

13. Complete the model. Then use the model to complete and solve the percent proportion.

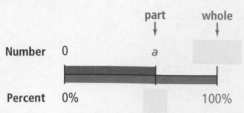

part   whole

Number   0   a   [ ]

Percent   0%   [ ]   100%

$$\frac{a}{\boxed{}} = \frac{\boxed{}}{100}$$

$$100a = \boxed{} \cdot \boxed{}$$

$$100a = \boxed{}$$

$$\frac{100a}{\boxed{}} = \frac{\boxed{}}{\boxed{}}$$

$$a = \boxed{}$$

14. Find the selling price of the car: $9000 - \boxed{} = \boxed{}$

 15. The family sold the car for $\$\boxed{}$.

✓ Problem 4 Finding a Base

Got It? 30% of what number is 12.5? Solve the problem using the percent equation. Then solve the problem using the percent proportion.

16. In the problem, the unknown quantity is base b / part a .

17. Solve the problem using the percent equation and the percent proportion.

Percent Equation
$$a = p\% \cdot b$$

Percent Proportion
$$\frac{a}{b} = \frac{p}{100}$$

18. 30% of $\boxed{}$ is about 12.5.

take note

Key Concept   Simple Interest Formula

Simple interest is interest you earn on only the principal in an account. The simple interest formula is given below, where I is the interest, P is the principal, r is the annual interest rate, written as a decimal, and t is the time in years.

$$I = Prt$$

19. You invest $100 at a simple interest rate of 2.5% per year for 6 years. Write an equation to show how much interest you will earn.

First, write the interest rate, 2.5%, as a decimal.

Remember to insert leading zeros. $2.5\% = \boxed{}$

Now write the equation. $I = \boxed{} \cdot \boxed{} \cdot \boxed{}$

Problem 5 Using the Simple Interest Formula

Got It? You deposited $125 in a savings account that earns a simple interest rate of 1.75% per year. You earned a total of $8.75 in interest. For how long was your money in the account?

20. Complete the model.

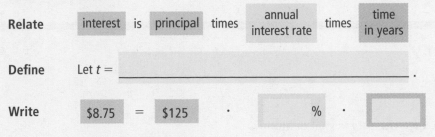

Relate | interest | is | principal | times | annual interest rate | times | time in years

Define | Let $t = $ _____ .

Write | $8.75 | = | $125 | · | % | · | [ ]

21. As a decimal, 1.75% = [ ] .

22. Now solve for t.

23. Your money was in the account for [ ] years.

Lesson Check • Do you UNDERSTAND?

Open-Ended Give an example of a percent problem where the part is greater than the base.

24. Place a ✓ if the situation has a part greater than the whole. Place an ✗ if the situation does NOT have a part greater than the whole.

| [ ] The green marbles in a jar of red, green, and blue marbles | [ ] Your math test score when you answer every question and the extra credit question correctly | ...rt of chicken stew that is chicken |

Math Success

Check off the vocabulary words that you understand.

☐ percent   ☐ part   ☐ base

Rate how well you can *solve percent problems*.

Need to review | 0 2 4 6 8 10 | Now I get it!

2-10 Change Expressed as a Percent

Vocabulary

● **Review**

1. What is a *percent*? Use the term *ratio* in your definition.

_____

_____

_____

2. Write the *percent* of a dollar each coin represents.

penny   nickel   dime   quarter

⬚ %   ⬚ %   ⬚ %   ⬚ %

● **Vocabulary Builder**

change (noun) **chaynj**

Main Idea: When a quantity increases or decreases, it undergoes a **change**.

Examples: If the temperature of a room **changes** from 78°F to 75°F, the **change** is a *decrease* of 3°F. If the temperature of the room **changes** from 65°F to 69°F, the **change** is an *increase* of 4°F.

● **Use Your Vocabulary**

Describe each *change* as an *increase* or a *decrease*.

3. 72 to 84   **4.** 25 to 16   **5.** $.99 to $1.02

_____   _____   _____

You can find the percent change when you know the original amount and how much it has changed.

If the new amount is greater than the original amount, the percent change is a *percent increase*. If the new amount is less than the original amount, the percent change is a *percent decrease*.

Key Concept   Percent Change

Percent change is the ratio of the **amount of change** to the original amount. The **amount of change** is the amount of increase or decrease.

> **Percent Change**
>
> $$p\% = \frac{\text{amount of increase or decrease}}{\text{original amount}}$$

6. Draw a line from each phrase in Column A to the correct subtraction expression in Column B.

Column A	Column B
amount of increase	original amount − new amount
amount of decrease	new amount − original amount

 Problem 1   Finding a Percent Decrease

Got It? The average monthly precipitation for Chicago, Illinois, peaks in June at 4.1 in. The average precipitation in December is 2.8 in. What is the percent decrease from June to December?

7. Write an expression to show the change in temperature from June to December.

☐ − ☐

8. Complete the equation.

$$\text{Percent change} = \frac{\boxed{} - \boxed{}}{4.1} \qquad \text{Substitute.}$$

$$= \frac{\boxed{}}{4.1} \qquad \text{Simpli}$$

$$\approx \boxed{}\,\% \qquad \text{W}\ldots \text{s a percent.}$$

9. The percent decrease in precipitation is about ☐%.

 Problem 2   Finding a Percent Increase

Got It? In one year, the toll for passenger cars to use a tunnel rose from $3 to $3.50. What was the percent increase?

10. The new amount of the toll is $ ☐ .

The original amount of the toll is $ ☐ .

11. Explain how you know you are finding a percent increase.

_____

_____

_____

Lesson 2-10

12. Substitute the values you know into the Percent Change formula.

Percent change = $\dfrac{\boxed{} - \boxed{}}{\boxed{}}$

13. Now solve the equation. Write the result as a percent.

14. The price of the toll increased by about ☐ %.

Problem 3 **Finding Percent Error**

Got It? You think that the distance between your house and a friend's house is 5.5 mi. The actual distance is 4.75 mi. What is the percent error in your estimation?

15. In the percent error ratio, you find an absolute value in the numerator. The absolute value of a number is always negative / nonnegative .

16. Complete the steps to solve the problem.

percent error $= \dfrac{|\text{estimated value} - \text{actual value}|}{\text{actual value}}$ Write the ratio.

$= \dfrac{|\,5.5 - \boxed{}\,|}{\boxed{}}$ Substitute.

$= \dfrac{\boxed{}}{\boxed{}}$ Simplify.

$\approx \boxed{}$, or about $\boxed{}$ %   Write the result as a percent.

Problem 5 **Finding the Greatest Possible Percent Error**

Got It? The diagram at the right shows the dimensions of a gift box to the nearest inch. Its measured volume is 360 in.^{3}, and the greatest possible error in volume is about 24%. If the gift box's dimensions were taken to the nearest half inch, how would the greatest possible error be affected?

5 in.

12 in.

6 in.

17. The greatest possible error in each measurement is half the unit of measure. Find the least and greatest possible measurements for each dimension.

$5 - 0.25 = \boxed{}$ $6 - 0.25 = \boxed{}$ $12 - \boxed{} = \boxed{}$

$5 + 0.25 = \boxed{}$ $6 + \boxed{} = \boxed{}$ $\boxed{} + \boxed{} = \boxed{}$

18. Find the minimum and maximum possible volumes. Use $V = \ell wh$.

$V = (11.75) \cdot (5.75) \cdot$ ⬚ $V = (12.25) \cdot (6.25) \cdot$ ⬚

$\approx$ ⬚ in.^{3} $\approx$ ⬚ in.^{3}

19. Now find the differences and circle the greater difference.

minimum volume difference   maximum volume difference

$360 -$ ⬚ $=$ ⬚   ⬚ $- 360 =$ ⬚

20. Complete the equation to determine the greatest possible percent error.

$$\frac{\text{greater difference in volume}}{\text{measured volume}} = \frac{⬚}{360} \approx ⬚ \text{, or about } ⬚ \%$$

21. Compare your answer from Exercise 20 to the original greatest possible error of about 24%. How is greatest possible error affected if you measure to the nearest half inch rather than to the nearest inch?

_____

_____

Lesson Check • Do you UNDERSTAND?

Vocabulary Determine whether each situation involves a *percent increase* or a *percent decrease*.

A hat that originally   You buy a CD for   A store buys glasses wholesale for
cost $12 sold for $9.50. $10 and sell it for $8.   per glass. The store sells them for $⬚.50.

Underline the correct word to complete each sentence.

22. When the new amount is greater than the original amount, the percent change is a

percent increase / decrease .

23. When the new amount is less than the original amount, the percent change is a

percent increase / decrease .

24. The price of the hat went down, so it is a percent increase / decrease .

25. The price of the CD went down, so it is a percent increase / decrease .

26. The price of the glasses went up / down , so it is a percent increase / decrease .

Math Success

Check off the vocabulary words that you understand.

☐ percent change   ☐ percent increase   ☐ percent decrease   ☐ percent error

Rate how well you can *solve percent increase and decrease problems*.

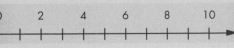

Lesson 2-10

3-1 Inequalities and Their Graphs

Vocabulary

● Review

1. Cross out any points that are NOT solutions of the *equation* $-5g = -15$.

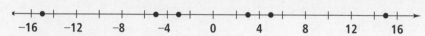

$$-16 \quad -12 \quad -8 \quad -4 \quad 0 \quad 4 \quad 8 \quad 12 \quad 16$$

2. Write two *equations* using 3, 13, and k.

● Vocabulary Builder

> **inequality symbols**
> $<, >, \geq, \leq, \neq$

inequality (noun) **in ee KWAL uh tee**

Definition: An **inequality** is a mathematical sentence that uses an **inequality** symbol to compare the values of two expressions.

Examples: The mathematical sentences $3 > 2$, $5 + 7 < 21$, and $x - 2 \leq 4$ are **inequalities.**

Nonexamples: The mathematical sentences $4 + 4 = 8$ and $x - 5 = 1$ are *not* **inequalities.** They are equations.

● Use Your Vocabulary

3. Where does each mathematical sentence belong? Write each *inequality* or equation in the correct box.

$17 \geq 5$ $\qquad$ $3x = 9$ $\qquad$ $2x > 5$ $\qquad$ $2(4) = 8$ $\qquad$ $8 < 3x$

Inequality	**Equation**

4. Complete each *inequality* with $<$, $>$, $\leq$, or $\geq$.

$z < 4$, so $4 \ \boxed{} \ z$ $\qquad$ $g \geq -2$ so $-2 \ \boxed{} \ g$ $\qquad$ $m < 7$, so $7 \ \boxed{} \ m$

Problem 1 Writing Inequalities

Got It? What is an inequality that represents the verbal expression?

> all real numbers *p* greater than or equal to 1.5

Use the verbal expression. Write T for *true* or F for *false*.

_____ **5.** A real number *p* could be less than 1.5.

_____ **6.** A real number *p* could be equal to 1.5.

_____ **7.** A real number *p* could be greater than 1.5.

8. Circle the symbol that represents "greater than or equal to."

$<$ $>$ $\leq$ $\geq$

9. Complete the inequality that represents the verbal phrase.

p ☐ 1.5

Problem 2 Identifying Solutions by Evaluating

Got It? Consider the numbers $-1, 0, 1,$ and 3. Which are solutions of $13 - 7y \leq 6$?

10. Check whether -1 is a solution of the inequality. Complete the steps below.

$13 - 7y \leq 6$	Write the original inequality.
$13 - 7 \cdot \boxed{} \overset{?}{\leq} 6$	Substitute the value for *y*.
$13 - \boxed{} \overset{?}{\leq} 6$	Multiply.
$\boxed{} \overset{?}{\leq} 6$	Simplify.

11. Underline the correct word(s) to complete each sentence.

When *y* is replaced with -1, the inequality is true / false .

So, -1 is / is not a solution.

12. Repeat with the other possible solutions: 0, 1, and 3.

13. Circle the numbers that are solutions of $13 - 7y \leq 6$.

-1 $\qquad$ 0 $\qquad$ 1 $\qquad$ 3

Lesson 3-1

A closed dot on a graph means the number is part of the solution. An open dot on a graph means the number is *not* part of the solution.

14. The endpoint of each graph is −3. Is −3 a solution of the inequality represented by the graph? Explain why or why not.

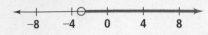

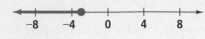

_____   _____

15. Write the endpoint of each graph of an inequality. Then explain why the endpoint *is* or *is not* a solution of the inequality.

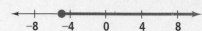

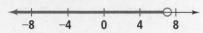

_____   _____

_____   _____

_____   _____

 Problem 3 Graphing an Inequality

Got It? What is the graph of the inequality $x > -4$?

16. Circle the words that complete the sentence.

The solutions of the inequality $x > -4$ are all numbers __?__ −4.

  greater than   less than   greater than or equal to   less than or equal to

17. Underline the correct word or words to complete each sentence.

The graph of $x > -4$ includes / does not include −4.

The graph of $x > -4$ will have an open / a closed dot at −4.

18. Graph the solutions of the inequality $x > -4$ on the number line.

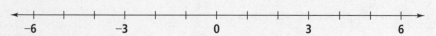

Problem 4 Writing an Inequality From a Graph

Got It? What inequality represents the graph?

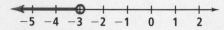

19. Circle all statements that describe the graph.

  open dot   shaded to the right of −3   numbers greater than −3 are included

  closed dot   shaded to the left of −3   numbers less than −3 are included

20. **Multiple Choice** Which inequality represents the graph?

  Ⓐ $x > -3$ Ⓑ $x < -3$ Ⓒ $x \geq -3$ Ⓓ $x \leq -3$

Problem 5 Writing Real-World Inequalities

Got It? **Reasoning** The inequality $s \le 8$ describes a situation where s is a legal speed. Can the speed be *all* real numbers less than or equal to 8? Explain.

21. Write *stopped, moving,* or *doesn't make sense* to describe each speed. Then circle a word to answer the question.

Speed	Description	Is it possible?
5	_____	Yes / No
0	_____	Yes / No
−3	_____	Yes / No

22. Can the speed be *all* real numbers less than or equal to 8? Explain.

_____

_____

Lesson Check • Do you UNDERSTAND?

Compare and Contrast What are some situations you could model with $x \ge 0$?
How do they differ from situations you could model with $x > 0$?

23. Use the situations at the right. Write each one on the correct line.

$x \ge 0$: _____

$x > 0$: _____

24. Describe how the situations for $x \ge 0$ differ from the situations for $x > 0$.

_____

_____

_____

- Counting numbers
- Length of a poster
- One baseball team's score
- Whole numbers
- Distance from your home to a park
- Inches of rain

Math Success

Check off the vocabulary words that you understand.

☐ inequality   ☐ solution of an inequality   ☐ graph of an inequality

Rate how well you can *write and graph inequalities.*

Need to review 0 2 4 6 8 10 Now I get it!

Lesson 3-1

3-2 Solving Inequalities Using Addition or Subtraction

Vocabulary

● Review

1. Write an *inequality symbol* to represent each verbal description.

Symbol	Verbal Description	Symbol	Verbal Description
	• less than, fewer than		• less than or equal to • at most, no greater than • as much as, no more than
	• greater than, more than		• greater than or equal to • at least, no less than • as little as, no fewer than

● Vocabulary Builder

equivalent (adjective) **ee KWIV uh lunt**

Related Word: equal

Main Idea: Numbers or expressions are **equivalent** when they have equal values.

Examples: $\frac{12}{4}$ is **equivalent** to 3.

The expression $1 + 6$ is **equivalent** to $9 - 2$.

● Use Your Vocabulary

Equivalent inequalities are inequalities that have the same solutions. Write an inequality that is *equivalent* to the inequality that is given.

2. Since $10 \geq -3, -3 \boxed{} 10$.

3. Since $-7 < -1, -1 \boxed{} -7$.

4. If $b > -10$, then $-10 \boxed{} b$.

5. If $h \leq 0$, then $0 \boxed{} h$.

6. Cross out the equations that are NOT *equivalent* to $x = 3$.

$3 = x$	$x = \frac{1}{3}$	$x + 2 = 5$	$x + 2 = 5 - 2$

7. Cross out the inequalities that are NOT *equivalent* to $x \leq 3$.

$3 \geq x$	$x \leq \frac{1}{3}$	$x + 2 \geq 5$	$x + 2 \leq 5 - 2$

Key Concept Addition and Subtraction Properties of Inequality

When you add or subtract the same number on each side of an inequality, the relationship between the two sides does not change.

Complete each inequality using either the *Addition Property of Inequality* or the *Subtraction Property of Inequality*.

8. Since $3 > -1$, $3 + 5 > -1 + $ $\boxed{}$.

9. Since $4 \leq 9$, $4 + n \leq 9 + $ $\boxed{}$.

10. If $z < 8$, then $z - (-4) < 8 - $ $\boxed{}$.

11. If $w \geq k$, then $w - t \geq k - $ $\boxed{}$.

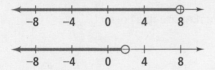

Problem 1 Using the Addition Property of Inequality

Got It? What are the solutions of $n - 5 < -3$? Graph the solutions.

12. First add 5 to both sides of $n - 5 < -3$. Then simplify.

$$n - 5 + \boxed{} < -3 + \boxed{}$$

$$n < \boxed{}$$

13. Circle the graph that shows the solutions of $n - 5 < -3$.

Problem 2 Solving an Inequality and Checking Solutions

Got It? What are the solutions of $m - 11 \geq -2$? Graph and check the solutions.

14. Underline the correct words to complete the sentence.

To isolate the variable, add 11 to / subtract −2 from each side of the equation.

15. Solve the inequality.

16. Graph the inequality on the number line below.

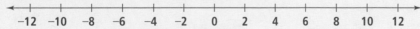

Lesson 3-2

17. Check the related equation.
Substitute for m in $m - 11 = -2$.

$$\boxed{} - 11 \overset{?}{=} -2$$

$$\boxed{} = -2$$

Does it check? Yes / No

18. Check the inequality symbol by replacing m with one of your solutions to Exercise 16.

$$m - 11 \geq -2$$

$$\boxed{} - 11 \overset{?}{\geq} -2$$

$$\boxed{} \geq -2$$

Does it check? Yes / No

 Problem 3 Using the Subtraction Property of Inequality

Got It? What are the solutions of $-1 \geq y + 12$? Graph the solutions.

19. Subtract 12 from both sides of the inequality. Then simplify.

$$-1 - \boxed{} \geq y + 12 - \boxed{}$$

$$\boxed{} \geq y$$

20. Graph the inequality on the number line.

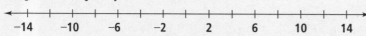

```
   -14   -10   -6   -2    2    6    10   14
```

21. Check your solution in the related equation and inequality to make sure it is correct.

Is your solution correct? Yes / No

Problem 4 Writing and Solving an Inequality

Got It? A club has a goal to sell at least 25 plants for a fundraiser. Club members sell 8 plants on Wednesday and 9 plants on Thursday. What are the possible numbers of plants the club can sell on Friday to meet their goal?

22. Circle the inequality that represents *at least*.

| $<$ | $>$ | $\leq$ | $\geq$ |

23. Complete the model below.

Relate plants sold Wednesday   plus   plants sold Thursday   plus   plants sold Friday   is at least   25

Define Let $p = $ _____

Write   8 $+$ $\boxed{}$ $+$ $\boxed{}$ $\boxed{}$ 25

24. Simplify and solve the inequality.

25. Club members must sell at least [ ] plants on Friday to meet their goal.

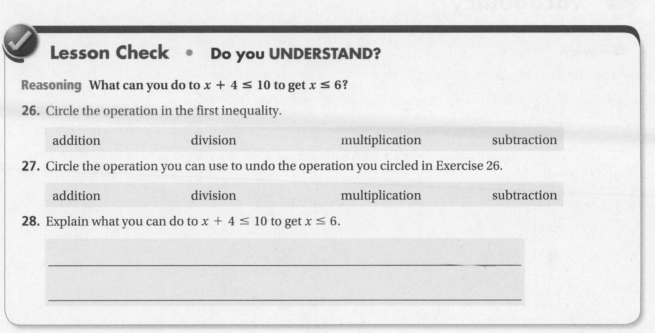

Lesson Check • Do you UNDERSTAND?

Reasoning What can you do to $x + 4 \leq 10$ to get $x \leq 6$?

26. Circle the operation in the first inequality.

addition   division   multiplication   subtraction

27. Circle the operation you can use to undo the operation you circled in Exercise 26.

addition   division   multiplication   subtraction

28. Explain what you can do to $x + 4 \leq 10$ to get $x \leq 6$.

_____

_____

Math Success

Check off the vocabulary words that you understand.

☐ equivalent inequalities   ☐ Addition and Subtraction Properties of Inequality

Rate how well you can *solve inequalities by adding or subtracting*.

Need to review   0   2   4   6   8   10   Now I get it!

Lesson 3-2

Vocabulary

● Review

1. Circle each *inequality*.

$5 + x < 6$ $\qquad$ $7 - y \geq 2$ $\qquad$ $a + b = 12$

$\qquad$ $m - 3 > 5$ $\qquad$ $2 + 3 = 3 + 2$ $\qquad$ $n + 3 \neq 8$

2. Draw a line from each *inequality* in Column A to an equivalent *inequality* in Column B.

Column A	Column B
$x + 7 < 11$	$11 \geq x + 7$
$x + 7 \geq 11$	$11 > x + 7$
$7 + x \leq 11$	$11 \leq x + 7$
$7 + x > 11$	$11 < x + 7$

● Vocabulary Builder

reverse

reverse (verb) rih VURS

Related Words: flip (verb), reversible (adjective), reverse (noun)

Definition: To **reverse** something means to turn it in an opposite direction.

Example: The Supreme Court has the power to **reverse** or uphold decisions made by the lower courts.

● Use Your Vocabulary

3. *Reverse* each inequality symbol below. Write the new symbol in the box.

$\leq$ $\qquad$ $>$ $\qquad$ $<$ $\qquad$ $\geq$

4. If the inequality symbol in $x < 2$ is *reversed*, tell how the solutions change.

_____

_____

Key Concept Multiplication Property of Inequality

When you multiply each side of an inequality by a positive number, *do not reverse* the direction of the inequality symbol.

Let a, b, and c be real numbers with $c > 0$.

If $a > b$, then $ac > bc$.   If $a < b$, then $ac < bc$.

Write $<$, $>$, $\leq$, or $\geq$ to complete each inequality.

5. $6 > 4$

$\dfrac{6}{2}$ ▢ $\dfrac{4}{2}$

3 ▢ 2

6. $2 \leq 3$

$2(5)$ ▢ $3(5)$

10 ▢ ▢

7. $-12 < -9$

$\dfrac{-12}{3}$ ▢ $\dfrac{-9}{3}$

▢ ▢ -3

8. If $p < q$ and $r > 0$, then pr ▢ qr.

When you multiply each side of an inequality by a negative number, *reverse* the direction of the inequality symbol.

Let a, b, and c be real numbers with $c < 0$.

If $a > b$, then $ac < bc$.   If $a < b$, then $ac > bc$.

Write $<$, $>$, $\leq$, or $\geq$ to complete each inequality.

9. $6 > 4$

$\dfrac{6}{-2}$ ▢ $\dfrac{4}{-2}$

-3 ▢ -2

10. $2 \leq 3$

$2(-5)$ ▢ $3(-5)$

-10 ▢ ▢

11. $-12 < -9$

$\dfrac{-12}{-3}$ ▢ $\dfrac{-9}{-3}$

▢ ▢ 3

12. If $g < h$ and $k < 0$, then $\dfrac{g}{k}$ ▢ $\dfrac{h}{k}$.

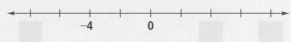

Problem 1 Multiplying by a Positive Number

Got It? What are the solutions of $\dfrac{c}{8} > \dfrac{1}{4}$? Graph the solutions.

13. Circle the first step in solving $\dfrac{c}{8} > \dfrac{1}{4}$.

Add 8 to each side.	Subtract 8 from each side.
Multiply each side by 8.	Divide each side by 8.

14. What must you do to the inequality symbol when solving $\dfrac{c}{8} > \dfrac{1}{4}$? Explain.

_____

15. Solve the inequality.

$\dfrac{c}{8} > \dfrac{1}{4}$

$\dfrac{c}{8}(8) > \dfrac{1}{4} \cdot$ ▢

c ▢ ▢

16. Graph the inequality on the number line.

$\leftarrow$ + + ▢ + + + ▢ + ▢ $\rightarrow$
             -4 0

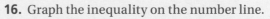

Lesson 3-3

Problem 2 Multiplying by a Negative Number

Got It? What are the solutions of $-\frac{n}{3} < -1$? Graph and check.

17. Circle the first step in solving $-\frac{n}{3} < -1$.

| Add -3 to each side. | Subtract -3 from each side. |
| Multiply each side by -3. | Divide each side by -3. |

18. What must you do to the inequality symbol when solving $-\frac{n}{3} < -1$? Explain.

_____

19. Solve the inequality.

$$-\frac{n}{3} < -1$$

$$-\frac{n}{3}(-3) > -1 \cdot \boxed{}$$

$$n \boxed{} \boxed{}$$

20. Graph the inequality.

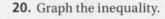

21. Check the solution by following the steps below.

$$-\frac{n}{3} < -1 \qquad \text{Write the original inequality.}$$

$$-\frac{\boxed{}}{3} \overset{?}{<} -1 \qquad \text{Substitute a value that makes the simplified inequality true.}$$

$$\boxed{} \overset{?}{<} -1 \qquad \text{Simplify and check.}$$

22. Is your solution correct? Yes / No

 Problem 3 Dividing by a Positive Number

Got It? A student club plans to buy food for a soup kitchen. A case of vegetables costs \$10.68. The club can spend at most \$50 for this project. What are the possible numbers of cases the club can buy?

23. Complete the model below.

| **Relate** | the cost of a case of vegetables | times | the number of cases | is at most | \$50 |

Define Let $c =$ the number of cases the club can buy.

| **Write** | $\boxed{}$ | $\cdot$ | $\boxed{}$ | $\leq$ | \$50 |

24. Now solve the inequality.

25. Circle the possible numbers of cases of vegetables the club can buy.

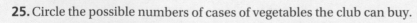

| 1 | 2 | 3 | 4 | 5 |

Got It? What are the solutions of $-5x > -10$? Graph the solutions.

26. To solve $-5x > -10$, will you reverse the inequality symbol? Why or why not?

_____

_____

27. Solve the inequality.

28. Graph the inequality on the number line.

Error Analysis Describe and correct the error in the solution.

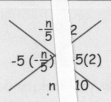

29. Describe the student's first step.

_____

30. What is the error in the student's solution?

_____

31. What is the correct solution?

Math Success

Check off the vocabulary words that you understand.

☐ inequality ☐ Multiplication Property of Inequality ☐ Division Property of Inequality

Rate how well you can *solve inequalities by multiplying or dividing*.

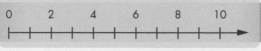

Vocabulary

● Review

1. Multiple Choice You must *reverse* the direction of an inequality symbol when you multiply both sides of an inequality by a number that is __?__ .

- Ⓐ less than 0
- Ⓑ greater than 0
- Ⓒ less than or equal to 0
- Ⓓ greater than or equal to 0

2. Write *reverse* if the inequality symbol will change when you solve the inequality. Write *same* if the symbol will remain the same.

$3t < 6$	$-8s < 4$	$5x \leq -10$	$-4 \leq -2a$
_____	_____	_____	_____

● Vocabulary Builder

at least (adverbial phrase) **at leest**; **at most** (adverbial phrase) **at mohst**

Main Idea: The phrase **at least** describes the least possible number that can be used. The phrase **at most** describes the greatest possible number that can be used.

Using Symbols: The inequality $x \geq 5$ means "x is **at least** 5." The inequality $x \leq 5$ means "x is **at most** 5."

● Use Your Vocabulary

3. Complete each sentence with the words *at least* or *at most*.

You must be __?__ 18 years of age to vote in a national election.

_____

An elevator can safely carry __?__ 15 people.

_____

When water boils, you know the temperature is __?__ 212°F.

_____

If all books cost $3 and Jane has $20, she can buy __?__ 6 books.

_____

4. Use your answers to Exercise 3. Complete each inequality with $\leq$ or $\geq$.

y ___ 18	e ___ 15	w ___ 212	$3b$ ___ 20

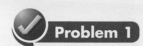

Problem 1 Using More Than One Step

Got It? What are the solutions of the inequality $-6a - 7 \leq 17$?
Check your solutions.

5. Circle the first step in solving the inequality. Then underline the second step.

Add 7 to each side.	Divide each side by 6.	Divide each side by -6 and reverse the inequality.
Subtract 7 from each side.	Multiply each side by 6.	Multiply each side by -6 and reverse the inequality.

6. Use your answers to Exercise 5 to solve the inequality.

7. Check the endpoint by substituting into the related equation, $-6a - 7 = 17$.

8. Check the inequality symbol by substituting into the original inequality, $-6a - 7 \leq 17$.

Problem 2 Writing and Solving a Multi-Step Inequality

Got It? You want to make a rectangular banner that is 18 ft long. You have no more
than 48 ft of trim for the banner. What are the possible widths of the banner?

9. Circle the formula for the perimeter of a rectangle.

$$C = 2\pi r \qquad\qquad A = \ell w \qquad\qquad d = rt \qquad\qquad P = 2\ell + 2w$$

10. Write an algebraic expression to describe the distance around a rectangular banner with a length of 18 ft and a width of w ft.

11. The distance around the banner should be at least / at most 48 feet.

12. Use the expression you wrote in Exercise 10 and the information from Exercise 11. Write an inequality to represent the situation described in the problem. Then solve your inequality.

13. The width of the banner should be at most ____ feet.

91

Problem 3 Using the Distributive Property

Got It? What are the solutions of $15 \le 5 - 2(4m + 7)$? Check your solutions.

14. Use the justifications at the right to solve the inequality.

$15 \le 5 - 2(4m + 7)$	Write the original inequality.
$15 \le 5 - \boxed{} - \boxed{}$	Distributive Property
$15 \le -8m - \boxed{}$	Subtract.
$15 + \boxed{} \le -8m - 9 + \boxed{}$	Addition Property of Inequality
$24 \le \boxed{}$	Add.
$\dfrac{24}{\boxed{}} \quad \dfrac{-8m}{\boxed{}}$	Division Property of Inequality
$-3 \boxed{} \ m$	Simplify.

15. Check your solutions by following the steps below.

$15 \overset{?}{\le} 5 - 2(4 \cdot \boxed{} + 7)$	Substitute one of your solutions to Exercise 14.
$15 \overset{?}{\le} 5 - 2(\boxed{} + 7)$	Multiply within parentheses.
$15 \overset{?}{\le} 5 - 2 \cdot \boxed{}$	Add within parentheses.
$15 \overset{?}{\le} 5 - \boxed{}$	Multiply.
$15 \le \boxed{}$	Simplify.

Problem 4 Solving an Inequality With Variables on Both Sides

Got It? What are the solutions of $3b + 12 > 27 - 2b$? Check your solutions.

16. The inequality is solved below. Write a justification for each step.

$3b + 12 > 27 - 2b$	_____
$2b + 3b + 12 > 27 - 2b + 2b$	_____ Property of Inequality
$5b + 12 - 12 > 27 - 12$	_____ Property of Inequality
$\dfrac{5b}{5} > \dfrac{15}{5}$	_____ Property of Inequality
$b > 3$	_____

17. Check your solutions in the original inequality.

18. Are your solutions correct?   Yes / No

Problem 5 Inequalities With Special Solutions

Got It? What are the solutions of the inequality $9 + 5n \le 5n - 1$?

19. Solve the inequality $9 + 5n \le 5n - 1$.

20. The inequality $9 + 5n \le 5n - 1$ is always / never true.

So, the solution is all real numbers / there is no solution .

 Lesson Check • **Do you UNDERSTAND?**

Error Analysis Your friend says that the solutions of the inequality $-2(3 - x) > 2x - 6$ are all real numbers. Do you agree with your friend? Explain. What if the inequality symbol were $\ge$?

21. The inequality $-2(3 - x) > 2x - 6$ is solved below. Write a justification from the box for each step.

$-2(3 - x) > 2x - 6$ _____

$-6 + 2x > 2x - 6$ _____

$-6 + 2x - 2x > 2x - 6 - 2x$ _____

$-6 > -6$ _____

> Distributive Prope...
> Simplify.
> Subtraction Proper...
> of Inequality
> Write the origina...
> inequality.

22. Look at the final inequality in Exercise 21. Is the inequality ever true?　　Yes / No

23. Do you agree with your friend? Explain. What if the inequality symbol were $\ge$?

_____

_____

_____

_____

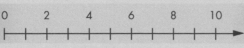 **Math Success**

Check off the vocabulary words that you understand.

☐ multi-step inequalities　　☐ properties of inequality　　☐ solutions

Rate how well you can *solve multi-step inequalities*.

 Need to review　0　2　4　6　8　10　Now I get it!

Vocabulary

● Review

1. Cross out the numbers below that are NOT *whole numbers*.

   | 12 | $\frac{2}{3}$ | 108 | 6.3 | 2 |

2. Describe the relationship between the set of *whole numbers* and the set of *real numbers*.

   _____

   _____

● Vocabulary Builder

> The **set** {0, 1, 2} contains the elements 0, 1, and 2.

set (noun) **set**

Definition: A **set** is a collection of distinct objects or elements. The *complement* of a **set** is the set of all objects or elements *not* in the set.

Using Symbols: The **set** of the first three whole numbers can be written in roster form as {0, 1, 2}. It can be written in set-builder form as $H = \{x \mid \text{whole numbers}, x < 3\}$.

Examples: The universal **set** of all meals in a day is {breakfast, lunch, snack, dinner}. Let A be the **set** {breakfast, lunch}. The *complement* of set A, written A', is the **set** of all meals *not* in A. So, $A' = \{\text{snack, dinner}\}$.

● Use Your Vocabulary

Complete each *set* with another element.

3. $A = \{\text{eyes, ears, nose, } \underline{?} \}$ 4. $B = \{\text{mother, father, brother, } \underline{?} \}$ 5. $C = \{\text{A, E, } \underline{?} \text{, O, U}\}$

   _____   _____   _____

6. Suppose that the universal set of coins is {penny, nickel, dime, quarter}. Let D be the set {penny, quarter}. What is the *complement* of set D?

   $D' = \{ \underline{\hspace{6cm}} \}$

Problem 1 Using Roster Form and Set-Builder Notation

Got It? N is the set of even natural numbers that are less than or equal to 12. How do you write N in roster form? In set-builder notation?

7. Circle the even natural numbers that are less than or equal to 12.

| 1 | 2 | 3 | 4 | 5 | 6 | 7 | 8 | 9 | 10 | 11 | 12 |

8. Write the numbers you circled in roster form below.

$N = \{$ ___ , ___ , ___ , ___ , ___ , ___ $\}$

9. Complete the set-builder notation below. Use the description of the circled numbers from Exercise 7 to help you.

$N = \{x \mid$ _____ $, x$ ___ $12\}$

 Problem 2 Inequalities and Set-Builder Notation

Got It? In set-builder notation, how do you write the solutions of $9 - 4n > 21$?

10. Solve the inequality.

11. In set-builder notation, the solutions are

$\{n \mid$ _____ $\}$.

The *empty set*, written $\{\ \}$, is the set that contains no elements. It is a *subset* of every set.

 Problem 3 Finding Subsets

Got It? What are the subsets of the set $P = \{a, b\}$? Of the set $S = \{a, b, c\}$?

12. List all of the subsets of set P. The first one is done for you.

The empty set:	$\{\}$
Two sets with one letter each:	$\{$ ___ $\}, \{$ ___ $\}$
The original set:	$\{$ ___ , ___ $\}$

13. List all of the subsets of set S.

The empty set:

Three sets with one letter each:

Three sets with two letters each:

The original set:

14. How many subsets does P have?

15. How many subsets does S have?

Lesson 3-5

Got It? Reasoning Let $A = \{x \mid x < -3\}$ and $B = \{x \mid x \leq 0\}$. Is A a subset of B? Explain your reasoning.

Use the graphs of $x < -3$ and $x \leq 0$ for Exercises 16–20.

16. The blue / red arrow represents the graph $x < -3$, or set A.

17. The blue / red arrow represents the graph of $x \leq 0$, or set B.

18. Is the graph of $x < -3$ part of the graph of $x \leq 0$?   Yes / No

19. Are the numbers from set A contained in set B?   Yes / No

20. Is set A a subset of set B?   Yes / No

 Problem 4 Finding the Complement of a Set

Got It? Universal set $U = \{$months of the year$\}$ and set $A = \{$months with exactly 31 days$\}$. What is the complement of set A? Write your answer in roster form.

21. Use the months from the universal set at the right. Write each month in the correct oval. Then label each set A or A'.

☐ = {exactly 31 days}   ☐ = {not exactly 31 days}

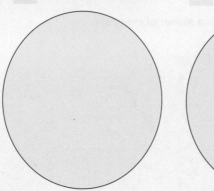

| January |
| February |
| March |
| April |
| May |
| June |
| July |
| August |
| September |
| October |
| November |
| December |

22. Write the complement of set A in roster form.

$A' = \{$ _____ $\}$

 Lesson Check • Do you know HOW?

Given the universal set $U = \{$seasons of the year$\}$ and $W = \{$winter$\}$, what is W'?

23. W' is __?__. Circle your answer.

the universal set   the complement of W a subset of W

24. Write the elements of U.

_____   _____   _____   _____

25. Use your answers to Exercise 24 and $W = \{winter\}$, to write W'.

$W' = \{$ _____ $\}$

Lesson Check • Do you UNDERSTAND?

Error Analysis A student says sets A and B below are the same. What error did the student make?

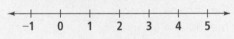 $A = \{x \mid x$ is a whole number less than 5$\}$  $B = \{1, 2, 3, 4\}$

26. Describe the set of whole numbers.

_____

_____

27. Graph the numbers that are in set A on the number line below.

$$\xleftarrow{\;\;}\overset{\displaystyle -1 \quad 0 \quad 1 \quad 2 \quad 3 \quad 4 \quad 5}{\rule{8cm}{0.4pt}}\xrightarrow{\;\;}$$

28. Graph the numbers that are in set B on the number line below.

$$\xleftarrow{\;\;}\overset{\displaystyle -1 \quad 0 \quad 1 \quad 2 \quad 3 \quad 4 \quad 5}{\rule{8cm}{0.4pt}}\xrightarrow{\;\;}$$

29. What error did the student make?

_____

_____

Math Success

Check off the vocabulary words that you understand.

☐ complement   ☐ empty set   ☐ universal set

☐ roster form   ☐ set-builder notation

Rate how well you can *work with sets.*

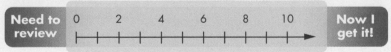

Need to review 0 2 4 6 8 10 Now I get it!

Compound Inequalities

Vocabulary

● Review

1. Write **I** if the math sentence is an *inequality*. Write **E** if it is an *equation*.

   _____ $15 > -12$ _____ $18 \leq 35$ _____ $5x = 15$ _____ $9 > 3x$

2. Write the *inequality* symbol that matches each description.

   greater than ▢   less than or equal to ▢   greater than or equal to ▢

● Vocabulary Builder

> **compound** (noun or adjective) KAHM **pownd**
>
> **Main Idea:** A **compound** (noun) is a whole formed by a union of two or more parts.
> A **compound** inequality (adjective) consists of two distinct inequalities joined by
> the word *and* or the word *or*.
>
> **Example:** You read $3 < x < 6$ as "*x* is less than 6 *and* greater than 3."

● Use Your Vocabulary

3. Cross out each inequality that is NOT a *compound inequality*.

   | $-2 > x$ or $x > 3$ | $x \geq 0$ | $5 < x \leq 10$ | $9 < x$ |

4. Draw a line from each description in Column A to the inequality it describes
   in Column B.

Column A	Column B
all numbers less than 9 or greater than 5	$x < 5$ or $x > 9$
all numbers less than 9 and greater than 5	$x < 9$ or $x > 5$
all numbers less than 5 and greater than 9	$x < 5$ and $x > 9$
all number less than 5 or greater than 9	$5 < x < 9$

5. **Reasoning** Which inequality in Exercise 4 describes an empty set? Explain.

   _____

   _____

98

 **Problem 1** Writing a Compound Inequality

Got It? Write a compound inequality to represent the phrase below. Graph the solutions.

> all real numbers that are greater than or equal to −4 and less than 6

6. Write the phrase as two phrases.

all real numbers that are _____ **and** all real numbers that are _____

_____ _____

7. Write an inequality to represent each statement from Exercise 6. Then write a compound inequality.

x ☐☐ x ☐☐

x ☐☐ and x ☐☐

8. Circle the graph of the compound inequality.

A solution of a compound inequality involving *and* is any number that makes *both* inequalities true.

 Problem 2 Solving a Compound Inequality Involving *And*

Got It? What are the solutions of $-2 < 3y - 4 < 14$? Graph the solutions.

9. Use the justifications at the right to solve the compound inequality.

☐ $< 3y - 4$	and ☐ < 14	Write two inequalities joined by *and*.
☐ $+$ ☐ $< 3y - 4 +$ ☐	and ☐ $+$ ☐ $< 14 +$ ☐	Addition Property of Inequality
☐ $< 3y$	and ☐ < 18	Add.
$\frac{☐}{☐} < \frac{☐}{☐}$	and $\frac{☐}{☐} < \frac{18}{☐}$	Division Property of Inequality
$\frac{☐}{☐} < y$	and ☐ $<$ ☐	Simplify.
☐ $< y <$ ☐		Write the solutions as a single inequality.

10. Underline the correct symbol(s) and words to complete the sentence.

Because the compound inequality includes $<$ / $>$ / $\geq$ / $\leq$, the graph of the compound inequality will include closed dots / open dots / one closed and one open dot .

11. Graph the compound inequality on the number line at the right.

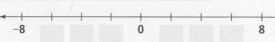

Copyright © by Pearson Education, Inc. or its affiliates. All Rights Reserved.

99 Lesson 3-6

Problem 3 Writing and Solving a Compound Inequality

Got It? Reasoning To earn a B in your algebra class, you must achieve an unrounded test average between 84 and 86, inclusive. You scored 78, 78, and 79 on the first three (out of four) tests. Is it possible for you to earn a B in the course? Assume that 100 is the maximum grade you can earn on the test. Explain.

12. Let $x =$ the score of the fourth test. Write a compound inequality.

$$\boxed{} \leq \frac{78 + 78 + 79 + x}{4} \leq \boxed{}$$

13. Now solve the compound inequality.

14. Is it possible for you to earn a B in the course? Explain.

_____

_____

_____

A solution of a compound inequality involving *or* is any number that makes *either* inequality true.

 Problem 4 Solving a Compound Inequality Involving *Or*

Got It? What are the solutions of $-2y + 7 < 1$ or $4y + 3 \leq -5$? Graph the solutions.

15. Complete the steps to solve the inequalities.

$$-2y + 7 < 1 \qquad\qquad \text{or} \qquad\qquad 4y + 3 \leq -5$$

$$-2y + 7 - \boxed{} < 1 - \boxed{} \qquad \text{or} \qquad 4y + 3 - \boxed{} \leq -5 - \boxed{}$$

$$-2y < \boxed{} \qquad\qquad \text{or} \qquad\qquad 4y \leq \boxed{}$$

$$\frac{-2y}{\boxed{}} > \frac{\boxed{}}{\boxed{}} \qquad \text{or} \qquad \frac{4y}{\boxed{}} \leq \frac{\boxed{}}{\boxed{}}$$

$$y \ \boxed{} \ \boxed{} \qquad\qquad \text{or} \qquad\qquad y \ \boxed{} \ \boxed{}$$

16. Graph the compound inequality on the number line below.
(*Hint:* Will you use open dots, closed dots, or one of each?)

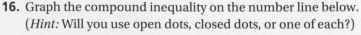
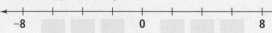

$-8 \qquad\qquad 0 \qquad\qquad 8$

You can use an inequality to describe an *interval* along the number line. In *interval notation*, you use three special symbols.

brackets	**parentheses**	**infinity**
Use [or] with ≤ or ≥ to indicate that the interval's endpoints are included.	Use (or) with < or > to indicate that the interval's endpoints are *not* included.	Use ∞ when the interval continues forever in a *positive* direction. Use −∞ when the interval continues forever in a *negative* direction.

Problem 5 Using Interval Notation

Got It? What is the graph of $(-2, 7]$? How do you write $(-2, 7]$ as an inequality?

Underline the correct word or words to complete each sentence.

17. In $(-2, 7]$, the parenthesis to the left of -2 means -2 is / is not included in the interval.

18. In $(-2, 7]$, the bracket to the right of 7 means 7 is / is not included in the interval.

19. Use your answers to Exercises 17 and 18 to write a compound inequality.

☐ ☐ x ☐

20. Graph the inequality.

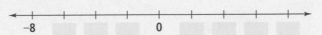

Lesson Check • Do you UNDERSTAND?

Error Analysis A student writes the inequality $x \geq 17$ in interval notation as $[17, \infty]$. Explain why this is incorrect.

21. Circle the correct interval notation for the inequality $x \geq 17$.

$(17, \infty)$	$(17, \infty]$	$[17, \infty)$	$(-\infty, 17]$ or $[17, \infty)$

22. Explain the student's error.

_____

_____

Math Success

Check off the vocabulary words that you understand.

☐ compound inequality ☐ inclusive ☐ interval ☐ interval notation

Rate how well you can *write and graph compound inequalities*.

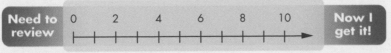

Absolute Value Equations and Inequalities

Vocabulary

● Review

Write T for *true* or F for *false*.

_____ **1.** To indicate the *absolute value* of −8, you write |−8|.

_____ **2.** The *absolute value* of −8 is −8, since −8 is 8 units to the left of 0 on the number line.

_____ **3.** The *absolute value* of −8 is 8, since −8 is 8 units away from 0 on the number line.

_____ **4.** According to the definition of absolute value, if |r| = 3, then r = 3 or r = −3.

● Vocabulary Builder

	numerical expression
	$18 \div (6 + 3)$

expression (noun) **ek SPRESH un**

algebraic expression
$4k - 7$

Related Words: express (verb), phrase (noun)

Main Idea: An **expression** is a word or phrase that communicates an idea. A mathematical **expression** is a mathematical phrase. A mathematical **expression** may be *numerical* or *algebraic*.

● Use Your Vocabulary

Write an *expression* for each word phrase.

5. *m* increased by 8   **6.** *y* divided by 9   **7.** *u* more than 7

m _____ y _____   _____ u

8. Cross out the *expression* that is NOT algebraic.

$3y - 12$	$4 + 18 - 3$	$12 + x$

9. Cross out the *expression* that is NOT numeric.

$3 - 12$	$4 + 18q - 3$	$12 + 5$

Problem 1 Solving an Absolute Value Equation

Got It? What are the solutions of $|n| - 5 = -2$? Graph and check the solutions.

10. Circle what you should do to solve $|n| - 5 = -2$.

| Change -2 to 2. | Isolate the variable. |

11. Complete the equation to solve for n.

$$|n| - 5 + \boxed{} = -2 + \boxed{}$$

$$|n| = \boxed{}$$

$$n = \boxed{} \quad \text{or } n = \boxed{}$$

12. Graph the solutions.

13. Check the solutions of the equation.

---

take note

Key Concept Solving Absolute Value Equations

To solve an equation in the form $|A| = b$, where A represents a variable expression and $b > 0$, solve $A = b$ and $A = -b$.

Complete.

14. To solve $|b| = 3$, solve $b = \boxed{}$ and $b = \boxed{}$.

15. To solve $|x - 5| = 6$, solve $x - 5 = \boxed{}$ and $x - 5 = \boxed{}$.

16. To solve $|h + 7| = 2h$, solve $h + 7 = \boxed{}$ and $h + 7 = \boxed{}$.

Problem 2 Solving an Absolute Value Equation

Got It? What are the solutions of $|3x - 1| = 8$? Check the solutions.

17. The absolute value equation is solved below. Write a justification for each step.

$3x - 1 = 8$	$3x - 1 = -8$	Write two equations.
$3x = 9$	$3x = -7$	
$x = 3$	$x = -\dfrac{7}{3}$	

18. Check the solutions in the original equation.

Lesson 3-7

Problem 3 Solving an Absolute Value Equation With No Solution

Got It? What are the solutions of $|3x - 6| - 5 = -7$?

19. To isolate the absolute value expression, you add 5 to each side of the equation. Circle the simplified value of the right side.

-12 -7 -6 -5 -3 -2

20. Underline the correct word to complete the sentence.

The absolute value of an expression cannot be negative / positive , so the inequality has no solution.

---

take note

Key Concept Solving Absolute Value Inequalities

Let A represent a variable expression and let $b > 0$.

To Solve an Inequality in the Form	Solve	
$|A| < b$	$-b < A < b$	(For $|A| \le b$, solve $-b \le A \le b$.)
$|A| > b$	$A < -b$ or $A > b$	(For $|A| \ge b$, solve $A \le -b$ or $A \ge b$.)

21. Circle the compound inequality you would use to solve $|5x| > 3$.

$-3 < 5x < 3$ $-3 \le 5x \le 3$ $5x < -3$ or $5x > 3$ $5x \le -3$ or $5x \ge 3$

22. Circle the compound inequality you would use to solve $|3x| < 5$.

$-5 < 3x < 5$ $-5 \le 3x \le 5$ $3x < -5$ or $3x > 5$ $3x \le -5$ or $3x \ge 5$

Problem 4 Solving an Absolute Value Inequality Involving ≥

Got It? What are the solutions of $|2x + 4| \ge 5$? Graph the solutions.

23. Write a compound inequality to solve the absolute value inequality.

$2x + 4$ ☐ -5 or $2x + 4$ ☐ 5

24. Solve the inequalities.

☐   or   ☐

25. Graph your solutions on the number line below.

Problem 5 Solving an Absolute Value Inequality Involving ≤

Got It? A food manufacturer makes 32-oz boxes of pasta. Not every box weighs exactly 32 oz. The allowable difference from the ideal weight is at most 0.05 oz. Write and solve an absolute value inequality to find the range of allowable weights.

26. Complete the model.

| Relate | difference between ideal and actual weights | is at most | 0.05 oz |

Define Let $w =$ the actual weight.

Write $\left| w - \boxed{} \right|$ $\boxed{}$ 0.05

27. Write the absolute value inequality as a compound inequality.

$-0.05 \boxed{} \quad w - \boxed{}$

28. Solve the compound inequality.

29. A box of pasta must weigh between $\boxed{}$ oz and $\boxed{}$ oz, inclusive.

 Lesson Check • **Do you UNDERSTAND?**

Reasoning How many solutions do you expect to get when you solve an absolute value equation? Explain.

30. Write how many solutions each absolute value equation has.

$|x| = 9$ $|x| = 0$ $|x| = -9$

$\boxed{}$ solution(s) $\boxed{}$ solution(s) $\boxed{}$ solution(s)

31. Explain how many solutions are possible for any absolute value equation.

 Math Success

Check off the vocabulary words that you understand.

☐ absolute value   ☐ equation   ☐ inequality

Rate how well you can *solve absolute value equations and inequalities.*

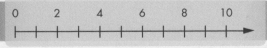

Lesson 3-7

Vocabulary

● Review

Write the elements of each *set*.

1. whole numbers less than 4

2. even numbers between 1 and 9

3. Two sets are *disjoint* when they have no elements in common.

Are the sets in Exercises 1 and 2 *disjoint*?   Yes / No

● Vocabulary Builder

> **union** (noun) YOON **yuhn**
>
> **Related Word:** intersection (noun), Venn diagram (noun)
>
> **Definition:** The **union** of two or more sets is the set that contains all the elements of the sets. The *intersection* of two or more sets is the set of elements that are in all of the sets.
>
> **Example:** Set A = {penny, nickel, dime} and set B = {nickel, dime, quarter}.
> $A \cup B$ = {penny, nickel, dime, quarter} and $A \cap B$ = {nickel, dime}

> $G \cup H$ means "the **union** of sets G and H."
>
> $G \cap H$ means "the **intersection** of sets G and H."

● Use Your Vocabulary

Write *union* or *intersection* to describe each set.

4. D = {cheese, milk, yogurt} and F = {apple, banana, pear}
the set {apple, banana, cheese, milk, pear, yogurt}

_____

5. D = {cheese, milk, yogurt} and M = {bread, cheese, egg}
the set {cheese}

_____

6. F = {apple, banana, pear} and M = {bread, cheese, egg}
the empty set

_____

Problem 1 Union of Sets

Got It? Write sets P and Q below in roster form. What is $P \cup Q$?

$P = \{x \mid x \text{ is a whole number less than 5}\}$
$Q = \{y \mid y \text{ is an even natural number less than 5}\}$

7. The symbol $\cup$ means the union / intersection of the sets.

8. Circle the numbers in set P.

> 0   1   2   3   4   5

9. Write set P in roster form.

$P = \{$ ___ , ___ , ___ , ___ , ___ $\}$

10. Circle the numbers in set Q.

> 0   1   2   3   4   5

11. Write set Q in roster form.

$Q = \{$ ___ , ___ $\}$

12. Write $P \cup Q$.

$P \cup Q = \{$ ___ , ___ , ___ , ___ , ___ $\}$

13. **Reasoning** What is true about the union of two distinct sets if one set is a subset of the other? (Assume that the subset is not the original set.)

_____

Problem 2 Intersection of Sets

Got It? Let $A = \{2, 4, 6, 8\}$, $B = \{0, 2, 5, 7, 8\}$, and
$C = \{n \mid n \text{ is an odd whole number}\}$. What is $A \cap B$?

14. The symbol $\cap$ means the union / intersection of the sets.

15. The numbers ____ and ____ are in both set A and set B.

16. Write $A \cap B$.

$A \cap B = \{$ ___ , ___ $\}$

17. Write $A \cap C$, and write $C \cap B$.

$A \cap C =$ _____ $C \cap B =$ _____

18. **Reasoning** What is true about the intersection of two distinct sets if one set is a subset of the other? (Assume that the subset is not the original set.)

_____

Lesson 3-8

✓ Problem 3 Making a Venn Diagram

Got It? Let $A = \{x \mid x$ is one of the first five letters in the English alphabet$\}$,
$B = \{x \mid x$ is a vowel$\}$, and $C = \{x \mid x$ is a letter in the word VEGETABLE$\}$. Which
letters are in all three sets?

19. List the elements of each set.

$A = \{A, \_\_, \_\_, \_\_, \_\_\}$ $\qquad\qquad$ $B = \{A, \_\_, \_\_, \_\_, \_\_\}$

$\qquad\qquad$ $C = \{V, \_\_, \_\_, \_\_, A, \_\_, \_\_\}$

20. Write the correct letters to complete each statement.

The letters that are in set A but are *not* in any other set are __?__.

The letters that are in set B that are *not* in any other set are __?__.

The letters that are in set C that are *not* in any other set are __?__.

The letter that is in both sets A and C, but *not* in B is __?__.

he letters that are in all three sets are __?__.

21. e your answers to Exercise 20 to complete the Venn diagram below.

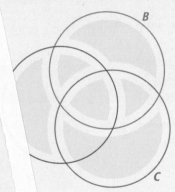

✓ Proble Using a Venn Diagram to Show Numbers of Elements

Got It? Of   students in student government, 20 are honor students and 9 are
officers and honor students. All of the students are officers, honor students, or both.
How many are officers but not honor students?

22. Use the information in the problem to complete each statement. Then complete
the Venn diagram.

Let $H = $ _____ and let $O = $ _____.

$H \cap O$ has ▢ students.

Only honor students: $20 - $ ▢ $ = $ ▢

Only officers: $30 - $ ▢ $ = $ ▢

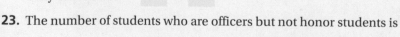

23. The number of students who are officers but not honor students is ▢.

Problem 5 Writing Solutions of an Inequality

Got It? Solve the inequality $8 \leq x + 5 < 11$. Write the solutions as either the union or the intersection of two sets.

24. Multiple Choice What is the first step in solving the inequality?

(A) Add 5 to each expression.

(C) Add 8 to each expression.

(B) Subtract 5 from each expression.

(D) Subtract 8 from each expression.

25. When you isolate the variable, the inequality becomes [ ] $\leq x <$ [ ].

26. Write two inequalities.

[ ] $\leq x$ and $x <$ [ ]

27. Now write the solutions of the inequality as the union or the intersection of two sets.

$\{x \mid$ [ ] $\leq x\}$ [ ] $\{x \mid x <$ [ ] $\}$

Lesson Check • Do you UNDERSTAND?

Compare and Contrast How are unions and intersections of sets different?

28. Write **U** if the statement describes a *union*. Write **I** if the statement describes an *intersection*.

_____   It contains the elements that belong to either set or both sets.

_____   In a Venn diagram, it is the part of the circles that overlap.

29. Use your answers to Exercise 28 to explain how unions and intersections are similar and how they are different.

_____

_____

_____

Math Success

Check off the vocabulary words that you understand.

☐ union   ☐ intersection   ☐ disjoint sets   ☐ subsets

Rate how well you can *find unions and intersections of sets.*

 Need to review 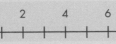 0 2 4 6 8 10 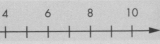 Now I get it!

4-1 | Using Graphs to Relate Two Quantities

Vocabulary

● Review

Use the *graph* at the right. Draw a line from each point in Column A to its coordinates in Column B.

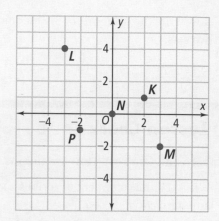

Column A	Column B
1. point K	$(-3, 4)$
2. point L	$(-2, -1)$
3. point M	$(0, 0)$
4. point N	$(2, 1)$
5. point P	$(3, -2)$

● Vocabulary Builder

analyze (verb) AN **uh lyz**

Other Word Forms: analyzed (verb), analysis (noun)

Definition: to examine carefully in detail; to identify the nature and relationship of its parts

What It Means: break down, dissect

Word Origin: from the Greek word *analusis*, meaning "a dissolving"

● Use Your Vocabulary

Complete each statement with the appropriate word from the list.

analyze   analysis   analyzed

6. The chemist _?_ the data to draw a conclusion.

7. Jean needed to _?_ the data she gathered in her experiment.

8. An _?_ of the traffic at an intersection showed the need for a traffic light.

Problem 1 Analyzing a Graph

Got It? What are the variables in the graph? Describe how the variables are related at various points on the graph.

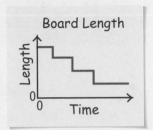

9. Circle the two variables being related in the graph.

time   cut   board   length

10. Show how the variables are related by underlining the correct word or words to complete each sentence.

The length of the board increases / decreases with time.

The length of the board is constant / decreasing while you are actually cutting the board.

During the time shown on the graph, there are three / four cuts.

There is / is not a piece of the board left at the end of the time shown.

Got It? What are the variables in the graph? Describe how the variables are related at various points on the graph.

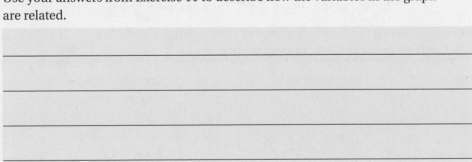

11. Show how the variables are related by underlining the correct word to complete each sentence.

The cost of the cell phone in June increases / decreases with number of minutes of calls.

The cost of the cell phone in June is constant / increasing for the first part of the month.

12. Use your answers from Exercise 11 to describe how the variables in the graph are related.

_____

_____

_____

_____

Lesson 4-1

Problem 2 Matching a Table and a Graph

Got It? The table shows the amount of sunscreen left in a can based on the number of times the sunscreen has been used. Which graph could represent the data shown in the table?

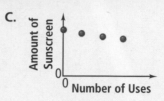

Sunscreen				
Number of Uses	0	1	2	3
Amount of Sunscreen (oz)	5	4.8	4.6	4.4

A.

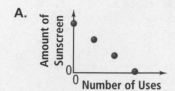

B.

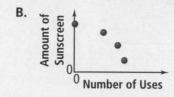

C.

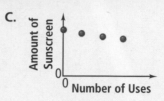

13. Analyze the data in the table. Complete each statement with the correct choice from the list. Use each word only once.

   slowly   fall   decreases

   The amount of sunscreen in the container ⎯?⎯ after each use.

   The amount of sunscreen in the container changes ⎯?⎯ .

   The graph should ⎯?⎯ at a slow rate.

14. The graph that could represent the data shown in the table is Graph ▢ .

Problem 3 Sketching a Graph

Got It? Suppose you start to swing yourself on a playground swing. You move back and forth and swing higher in the air. Then you slowly swing to a stop. What sketch of a graph could represent how your height from the ground might change over time? Label each section.

15. **Multiple Choice** The two variables being related are time and ⎯?⎯ .

   Ⓐ length of swing   Ⓑ distance from top of swing   Ⓒ your height from ground   Ⓓ your height

16. Consider the three cycles during the middle of your time on the swing. Circle the best sketch of your height from the ground during that time.

constant distance from ground

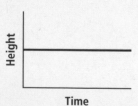

start high, swing low, end high

start low, swing high, end low

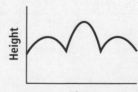

Lesson Check • Do you UNDERSTAND?

Reasoning Describe a real-world relationship that could be represented by the graph sketched at the right.

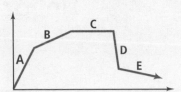

17. Draw a line from the name of each segment in Column A to its verbal description in Column B.

Column A	Column B
A	spilling water from a cup
B	pouring water into a cup quickly
C	stop pouring water into a cup
D	water leaking from a hole in a cup
E	pouring water into a cup slowly

18. Use the verbal descriptions above to help you write a situation that could be represented by the sketch.

_____

_____

_____

_____

Math Success

Check off the vocabulary words that you understand.

☐ variable quantities   ☐ increase   ☐ decrease

Rate how well you can *use graphs*.

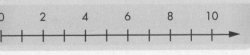

Lesson 4-1

4-2

Patterns and Linear Functions

Vocabulary

● Review

1. A *function* is a relationship that pairs each input value with exactly one output value. Cross out the relationship below that does NOT show a *function*.

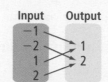

Input	Output
−1	
−2	1
1	2
2	

● Vocabulary Builder

independent (adjective) **in dee PEN dunt**

Related Words: dependent, input, output

Definition: An **independent** variable is a variable whose value determines the value of another variable, called the *dependent* variable.

```
                          ┌─────────────┐
   x →                    │  function   │
independent               └──────┬──────┘
variable                         │
(input)                          ↓
                                 y
                    dependent variable
                         (output)
```

Math Usage: In the diagram, the **independent** variable, *x*, is called the *input* of the function. The dependent variable, *y*, is called the *output* of the function.

Example: When showing the relationship between amount of sunlight and amount of plant growth, the *independent* variable is the amount of sunlight.

● Use Your Vocabulary

Write **I** if the first value is *independent* of the second value. Write **D** if the first value is *dependent* on the second value.

_____ **2.** the growth of a plant and the light the plant receives

_____ **3.** the speed of a swimmer and the depth of a pool

_____ **4.** the number of books a shelf holds and the length of the shelf

Got It? In the diagram below, what is the relationship between the number of triangles and the perimeter of the figure they form? Represent this relationship using a table, words, an equation, and a graph.

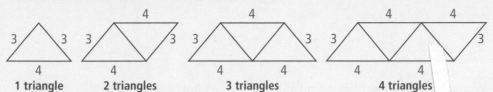

1 triangle   2 triangles   3 triangles   4 triangles

5. Define the variables.

Let $x =$ _____ .   Let $y =$ _____ .

6. Complete the table.

Number of Triangles	1	2	3	
Perimeter	☐	☐	☐	☐

7. Complete the model below.

Relate   perimeter   is   ☐   times   number of triangles   plus   ☐

Write   ☐   =   ☐   •   ☐   +   ☐

8. Write an equation to represent the relationship you wrote in Exercise 7.

_____

9. Use the table to list the points you will plot.

(1, ☐)   (2, ☐)   (3, ☐)   (4, ☐)

10. Now plot the points on the graph.

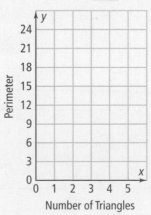

You have seen that one way to represent a function is with a graph. A **linear function** is a function whose graph is a line or a part of a line.

Lesson 4-2

Got It? Is the relationship in the table at the right a linear function? Describe the relationship using words, an equation, and a graph.

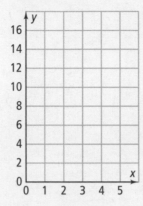

Input, x	0	1	2	3
Output, y	8	10	12	14

11. Describe the pattern in the table in words.

_____

12. Multiple Choice Which equation describes the relationship in the table?

Ⓐ $y = 2x + 8$ Ⓑ $y = 2x - 8$ Ⓒ $y = x \div 2 + 8$ Ⓓ $y = x \div 2 - 8$

13. Plot the points from the table on the graph.

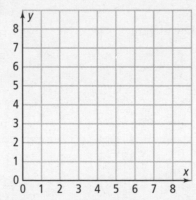

14. Underline the correct word or words to complete the sentence.

The points lie / do not lie on a line, so, the relationship is / is not a linear function.

Got It? Reasoning Does the set of ordered pairs (0, 2), (1, 4), (3, 5), and (1, 8) represent a linear function? Explain.

15. Plot the points on the graph.

16. Do the ordered pairs represent a linear function? Explain.

_____

_____

Lesson Check • Do you UNDERSTAND?

Vocabulary The amount of toothpaste in a tube decreases each time you brush your teeth. Identify the independent and dependent variables in this relationship.

17. Complete each phrase to identify the variables.

Let A = the amount of toothpaste in a __?__ .   Let B = the number of times you __?__ your teeth.

_____   _____

18. Underline the correct word to complete each sentence.

A is the independent / dependent variable. B is the independent / dependent variable.

Lesson Check • Do you UNDERSTAND?

Reasoning Does the graph at the right represent a linear function? Explain.

19. Draw a line from each word in Column A to its definition in Column B.

Column A	Column B
relation	function whose graph is a line or part of a line
function	pairing of input and output values
linear function	relationship that pairs each input value with exactly one output value

20. Use the terms above to explain if the graph represents a linear function.

_____

_____

_____

Math Success

Check off the vocabulary words that you understand.

☐ dependent variable   ☐ independent variable   ☐ linear function

Rate how well you can *describe linear functions*.

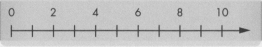

Need to review 0 2 4 6 8 10 Now I get it!

Lesson 4-2

Vocabulary

● **Review**

Find the next number in each *pattern*.

1. 1, 2, 4, 8, ▢

2. −8, 4, −2, ▢

3. 1, 3, 9, 27, ▢

4. $\frac{1}{2}, \frac{1}{4}, \frac{1}{8},$ ▢

5. The next shape in the *pattern* below has ▢ blocks.

● **Vocabulary Builder**

nonlinear (adjective) **nahn LIN ee ur**

Related Words: line (noun), linear (adjective)

Definition: Something that is **nonlinear** is not in a straight line.

Math Usage: A **nonlinear** function is a function whose graph is not a line or part of a line. A *linear* function is a function whose graph is a line or part of a line.

Common Usage: A **nonlinear** narrative is a story where the events are told out of chronological order.

● **Use Your Vocabulary**

6. Circle each graph of a *nonlinear* function.

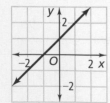 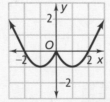 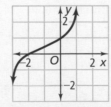 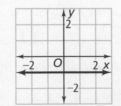

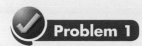 **Problem 1** **Classifying Functions as Linear or Nonlinear**

Got It? The table below shows the fraction A of the original area of a piece of paper that remains after the paper has been cut in half n times. Graph the function represented by the table. Is the function *linear* or *nonlinear*?

Cutting Paper				
Number of Cuts, n	1	2	3	4
Fraction of Original Area Remaining, A	$\frac{1}{2}$	$\frac{1}{4}$	$\frac{1}{8}$	$\frac{1}{16}$

7. Complete each ordered pair.

(1,   )   (2,   )   (3,   )   (4,   )

8. Graph the ordered pairs from Exercise 7 on the coordinate plane.

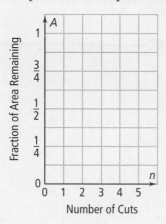

9. Complete the sentence with *linear* or *nonlinear*: The function is ___?___.

Got It? **Reasoning** Will the area A in Exercise 8 ever reach zero? Explain.

10. If you start with a piece of paper in your hand and repeatedly cut the paper in half, will your hand ever be empty?   Yes / No

11. Will the remaining area A ever reach zero? Explain.

Got It? The table shows the number of new branches in each figure of the pattern below. What is a pattern you can use to complete the table? Represent the relationship using words, an equation, and a graph.

Number of Figure, x	1	2	3	4	5
Number of New Branches, y	3	9	27	▪	▪

12. Look for a pattern in the table. Describe it below.

_____

_____

13. Use the words *the figure* and *new branches* to complete the diagram below.

the number of _____

the number of _____ = 3^{the number of _____}

14. Circle the equation that represents the function.

$y = 2^x$ $y = x^2$ $y = 3^x$ $y = x^3$

15. Complete each statement.

When $x = 4$, $y = $ ▢ .   When $x = 5$, $y = $ ▢ .

16. Write ordered pairs to represent the data in the table and your results from Exercise 15. Then graph the data.

(1, ▢)   (▢ , 9)   (▢ , 27)

(4, ▢)   (5, ▢)

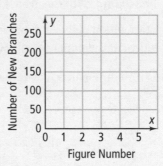

You can think of a function as a rule that you apply to the *input* in order to get the *output*. You can describe a nonlinear function with words or with an equation, just as you did with linear functions.

Problem 3 Writing a Rule to Describe a Nonlinear Function

Got It? What is a rule for the function represented by the ordered pairs (1, 1), (2, 4), (3, 9), (4, 16), and (5, 25)?

17. Make a table to organize the *x*- and *y*-values.

x	1	2	☐	4	☐
y	☐	☐	9	☐	25

18. Use words to explain the relationship between the *x*- and *y*-values.

_____

19. Now use the relationship you described to write an equation that is a rule for the function.

Lesson Check • Do you UNDERSTAND?

Error Analysis A classmate says that the function in the table at the right can be represented by the rule $y = x + 1$. Describe and correct your classmate's error.

x	y
0	1
1	2
2	5
3	10
4	1

20. Use the ordered pairs below. Cross out the ordered pairs that are NOT described by the equation $y = x + 1$.

(0, 1)   (1, 2)   (2, 5)   (3, 10)   (4, 17)

21. Explain your classmate's error in using $y = x + 1$ to describe the function.

_____

_____

_____

22. Circle the equation that correctly describes the function.

$y = 2x$ $y = x^2 + 1$ $y = 2^x + 1$

Math Success

Check off the vocabulary words that you understand.

☐ linear function   ☐ nonlinear function

Rate how well you can *describe nonlinear functions*.

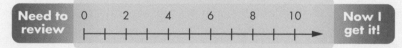

Need to review 0 2 4 6 8 10 Now I get it!

Graphing a Function Rule

Vocabulary

● **Review**

Find each *input* or *output*.

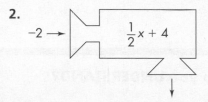

1.
$3 \rightarrow$ | $2x + 1$

2.
$-2 \rightarrow$ | $\frac{1}{2}x + 4$

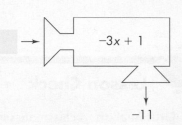

3.
$\rightarrow$ | $-3x + 1$
$\rightarrow -11$

Write T for *true* or F for *false*.

_____ **4.** The *inputs* of a function are the domain of the function.

_____ **5.** A function pairs every *input* with exactly one *output*.

● **Vocabulary Builder**

discrete (adjective) **dih SKREET**

Related Words: separate (adjective), distinct (adjective)

Main Idea: Discrete describes something consisting of distinct or unconnected elements.

Example: The set of integers is a **discrete** set.

Nonexample: The set of real numbers is *not* a **discrete** set.

● **Use Your Vocabulary**

6. Circle the word or words that mean the opposite of *discrete*.

| separate | continuous | infinite | countable |

7. Circle the situation below that describes a *discrete* set.

| the possible temperatures in Florida | the number of oranges sold at a fruit stand each day |

Problem 1 Graphing a Function Rule

Got It? What is the graph of the function rule $y = \frac{1}{2}x - 1$?

8. Complete the table below. Then graph each ordered pair on the coordinate plane at the right. Connect the points with a line.

x	$y = \frac{1}{2}x - 1$	(x, y)
−1	$y = \frac{1}{2} \cdot \boxed{} - 1 = \boxed{}$	
0	$y = \frac{1}{2} \cdot \boxed{} - 1 = \boxed{}$	
1	$y = \frac{1}{2} \cdot \boxed{} - 1 = \boxed{}$	
2	$y = \frac{1}{2} \cdot \boxed{} - 1 = \boxed{}$	

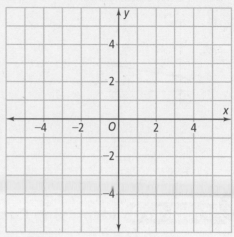

When you graph a real-world function rule, choose appropriate intervals for the units on the axes. Every interval on an axis should represent the same change in value. If all the data are nonnegative, show only the first quadrant.

Problem 2 Graphing a Real-World Function Rule

Got It? The function rule $W = 8g + 700$ represents the total weight W, in pounds, of a spa that contains g gallons of water. What is a reasonable graph of the function rule given that the capacity of the spa is 250 gal?

9. Use the values of g to complete the table.

g	$W = 8g + 700$	(g, W)
0		
50		
150		
250		

10. Graph the ordered pairs on the coordinate plane at the right. Connect the points with a line segment.

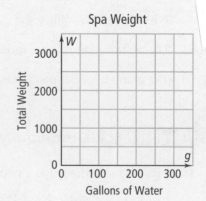

Spa Weight

123

Lesson 4-4

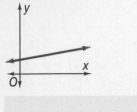

Key Concept   Continuous and Discrete Graphs

A *continuous graph* is a graph that is unbroken.

A *discrete graph* is a graph composed of distinct, isolated points.

Label each graph as *discrete* or *continuous*.

11.

12.

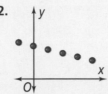

_____

_____

 Problem 3   Identifying Continuous and Discrete Graphs

Got It? The amount of water *w* in a wading pool, in gallons, depends on the amount of time *t*, in minutes, the wading pool has been filling, as related by the function rule $w = 3t$. Graph the function rule. Is the graph *continuous* or *discrete*? Justify your answer.

13. Complete the table to find each value of *w*.

t	1	2	3	4
w				

14. Graph each ordered pair on the coordinate plane.

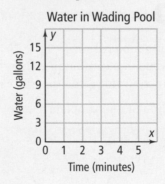

Water in Wading Pool

15. Underline the correct word or words to complete each sentence.

While the pool is filling, the water will / will not enter throughout a given minute.

The points on the graph should / should not be connected by a line.

The graph is continuous / discrete .

 Problem 4   Graphing Nonlinear Function Rules

Got It? What is the graph of the function rule $y = x^3 + 1$?

16. Cross out any ordered pair that does not lie on the graph of $y = x^3 + 1$.

$(-2, -9)$ $\qquad$ $(-1, 0)$ $\qquad$ $(0, -1)$ $\qquad$ $(1, 2)$ $\qquad$ $(2, 9)$

17. Circle the letter of the correct graph of the function.

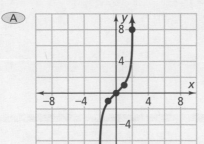 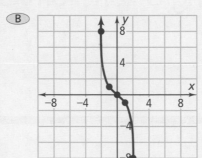 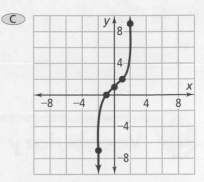

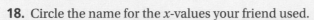

Lesson Check • Do you UNDERSTAND?

Error Analysis Your friend graphs $y = x + 3$ at the right. Describe and correct your friend's error.

18. Circle the name for the *x*-values your friend used.

| integers | rational numbers | real numbers | whole numbers |

19. Circle the best name for the *x*-values of $y = x + 3$.

| integers | rational numbers | real numbers | whole numbers |

20. Describe your friend's error.

21. Graph the function correctly on the coordinate plane at the right.

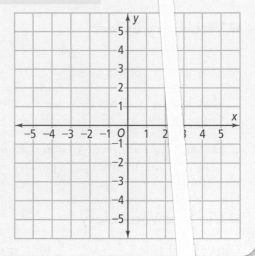

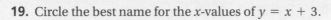

Math Success

Check off the vocabulary words that you understand.

☐ continuous graph   ☐ discrete graph

Rate how well you can *graph function rules*.

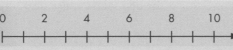

4-5   Writing a Function Rule

Vocabulary

● Review

In *function* notation, you read $f(x)$ as "f of x." You can think of the value "$f(x)$" as another way of writing "y."

1. Write how you would read $h(g)$ aloud. _____

2. Circle the equation that shows *function* notation.

$f(x) = 2x + 1$ $xy = f$ $f(x) - 1$ $0.8x$

3. Carmine wants to buy some peaches. Each peach costs $.25. Circle the *function* Carmine could use to find the cost of any number of peaches p.

$0.25c = p(c)$ $c(p) = 0.25$ $c(p) = 0.25p$ $0.25 = c \cdot p(c)$

● Vocabulary Builder

> **rule** (noun) **rool**
>
> **Main Idea:** A mathematical **rule** is a method or procedure that describes how to solve a problem.
>
> **Example:** A **rule** of integer multiplication is that a negative integer multiplied by a negative integer produces a positive integer.

● Use Your Vocabulary

Consider the *rule* $\frac{a}{b} \div \frac{c}{d} = \frac{a}{b} \cdot \frac{d}{c}$, for $b, c, d \neq 0$.

4. Circle the equation that is an example of this *rule*.

$\frac{2}{1} \div \frac{1}{2} = \frac{2}{5} \cdot \frac{1}{2}$ $\frac{2}{5} \div \frac{1}{2} = \frac{2}{5} \cdot \frac{2}{1}$ $\frac{2}{5} \div \frac{1}{2} = \frac{5}{2} \cdot \frac{1}{2}$

5. According to this *rule*, $\frac{2}{3} \div \frac{6}{9} = \boxed{} \cdot \boxed{}$.

6. Circle the correct words to complete the sentence.

The reason that this *rule* states that $b, c, d \neq 0$ is because ___?___ .

you cannot multiply by 0   you cannot divide by 0   the dividend cannot be 0

Problem 1 **Writing a Function Rule**

Got It? A landfill has 50,000 tons of waste in it. Each month it accumulates an average of 420 more tons of waste. What is a function rule that represents the total amount of waste after *m* months?

7. Complete the model below.

| Relate | total waste | is | 50,000 tons of waste | plus | 420 tons of waste each month | times | number of months |

Define Let $T =$ the total waste, and let $m =$ the number of months.

Write ☐ = ☐ + ☐ · ☐

8. Write an equation to represent the situation.

Problem 2 **Writing and Evaluating a Function Rule**

Got It? A kennel charges $15 per day to board dogs. Upon arrival, each dog must have a flea bath that costs $12. Write a function rule for the total cost for *n* days of boarding plus a bath. How much does a 10-day stay cost?

9. Define your variables.

Let $T =$ _____.   Let $n =$ _____.

10. Now complete the reasoning model below.

Think	Write
I will have to pay $15 per day to board my dog. How much will that cost for *n* days?	☐ · ☐
I also have to pay $12 for the flea bath.	+ ☐
If I put those together, I can write a formula for the total cost, *T*.	$T =$ ☐ · ☐ + ☐

11. Now evaluate *T* for $n = 10$.

12. The cost of a 10-day stay is $ ☐ .

Lesson 4-5

Got It? Write a function rule for the area of a triangle whose height is 4 in. more than twice the length of its base. What is the area of the triangle when the length of its base is 16 in.?

13. Use the given information to write an equation for the height of the triangle.

Let h = the height of the triangle.

Let b = the length of the base of the triangle.

Relate $h =$ 4 in.   more than   twice the length of its base

Write $h = $ ☐ $+$ ☐

14. Use the justifications at the right to find a function rule for the area of the triangle.

$A = \frac{1}{2} \cdot b \cdot h$ 　　　　　　　Formula for area of a triangle

$A = \frac{1}{2} \cdot b \cdot $ ☐ 　　　　　Substitute for h.

$A = \frac{1}{2} \cdot 2b$ ☐ $+ \frac{1}{2} \cdot$ ☐ 　　Distribute $\frac{1}{2} b$.

$A = b$ ☐ $+$ ☐ 　　　　　　　Simplify.

15. Now find the area of the triangle when its base is 16 in.

$A = $ ☐ $^2 + 2 \cdot$ ☐ 　　　Substitute 16 for b.

$A = $ ☐ $+$ ☐ 　　　　　Evaluate the exponent and the multiplication.

$A = $ ☐ 　　　　　　　Add.

16. The area of the triangle is ☐ in.^{2}

Got It? **Reasoning** Graph the function rule from Exercise 14. How do you know the rule is nonlinear?

17. Complete the table of values.

b	$A = b^2 + $ ☐	A
1		
4		
7		
10		

18. Graph the ordered pairs (b, A) that you found in Exercise 17. Use the points to graph the function rule.

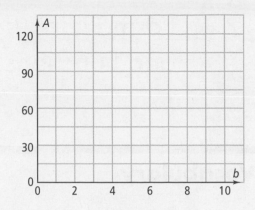

19. How do you know the rule is nonlinear? Explain.

_____

_____

Lesson Check • Do you UNDERSTAND?

Reasoning Is the graph of a function rule that relates a square's area to its side length *continuous* or *discrete*? Explain.

20. Underline the correct word to complete each sentence.

A *continuous / discrete* graph is unbroken.

A *continuous / discrete* graph is composed of isolated points.

The number of possible values for the length of a side of a square is finite / infinite .

21. Is the graph *continuous* or *discrete*? Explain.

_____

_____

_____

Math Success

Check off the vocabulary words that you understand.

☐ function notation   ☐ function rule

Rate how well you can *write function rules*.

| Need to review | 0 | 2 | 4 | 6 | 8 | 10 | Now I get it! |

Lesson 4-5

4-6 Formalizing Relations and Functions

Vocabulary

● Review

1. Use the words below to label the function machine at the right. Use each word once.

function rule   *y*-values   output

x-values   input   range

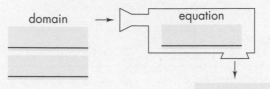

domain

equation

● Vocabulary Builder

reasonable (adjective) **ree zun uh bul**

Definition: Something is **reasonable** if it makes sense or is sensible.

Example: It is **reasonable** to expect warm weather in Miami in July.

Nonexample: It is *not* **reasonable** to expect snow in Miami in July.

Other Word Forms: reasonableness (noun); reasonably (adverb)

Opposite: unreasonable (adjective)

● Use Your Vocabulary

Complete each sentence with the appropriate word from the list.

reasonable   reasonableness   unreasonable

2. The student estimated to check the __?__ of her answer.

3. Sales tax of $32 on an $85 item is __?__ .

4. A price of $14 is __?__ for a pizza.

Problem 1 Identifying Functions Using Mapping Diagrams

Got It? Identify the domain and range of the following relation:

$$\{(4.2, 1.5), (5, 2.2), (7, 4.8), (4.2, 0)\}$$

Represent the relation with a mapping diagram. Is the relation a function?

5. Use the words *domain* and *range* to label the mapping diagram. Then draw arrows to represent the relation.

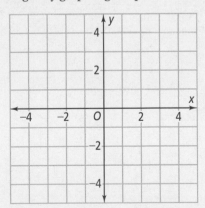

4.2	0
5	1.5
7	2.2
	4.8

6. Does the relation map each domain value to exactly one range value?   Yes / No

7. Is the relation a function?   Yes / No

You can use the **vertical line test** to decide whether a relation is a function. If any vertical line passes through more than one point of the graph, then the relation is *not* a function.

Problem 2 Identifying Functions Using the Vertical Line Test

Got It? Is the relation $\{(4, 2), (1, 2), (0, 1), (-2, 2), (3, 3)\}$ a function? Use the vertical line test.

8. Begin by graphing the points from the relation on the coordinate plane.

9. Can you draw a vertical line that intersects more than one point? If so, draw it.   Yes / No

10. Is the relation a function?   Yes / No

Lesson 4-6

Problem 3 Evaluating a Function

Got It? The function $w(x) = 250x$ represents the number of words $w(x)$ you can read in x minutes. How many words can you read in 6 min?

11. You should substitute ▢ for x.

12. The function is evaluated below. Write the justification for each step.

$w(x) = 250x$ _____

$w(6) = 250 \cdot 6$ _____

$w(6) = 1500$ _____

13. You can read ▢ words in 6 minutes.

Problem 4 Finding the Range of a Function

Got It? The domain of $g(x) = 4x - 12$ is $\{1, 3, 5, 7\}$. What is the range?

14. Underline the correct word to complete each sentence.

The domain / range is the set of input values.

The domain / range is the set of output values.

15. Use the function $g(x) = 4x - 12$ with domain $\{1, 3, 5, 7\}$. Find each output.

$g(1)$

$g(3)$

$g(5)$

$g(7)$

16. The range of $g(x) = 4x - 12$ with domain $\{1, 3, 5, 7\}$ is

$\{$ ▢ , ▢ , ▢ , ▢ $\}$.

Problem 5 Identifying a Reasonable Domain and Range

Got It? You have 7 qt of paint to paint the trim in your house. A quart of paint covers 100 ft^2. The function $A(q) = 100q$ represents the area $A(q)$, in square feet, that q quarts of paint cover. What domain and range are reasonable for the function?

17. Complete the reasoning model below.

Think	Write
The least amount of paint I can use is 0 qt. So, that is the least domain value.	$A() = 100 \cdot $ $A() = $
The greatest amount of paint I can use is 7 qt. So, that is the greatest domain value.	$A() = 100 \cdot $ $A() = $

18. A reasonable domain is $\boxed{} \le q \le \boxed{}$.

19. A reasonable range is $\boxed{} \le A(q) \le \boxed{}$.

Lesson Check • Do you UNDERSTAND?

Error Analysis A student drew the dashed line on the graph shown and concluded that the graph represented a function. Is the student correct? Explain.

20. Describe how the vertical line test helps you decide whether a relation is a function.

_____

_____

21. Underline the correct word or words to complete each sentence about the graph.

I can draw a vertical line that passes through only one point / more than one point

Therefore the graph does / does not represent a function.

22. Describe the student's error.

_____

_____

_____

Math Success

Check off the vocabulary words that you understand.

☐ relation ☐ domain ☐ range ☐ vertical line test ☐ function notation

Rate how well you *understand functions*.

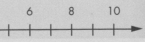

| Need to review | 0 | 2 | 4 | 6 | 8 | 10 | Now I get it! |

Lesson 4-6

Vocabulary

● **Review**

1. Circle the name of the next shape in the *pattern* at the right.

| rectangle | circle | hexagon | octagon |

   ...

Find the next number in each *pattern*.

2. $1, \frac{1}{3}, \frac{1}{9},$

3. $6, 4, 2, 0,$

4. $2, 10, 50, 250,$

● **Vocabulary Builder**

> Fibonacci **sequence**
>
> 0, 1, 1, 2, 3, 5, 8, 13, 21, ...

sequence (noun) SEE **kwuns**

Definition: A **sequence** is an ordered list of numbers that often form a pattern. Each number in the list is called a *term* of the **sequence**.

Example: The Fibonacci sequence is a **sequence** of numbers where the first number is 0, the second number is 1, and each subsequent number is equal to the sum of the previous two numbers.

Origin: from the Latin word *sequentia*, which means "to follow"

● **Use Your Vocabulary**

The following sets of numbers are *sequences*. Explain each pattern.

5. set of whole numbers greater than or equal to 5: {5, 6, 7, 8, 9, ...}

_____

_____

6. {40, 42, 44, 46, 48, ...}

_____

_____

Problem 1 Extending Sequences

Got It? Describe a pattern in the sequence 5, 11, 17, 23, ... What are the next two terms of the sequence?

7. Complete the diagram. What number is added to each term?

+ ☐   + ☐   + ☐

5   11   17   23

8. Describe the pattern in the sequence.

_____

9. Find the next two terms in the sequence.

5, 11, 17, 23, ☐ , ☐ , . . .

In an **arithmetic sequence**, the difference between consecutive terms is constant. This difference is called the **common difference**.

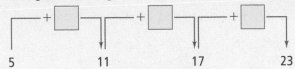

Problem 2 Identifying an Arithmetic Sequence

Got It? Tell whether the sequence 8, 15, 22, 30, ... is arithmetic. If it is, what is the common difference?

10. Complete the table.

Consecutive Terms	8 and 15	15 and ☐	22 and ☐
Difference	☐	☐	☐

11. Do the consecutive terms have a common difference?　　Yes / No

12. Is the sequence an arithmetic sequence? If so, what is the common difference?

_____

_____

Got It? Tell whether the sequence 7, 9, 11, 13, ... is arithmetic. If it is, what is the common difference?

13. Complete the table.

Consecutive Terms	7 and 9	9 and ☐	11 and ☐
Difference	☐	☐	☐

Lesson 4-7

14. Do the consecutive terms have a common difference?   Yes / No

15. Is the sequence an arithmetic sequence? If so, what is the common difference?

_____

Got It? Tell whether the sequence 10, 4, −2, −8, . . . is arithmetic. If it is, what is the common difference?

16. Do the consecutive terms have a common difference?   Yes / No

17. Is the sequence an arithmetic sequence? If so, what is the common difference?

_____

Key Concept   Rule for an Arithmetic Sequence

The nth term of an arithmetic sequence with the first term $A(1)$ and common difference d is given by this rule:

$$A(n) = A(1) + (n - 1)d$$

nth term   first term   term number   common difference

18. The equation $A(5) = 3 + (5 - 1)7$ generates the fifth term in a sequence.
Draw a line from each number in Column A to its description in Column B.

Column A	Column B
7	first term of the sequence
5	term number
3	common difference

Problem 3   Writing a Rule for an Arithmetic Sequence

Got It? A subway pass has a starting value of $100. After one ride, the value of the pass is $98.25. After two rides, its value is $96.50. After three rides, its value is $94.75. Write a rule to represent the remaining value on the card as an arithmetic sequence. What is the value of the pass after 15 rides?

19. Complete the diagram.

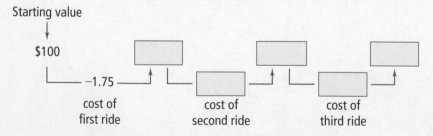

Starting value

$100

−1.75

cost of
first ride

cost of
second ride

cost of
third ride

20. Complete each sentence. Then complete the formula.

The first term of the sequence is ▢ .   The common difference is ▢ .

$$A(n) = \boxed{} + (n - 1) \cdot (\boxed{})$$

21. Use the formula from Exercise 20 to find the value of the pass after 15 rides. Note that the term *after* 15 rides are used is the *16th* term.

22. The value of the pass after 15 rides is $ ▢ .

Lesson Check • Do you UNDERSTAND?

Reasoning Can you use the rule below to find the *n*th term of an arithmetic sequence with a first term $A(1)$ and a common difference d? Explain.

$$A(n) = A(1) + nd - d$$

23. Use the Distributive Property to write an equivalent formula.

$$A(n) = A(1) + nd - d$$

24. Can you use the rule $A(n) = A(1) + nd - d$ to find the *n*th term of an arithmetic sequence? Explain.

_____

_____

_____

Math Success

Check off the vocabulary words that you understand.

☐ sequence   ☐ term of a sequence   ☐ arithmetic sequence   ☐ common difference

Rate how well you can *understand arithmetic sequences.*

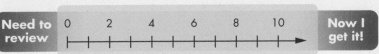

Lesson 4-7

Vocabulary

● **Review**

1. Circle the *rate* that matches this situation: Ron reads 5 books every 2 weeks.

$\dfrac{5 \text{ weeks}}{2 \text{ books}}$ $\dfrac{2 \text{ books}}{5 \text{ weeks}}$ $\dfrac{5 \text{ books}}{2 \text{ weeks}}$

2. Write *always, sometimes,* or *never.*

A *rate* is _?_ a ratio.   _____

A *ratio* is _?_ a *rate.*   _____

3. Underline the correct word to complete each sentence.

A *rate* compares two quantities by   division / multiplication .

A *rate* compares quantities in   different / the same   unit(s).

● **Vocabulary Builder**

$$\text{slope} = \frac{\text{vertical change}}{\text{horizontal change}} = \frac{\text{rise}}{\text{run}}$$

slope (noun) **slohp**

Definition: **Slope** is the ratio of the vertical change (or rise) to the horizontal change (or run) between two points on a line. **Slope** is also called the rate of change.

Main Idea: **Slope** describes the steepness of a line in the coordinate plane.

Examples: You can measure the **slope** of a hill, mountain, road, or roof.

● **Use Your Vocabulary**

4. How does the *slope* of a road affect a person's driving?

_____

_____

5. What kind of ski *slope* would a beginner skier use?

_____

_____

Problem 1 Finding Rate of Change Using a Table

Got It? The table at the right shows the distance a band marches over time. The rate of change from one row of the table to the next is 260 feet per minute. Do you get the rate of change of 260 feet per minute if you use nonconsecutive rows of the table? Explain.

Distance Marched

Time (min)	Distance (ft)
1	260
2	520
3	80
4	040

6. Use the values from the second and fourth rows to find the rate of change.

$$\text{rate of change} = \frac{\text{change in distance}}{\text{change in time}}$$

$$= \frac{\boxed{} - 520}{4 - \boxed{}}$$

$$= \frac{\boxed{}}{2}$$

$$= \frac{\boxed{}}{1}$$

When you use nonconsecutive rows, the rate of change is ⬜ ft per min.

7. Is the rate of change you found in Exercise 6 the same as if you had used two consecutive rows? Explain why or why not.

_____

_____

Problem 2 Finding Slope Using a Graph

Got It? What is the slope of the line?

8. Label each point on the graph with its coordinates.

9. Draw a vertical arrow to represent the rise.

rise = ⬜

10. Draw a horizontal arrow to represent the run.

run = ⬜

11. Underline the correct word to complete the sentence.

Because the points are on the same line, the rate of change from point to point

is constant / differs .

12. Write the slope of the line.

$$\text{slope} = \frac{\text{vertical change}}{\text{horizontal change}} = \frac{\text{rise}}{\text{run}} = \frac{\boxed{}}{\boxed{}}$$

Lesson 5-1

take note

Key Concept   The Slope Formula

In the diagram, (x_1, y_1) are the coordinates of point A, and (x_2, y_2) are the coordinates of point B. To find the slope of $\overleftrightarrow{AB}$, you can use the *slope formula*.

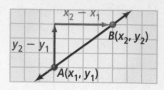

$$\text{slope} = \frac{\text{rise}}{\text{run}} = \frac{y_2 - y_1}{x_2 - x_1}, \text{ where } x_2 - x_1 \neq 0$$

When using the *slope formula*, the x–coordinate you use first in the denominator must belong to the same ordered pair as the y-coordinate you use first in the numerator.

13. To find the change in x- or y-coordinates, do you add or subtract?

_____

14. What number will you get in the denominator if the x-coordinates are the same? Explain how that will affect the answer you find for the slope.

_____

 Problem 3   **Finding Slope Using Points**

Got It? What is the slope of the line through $(1, 3)$ and $(4, -1)$?

15. You can use either pair for (x_2, y_2).

For example, use $(4, \quad)$ for (x_2, y_2). Then use $(1, \quad)$ for (x_1, y_1).

16. Complete the equation.

$$\text{slope} = \frac{y_2 - y_1}{x_2 - x_1} = \frac{-1 - \boxed{}}{4 - \boxed{}} = \frac{\boxed{}}{\boxed{}}$$

17. The slope of the line through $(1, 3)$ and $(4, -1)$ is $\boxed{}$.

Problem 4   **Finding Slopes of Horizontal and Vertical Lines**

Got It? What is the slope of the line through $(4, -3)$ and $(4, 2)$?

18. Graph the points $(4, -3)$ and $(4, 2)$ and draw the line that goes through the points.

19. Is the line that you drew *horizontal* or *vertical*?

_____

20. What is the slope of the line through $(4, -3)$ and $(4, 2)$?

_____

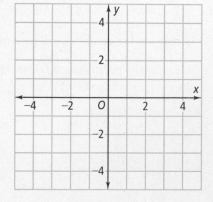

Problem 1 Finding Rate of Change Using a Table

Got It? The table at the right shows the distance a band marches over time. The rate of change from one row of the table to the next is 260 feet per minute. Do you get the rate of change of 260 feet per minute if you use nonconsecutive rows of the table? Explain.

Distance Marched

Time (min)	Distance (ft)
1	260
2	520
3	780
4	1040

6. Use the values from the second and fourth rows to find the rate of change.

$$\text{rate of change} = \frac{\text{change in distance}}{\text{change in time}}$$

$$= \frac{\boxed{} - 520}{4 - \boxed{}}$$

$$= \frac{\boxed{}}{2}$$

$$= \frac{\boxed{}}{1}$$

When you use nonconsecutive rows, the rate of change is ⬚ ft per min.

7. Is the rate of change you found in Exercise 6 the same as if you had used two consecutive rows? Explain why or why not.

_____

_____

Problem 2 Finding Slope Using a Graph

Got It? What is the slope of the line?

8. Label each point on the graph with its coordinates.

9. Draw a vertical arrow to represent the rise.

rise = ⬚

10. Draw a horizontal arrow to represent the run.

run = ⬚

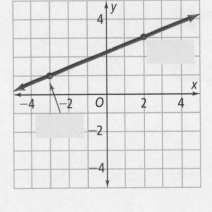

11. Underline the correct word to complete the sentence.

Because the points are on the same line, the rate of change from point to point

is constant / differs .

12. Write the slope of the line.

$$\text{slope} = \frac{\text{vertical change}}{\text{horizontal change}} = \frac{\text{rise}}{\text{run}} = \frac{\boxed{}}{\boxed{}}$$

Lesson 5-1

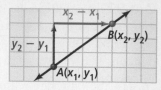

Key Concept   The Slope Formula

In the diagram, (x_1, y_1) are the coordinates of point A, and (x_2, y_2) are the coordinates of point B. To find the slope of $\overleftrightarrow{AB}$, you can use the *slope formula*.

$$\text{slope} = \frac{\text{rise}}{\text{run}} = \frac{y_2 - y_1}{x_2 - x_1}, \text{ where } x_2 - x_1 \neq 0$$

When using the *slope formula*, the x–coordinate you use first in the denominator must belong to the same ordered pair as the y–coordinate you use first in the numerator.

To find the change in x– or y–coordinates, do you add or subtract?

14. What number will you get in the denominator if the x-coordinates are the same? Explain how that will affect the answer you find for the slope.

Problem 3   Finding Slope Using Points

Got It? What is the slope of the line through $(1, 3)$ and $(4, -1)$?

15. You can use either pair for (x_2, y_2).

For example, use $(4, \quad)$ for (x_2, y_2). Then use $(1, \quad)$ for (x_1, y_1).

16. Complete the equation.

$$\text{slope} = \frac{y_2 - y_1}{x_2 - x_1} = \frac{-1 - \boxed{}}{4 - \boxed{}} = \frac{\boxed{}}{\boxed{}}$$

17. The slope of the line through $(1, 3)$ and $(4, -1)$ is $\boxed{}$.

Problem 4   Finding Slopes of Horizontal and Vertical Lines

Got It? What is the slope of the line through $(4, -3)$ and $(4, 2)$?

18. Graph the points $(4, -3)$ and $(4, 2)$ and draw the line that goes through the points.

19. Is the line that you drew *horizontal* or *vertical*?

20. What is the slope of the line through $(4, -3)$ and $(4, 2)$?

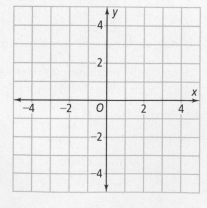

Concept Summary   Slopes of Lines

21. Label each graph with one of the descriptions in the box at the right.

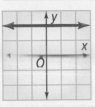

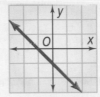

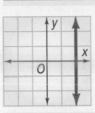

negative slope
positive slope
slope of 0
undefined slope

_____   _____

_____   _____

Lesson Check • Do you UNDERSTAND?

Error Analysis A student calculated the slope of the line at
the right to be 2. Explain the mistake. What is the correct slope?

22. The rise of the graphed line is ☐ .

23. The run of the graphed line is ☐ .

24. What mistake did the student make by calculating the
slope to be 2? Explain how to find the correct slope.

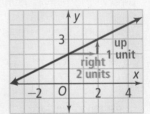

_____

_____

Math Success

Check off the vocabulary words that you understand.

☐ rate of change   ☐ slope

Rate how well you can *find the slope of a line*.

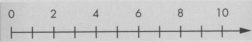

Need to review   0   2   4   6   8   10   Now I get it!

Vocabulary

● Review

1. Cross out the expression below that does NOT show a formula for *slope*.

$$\frac{\text{horizontal change}}{\text{vertical change}} \qquad\qquad \frac{y_2 - y_1}{x_2 - x_1} \qquad\qquad \frac{\text{rise}}{\text{run}}$$

2. Underline the correct word in each sentence about *slope*.

The *slope* of a horizontal line is undefined / zero .

The *slope* of a vertical line is undefined / zero .

● Vocabulary Builder

> $y = kx$, where $k \neq 0$, is a **direct variation**.
>
> In the above, k is called the *constant of variation*.

direct (adjective) **duh** REKT

Definition: **Direct** means straightforward in language or action.

Other Word Forms: directly (adverb), direction(s) (noun)

Math Usage: If the ratio of two variables is constant, then the variables form a **direct** variation.

What It Means: In a **direct** variation, one variable *directly* affects another by multiplying it by a constant value.

Both variables increase: The more expensive the car, the more sales tax you pay.

One variable increases, the other variable decreases: As a candle burns longer, its height gets smaller.

● Use Your Vocabulary

Choose the correct word from the list to complete each sentence.

| directly | direct | directions |

3. Renee gave the visitor __?__ to the museum.

4. The fans went __?__ to their seats.

5. There is a __?__ connection between the outside temperature and the number of people at the beach.

A function in the form $y = kx$, where $k \neq 0$, represents a **direct variation**. The **constant of variation** k is the coefficient of x.

To determine whether an equation represents a direct variation, solve it for y. If you can write the equation in the form $y = kx$, where $k \neq 0$, it represents a direct variation.

 Problem 1 **Identifying a Direct Variation**

Got It? Does $4x + 5y = 0$ represent a direct variation? If so, find the constant of variation.

6. Circle the equation that shows direct variation.

$$y = \frac{k}{x} \qquad\qquad y = kx \qquad\qquad yx = k$$

7. Complete the steps to solve $4x + 5y = 0$ for y.

$4x + 5y = 0$ Write the original equation.

$5y = 0 - \boxed{}$ Subtract $\boxed{}$ from each side.

$y = \boxed{}$ Divide each side by $\boxed{}$.

8. Does $4x + 5y = 0$ represent a direct variation? Explain.

_____

_____

9. In the equation $4x + 5y = 0$, $\boxed{}$ is the constant of variation.

 Problem 2 **Writing a Direct Variation Equation**

Got It? Suppose y varies directly with x, and $y = 10$ when $x = -2$. What direct variation equation relates x and y? What is the value of y when $x = -15$?

10. Complete the reasoning model below.

Think	Write
I start with the function form of direct variation.	$y = \boxed{} \cdot x$
Then I substitute 10 for y and -2 for $\boxed{}$.	$10 = \boxed{} \cdot (-2)$
Now I divide each side by $\boxed{}$ to solve for k.	$\boxed{} = \boxed{}$
Next, I write an equation by substituting $\boxed{}$ for k.	$y = \boxed{} \cdot x$
Finally, I determine the value of y when $x = -15$.	$y = \boxed{} \cdot \boxed{} = \boxed{}$

Lesson 5-2

Problem 3 Graphing a Direct Variation

Got It? Weight on the moon y varies directly with weight on Earth x. A person who weighs 100 lb on Earth weighs 16.6 lb on the moon. What is an equation that relates weight on Earth x and weight on the moon y? What is the graph of this equation?

11. Find the value of k. Round k to the nearest hundredth if necessary.

$$y = kx$$

$$\boxed{} = k \cdot \boxed{}$$

$$\boxed{} = k$$

12. To the nearest hundredth, $k = \boxed{}$. So, $y \approx \boxed{} \cdot x$.

13. Make a table of values.

x	$y = \boxed{}\, x$
0	$y = \boxed{} \cdot 0 = 0$
25	$y = \boxed{} \cdot 25 = \boxed{}$
50	$y = \boxed{} \cdot 50 = \boxed{}$
100	$y = \boxed{} \cdot 100 = \boxed{}$
125	$y = \boxed{} \cdot 125 = \boxed{}$

14. Graph the values from the table.

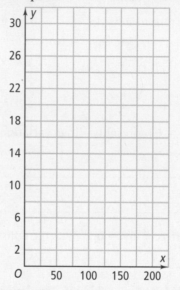

---

take note

Concept Summary Graphs of Direct Variations

The graph of a direct variation equation $y = kx$ is a line with the following properties.

- The line passes through (0, 0).
- The slope of the line is k.

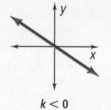

$k > 0$ $k < 0$

15. Substitute $x = 0$ and $y = 0$ in the equation $-2x + y = 3$.

$$-2x + y = 3$$

$$-2 \cdot \boxed{} + \boxed{} = 3$$

$$\boxed{} + \boxed{} = 3$$

$$\boxed{} \overset{?}{=} 3$$

16. Because the graph of $-2x + y = 3$ passes / does not pass through (0, 0), the equation is / is not a direct variation.

Problem 4 **Writing a Direct Variation From a Table**

x	y
−3	2.25
1	−0.75
4	−3

Got It? For the data in the table at the right, does y vary directly with x? If it does, write an equation for the direct variation.

18. Write each ordered pair as the ratio of the y-coordinate to the x-coordinate. Then write the ratio of y to x as a decimal.

$(-3, 2.25)$ $(1, -0.75)$ $(4, -3)$

_____ = [ ]   _____ = [ ]   ____ = [ ]

19. For the data in the table, does y vary directly with x?   Yes / No

20. The equation for the direct variation shown is $y = $ [ ] $\cdot x$.

 Lesson Check • **Do you UNDERSTAND?**

Vocabulary Determine whether each statement is *always*, *sometimes*, or *never* true.

The ordered pair $(0, 0)$ is a solution of the direct variation equation $y = kx$.

21. Substitute $(0, 0)$ into $y = kx$.

[ ] $\overset{?}{=} k \cdot$ [ ]

22. The statement is __?__ true.

_____

You can write a direct variation in the form $y = k + x$, where $k \neq 0$.

23. Is $y = k + x$ of the form $y = kx$?

Yes / No

24. The statement is __?__ true.

_____

The constant of variation for a direct variation represented by $y = kx$ is $\frac{y}{x}$.

25. When you divide each side of $y = kx$ by x, you obtain $k = $ [ ].

26. Because you cannot divide by 0, the statement is __?__ true.

_____

 Math Success

Check off the vocabulary words that you understand.

☐ direct variation   ☐ constant of variation for a direct variation

Rate how well you can *work with direct variation.*

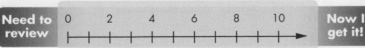

Lesson 5-2

Vocabulary

● Review

1. **Multiple Choice** Which equation is NOT a *linear* equation?

   Ⓐ $y = -3x + 4$ Ⓑ $y = x$ Ⓒ $y = \dfrac{x}{5} - 7$ Ⓓ $y = 5^x$

2. Place a ✓ in the box if the statement applies to the graph of a *linear* equation.
   Place an ✗ if it does NOT apply to the graph of a *linear* equation.

   ☐ The graph of a linear equation is always a horizontal line.

   ☐ The graph of a linear equation is always a straight line.

   ☐ The graph of a linear equation may be shaped like a "U."

● Vocabulary Builder

> A **y-intercept** is the y-coordinate of a point where a graph crosses the y-axis.

intercept (noun) ɪN **tur sept**

Other Word Forms: intercepted (verb), interception (noun)

Definition: An **intercept** is a point where someone or something is stopped along its way from one place to another.

Main Idea: You can find the **intercept(s)** of a graph by finding the point(s) where the graph crosses a coordinate axis.

Related Words: *x*-intercept; *y*-intercept

● Use Your Vocabulary

Choose the correct word from the list to complete each sentence.

intercept   intercepted   interception

3. During a football game, the home team's quarterback threw an __?__ .

4. The *y*-coordinate of a point where a graph crosses the *y*-axis is a *y*-__?__ .

5. The teacher __?__ the message Charlie was passing to his friend.

Key Concept   Slope-Intercept Form of a Linear Equation

The **slope-intercept** form of a linear equation of a nonvertical line is $y = mx + b$.

The slope of the line is m. The y-intercept is b.

6. Use the words *slope, y-intercept*, and *slope-intercept form* to complete the diagram at the right.

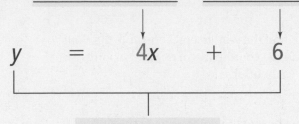

$$y = 4x + 6$$

Problem 2   Writing an Equation in Slope-Intercept Form

Got It? What is an equation of the line with slope $\frac{3}{2}$ and y-intercept -1?

7. Write the numbers $\frac{3}{2}$ and -1 in the correct boxes below.

$$y = \; m \cdot x + \; b$$

$$y = \boxed{} \cdot x + \boxed{}$$

8. An equation in slope-intercept form is _____ .

Problem 3   Writing an Equation From a Graph

Got It? What is an equation of the line shown at the right?

9. Find two points on the graph to find the slope of the line. What two points will you use?

$(\quad , \quad)$ and $(\quad , \quad)$

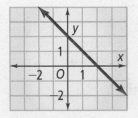

10. Use the points to find the slope of the line.

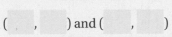

11. The slope of the line is _____ .

12. Use the graph to find the y-intercept.
   The y-intercept is _____ .

13. Write the slope-intercept form of the equation.

Problem 4   Writing an Equation From Two Points

Got It? What equation in slope-intercept form represents the line that passes through the points $(3, -2)$ and $(1, -3)$?

14. Circle the first step to solve this problem. Underline the second step.

| Solve for b. | Find the slope. | Write the slope-intercept form. |

Lesson 5-3

15. Use the points $(3, -2)$ and $(1, -3)$ to find the slope of the line.

$$m = \frac{\boxed{} - (-3)}{3 - \boxed{}} = \frac{1}{\boxed{}}$$

16. Next, find the *y*-intercept. Substitute the slope for *m* and the coordinates of one of the points for *x* and *y*. Then solve for *b*.

$$y = m \cdot x + b$$

17. Write the equation of the line in slope-intercept form. Substitute the slope for *m* and the *y*-intercept for *b*.

$$y = \boxed{} \cdot x + \boxed{}$$

Problem 5 Graphing a Linear Equation

Got It? What is the graph of $y = -3x + 4$?

18. The ordered pair for the *y*-intercept, 4, is ($\boxed{}$, $\boxed{}$).

19. Explain how you will use the slope to find another point on the line.

_____

20. Use the slope, -3, to find another point on the line.

21. Use the points you found in Exercises 18 and 20. What is the graph of $y = -3x + 4$?

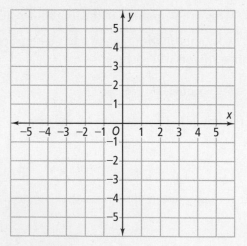

Problem 6 Modeling a Function

Got It? A plumber charges a $65 fee for a repair plus $35 per hour. Write an equation to model the total cost *y* of a repair that takes *x* hours. What graph models the total cost?

22. Let $x =$ the number of hours the plumber works. Let $y =$ the total cost of a repair.

When $x = 0$, $y = \boxed{}$. So the *y*-intercept is $\boxed{}$.

23. The slope is the amount of change each hour.

So, the slope is [ ].

24. Write an equation to model the cost of a repair.

25. Complete the table for your equation.

Hours (*x*)	0	1			
Total Cost (*y*)	65				

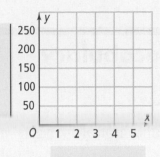

26. Graph the data from the table to model the total cost.
Be sure to label the axes.

Lesson Check • **Do you UNDERSTAND?**

Vocabulary Is $y = 5$ a linear equation? Explain.

27. Does $y = 5$ have a slope? Explain.

28. Find three points that satisfy $y = 5$.

(,)　　　　　　(,)　　　　　　(,)

29. Is $y = 5$ a linear equation? Explain.

Math Success

Check off the vocabulary words that you understand.

☐ linear function　　　　☐ *y*-intercept　　　　☐ slope-intercept form

Rate how well you can *find the slope-intercept form of a linear equation.*

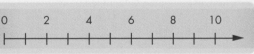

Lesson 5-3

Point-Slope Form

Vocabulary

● Review

1. Circle the equation that has a *y-intercept* of 3.

| $y = 3x + 4$ | $y = 4x - 3$ | $y = 5x + 3$ | $y = -3x + 2$ |

2. Circle the equation that is in *slope-intercept* form.

| $2x - y = 10$ | $x + 3y + 11 = 0$ | $y - 4 = \frac{2}{3}(x + 7)$ | $y = 2x + 6$ |

3. Circle the statement that is true about the *y-intercept* of any graph.

| occurs where $y = 0$ on the graph | occurs where $x = 0$ on the graph | occurs where graph touches the *x*-axis |

● Vocabulary Builder

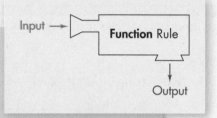

function (noun) FUNGK **shun**

Related Words: input, output, function rule

Definition: A **function** is a relationship that assigns exactly one output value to each input value.

Main Idea: A **function** is used to describe how one value depends on another.

Example: The function machine above shows that the **function** assigns an output to every input according to a specified rule.

● Use Your Vocabulary

Complete each sentence with the appropriate word from the list.

| price | sun | time |

4. The length of a shadow is a *function* of the angle of the __?__ .

5. The amount of water that has leaked from a leaky faucet is a *function* of __?__ .

6. The amount of sales tax you pay is a *function* of the item's __?__ .

Key Concept   Point-Slope Form of a Linear Equation

The **point-slope form** of an equation of a nonvertical line with slope m and through point (x_1, y_1) is $y - y_1 = m(x - x_1)$.

7. In the above, what does (x_1, y_1) represent?

8. What does m represent?

Problem 1   Writing an Equation in Point-Slope Form

Got It? A line passes through $(8, -4)$ and has slope $\frac{2}{3}$. What is an equation in point-slope form of the line?

9. Use the point-slope form of an equation. For a line that passes through $(8, -4)$ and has slope $\frac{2}{3}$, circle x_1 and underline y_1.

-4	$\frac{2}{3}$	8	12

10. Now substitute into point-slope form.

$$y - y_1 = m \cdot (x - x_1)$$

$$y - \boxed{} = \boxed{} \cdot (x - \boxed{})$$

11. An equation of the line is _____ .

Problem 2   Graphing Using Point-Slope Form

Got It? What is the graph of the equation $y + 7 = -\frac{4}{5}(x - 4)$?

12. Circle the ordered pair of a point on the graph of $y + 7 = -\frac{4}{5}(x - 4)$.

$(7, 4)$	$(4, 7)$	$(-4, -7)$	$(4, -7)$

13. Circle the correct description of the slope.

Go up 4 units and left 5 units   Go down 4 units and left 5 units   Go up 4 units and right 5 units

14. Use your answers to Exercises 12 and 13 to graph the line.

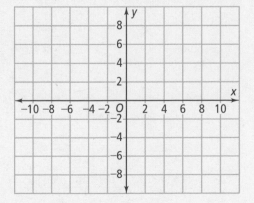

Lesson 5-4

Using Two Points to Write an Equation

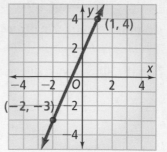

Got It? Use the point $(-2, -3)$ to write an equation of the line shown.

15. Follow the steps to write the equation of the line shown.

> **1** Find the slope of the line. Use two points and the
> slope formula, $m = \dfrac{y_2 - y_1}{x_2 - x_1}$.

> **2** Use the slope and the point $(-2, -3)$ to write
> an equation of the line in point-slope form.
>
> $$y - y_1 = m(x - x_1)$$
>
> $$y - \boxed{} = \boxed{} \cdot (x - \boxed{})$$
>
> An equation of the line is $\boxed{}$.

Problem 4 **Using a Table to Write an Equation**

Volume of Water in Tank

Time, x (h)	Water, y (gal)
2	3320
3	4570
5	7070
8	10,820

Got It? The table shows the number of gallons of water y in a tank after x hours. The relationship is linear. What is an equation in point-slope form that models the data? What does the slope represent?

16. Complete the reasoning model below.

Think	Write
I can use any two points from the table to find the slope.	$m = \dfrac{4570 - \boxed{}}{3 - \boxed{}} = \dfrac{\boxed{}}{\boxed{}}$
Then I can substitute one point and the slope into the point-slope equation.	$y - y_1 = m \cdot (x - x_1)$ $y - \boxed{} = \boxed{} \cdot (x - \boxed{})$
Finally, I can tell what the slope represents.	The slope represents a rate of __?__. $\boxed{}$

Got It? Reasoning Write the equation from Exercise 16 in slope-intercept form. What does the *y*-intercept represent?

17. Write the equation in point-slope form from Exercise 16. Use it to write the equation in slope-intercept form.

18. What does the *y*-intercept in your answer to Exercise 17 represent?

_____

_____

Lesson Check • Do you UNDERSTAND?

Reasoning Can any equation in point-slope form also be written in slope-intercept form? Give an example to explain.

19. Use point-slope form, $y - y_1 = m(x - x_1)$, and any point and slope to write an equation in point-slope form.

20. Now write your equation in slope-intercept form.

21. Can any equation in point-slope form also be written in slope-intercept form?   Yes / No

Math Success

Check off the vocabulary words that you understand.

☐ point-slope form   ☐ equation   ☐ graph

Rate how well you can *write equations in point-slope form.*

Need to review   0   2   4   6   8   10   Now I get it!

5-5 Standard Form

🔊 Vocabulary

● Review

Underline the correct word to complete each sentence.

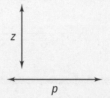

1. Line z is a *horizontal / vertical* line.

2. Line p is a *horizontal / vertical* line.

3. A line with a slope of 0 is *horizontal / vertical*.

4. A line with an undefined slope is *horizontal / vertical*.

● Vocabulary Builder

standard (adjective) STAN durd

Other Word Forms: standards (plural noun), standardized (adjective)

Main Idea: Something that is **standard** is well known and widely used.

Example: The **standard** measure of weight used in the U.S. is the pound.

Math Usage: The **standard** form of a linear equation is $Ax + By = C$, where A, B, and C are real numbers, and A and B are not both zero.

Opposites: different, irregular

● Use Your Vocabulary

Underline the correct word(s) to complete each sentence.

5. In gymnastics, judges use a set of *standards / standardized* to award a score.

6. Most English words have a *standard / standardized* pronunciation.

7. Many states use *standard / standardized* tests to assess their students' performance.

8. Multiple Choice Which linear equation is in *standard* form?

Ⓐ $y = -6x + 4$ Ⓒ $3x - 7y = 42$

Ⓑ $y = -7x - 3$ Ⓓ $y - 6 = 2(x + 7)$

Problem 1 Finding *x*- and *y*-Intercepts

Got It? What are the *x*- and *y*-intercepts of the graph of $5x - 6y = 60$?

Complete each sentence.

9. To find the *x*-intercept, let $y = $ ☐ .

10. To find the *y*-intercept, let $x = $ ☐ .

11. Find the *x*-intercept.

$$5x - 6 \cdot \boxed{} = 60$$

$$5x - \boxed{} = 60$$

$$\boxed{} = 60$$

$$\frac{\boxed{}}{5} = \frac{60}{5}$$

$$x = \boxed{}$$

12. Find the *y*-intercept.

$$5 \cdot \boxed{} - 6y = 60$$

$$\boxed{} - 6y = 60$$

$$\boxed{} = 60$$

$$\frac{\boxed{}}{-6} = \frac{60}{-6}$$

$$y = \boxed{}$$

Got It? What are the *x*- and *y*-intercepts of the graph of $3x + 8y = 12$?

13. Find the *x*-intercept.

$$3x + 8 \cdot \boxed{} = 12$$

$$\boxed{} = 12$$

$$\boxed{} = 12$$

$$x = \boxed{}$$

14. Find the *y*-intercept.

$$3 \cdot \boxed{} + 8y = 12$$

$$\boxed{} = 12$$

$$\boxed{} = 12$$

$$y = \boxed{}$$

 Problem 2 Graphing a Line Using Intercepts

Got It? What is the graph of $2x + 5y = 20$?

15. Circle the *x*-intercept of $2x + 5y = 20$.

| $x = 1$ | $x = 10$ | $x = 20$ |

16. Circle the *y*-intercept of $2x + 5y = 20$.

| $y = -5$ | $y = -4$ | $y = 4$ |

17. Use the intercepts to graph the line $2x + 5y = 20$.

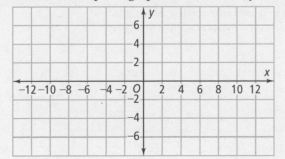

Lesson 5-5

Problem 3 Graphing Horizontal and Vertical Lines

Got It? What is the graph of the equation $x = 4$?

18. The equation $x = 4$ means that for all values of y, the value of x is [　].

19. For the reason given above, the graph of $x = 4$ is a horizontal / vertical line.

20. Graph the equation $x = 4$.

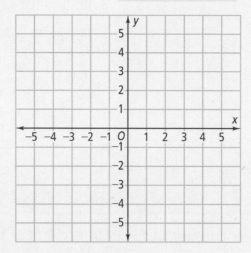

Problem 4 Transforming to Standard Form

Got It? Write $y - 2 = -\frac{1}{3}(x + 6)$ in standard form using integers.

21. Circle the first step to put $y - 2 = -\frac{1}{3}(x + 6)$ in standard form.

| Solve for y. | Multiply both sides by -3. | Add x to both sides. |

22. Now find the standard form of the equation using integers.

23. The standard form of the equation is [　] $\cdot x +$ [　] $\cdot y = 0$.

Problem 5 Using Standard Form as a Model

Got It? A media download store sells songs for $1 each and movies for $15 each. You have $60 to spend. Write and graph an equation that describes the numbers of songs and movies you can purchase for $60.

24. You cannot buy a fraction of a song or movie. Describe how you will use the graph of the equation to find solutions that make sense.

25. Use the model to help you complete the equation.

Relate | cost of a song | · | number of songs | + | cost of a movie | · | number of movies | is | $60

Define   Let $x =$ the number of songs purchased.

Let $y =$ _____ .

Write   ☐ · x + ☐ · y = 60

26. Find the intercepts of the equation.

27. Use the intercepts to graph the equation.

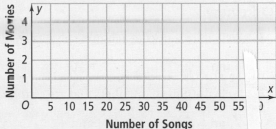

Number of Songs

Lesson Check • Do you UNDERSTAND?

Vocabulary Tell whether each linear equation is in *slope-intercept form, point-slope form,* or *standard form.*

$y + 5 = -(x - 2)$ $y = -2x + 5$ $y - 10 = -2(x - 1)$ $2x + 4y = 12$

28. Draw a line from each equation in Column A to the form of the equation in Column B.

Column A

$y + 5 = -(x - 2)$

$y = -2x + 5$

$y - 10 = -2(x - 1)$

$2x + 4y = 12$

Column B

$y = mx + b$ (Slope-Intercept Form)

$y - y_1 = m(x - x_1)$ (Point-Slope Form)

$Ax + By = C$ (Standard Form)

Math Success

Check off the vocabulary words that you understand.

☐ linear equation   ☐ x-intercept   ☐ standard form

Rate how well you can *graph a linear equation using intercepts.*

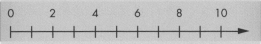

Need to review   0   2   4   6   8   10   Now I get it!

5-6 | Parallel and Perpendicular Lines

Vocabulary

● Review

1. Circle the product of a number and its *reciprocal*.

100	1	0	−1

2. Circle the pairs of numbers that are *reciprocals*.

7 and $\frac{1}{7}$	1 and −1	0 and $\frac{0}{12}$	$-\frac{3}{4}$ and $-\frac{4}{3}$

● Vocabulary Builder

parallel (adjective) PA ruh lel

Related Word: perpendicular (adjective)

Math Usage: Lines that are **parallel** are lines in the same plane that never intersect.

Using symbols: $\overleftrightarrow{AB} \parallel \overleftrightarrow{CD}$ means line AB is parallel to line CD.

Example: The stripes on the American flag are **parallel**.

● Use Your Vocabulary

Picture A

Picture B

Picture C

Complete each sentence with *parallel* or *perpendicular*.

3. The railroad tracks in Picture A are   ? .

4. The window bars in Picture B that do NOT meet are   ? .

5. The roads in Picture C are   ? .

Key Concept Slopes of Parallel Lines

Nonvertical lines are parallel if they have the same slope and different y-intercepts. Vertical lines are parallel if they have different x-intercepts.

6. Draw a line from each equation in Column A to an equation whose graph is parallel in Column B.

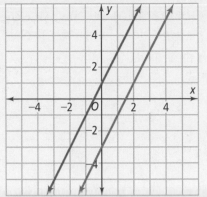

Column A	Column B
$y = 2x + 4$	$x = 2$
$y = \frac{1}{3}x - 2$	$y = 2x - 4$
$x = 3$	$y - \frac{1}{3}x - 1$

Problem 1 Writing an Equation of a Parallel Line

Got It? A line passes through $(-3, -1)$ and is parallel to the graph of $y = 2x + 3$. What equation represents the line in slope-intercept form?

7. The slope of the graph of $y = 2x + 3$ is ⬜.

8. The slope of any line parallel to the graph of $y = 2x + 3$ is ⬜.

9. Use point-slope form to find an equation of the line that passes through $(-3, -1)$ and uses the slope from Exercise 8.

$$y - y_1 = m(x - x_1)$$

Key Concept Slopes of Perpendicular Lines

Two nonvertical lines are perpendicular if the product of their slopes is -1. Two numbers whose product is -1 are called **opposite reciprocals**. A vertical line and a horizontal line are also perpendicular.

10. **Multiple Choice** The slope of a line is 2. What is the slope of a line perpendicular to that line?

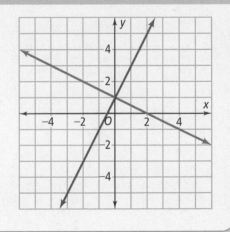

  Ⓐ 2   Ⓒ -2

  Ⓑ $\frac{1}{2}$ Ⓓ $-\frac{1}{2}$

Lesson 5-6

Problem 2 **Classifying Lines**

Got It? Are the graphs of the equations $y = \frac{3}{4}x + 7$ and $4x - 3y = 9$ *parallel,*
perpendicular, or *neither*? Explain.

11. Write the equation $4x - 3y = 9$ in slope-intercept form.

12. The slope of the line $y = \frac{3}{4}x + 7$ is ____.   **13.** The slope of the line $4x - 3y = 9$ is ____.

14. Are the lines *parallel, perpendicular,* or *neither*? Explain.

_____

_____

_____

_____

Problem 3 **Writing an Equation of a Perpendicular Line**

Got It? A line passes through $(1, 8)$ and is perpendicular to the graph of
$y = 2x + 1$. **What equation represents the line in slope-intercept form?**

15. Find the slope of the perpendicular line.

Slope of the given line = ⬜   ⬜ = opposite reciprocal
(slope of perpendicular line)

⬜ × ⬜ = −1

16. The slope of the perpendicular line is ____.

17. Use point-slope form and the point $(1, 8)$ to write an equation of the perpendicular line.

$y - y_1 = m \cdot (x - x_1)$

Problem 4 Solving a Real-World Problem

Got It? An architect uses software to design a ceiling. The architect needs to enter an equation that represents a new beam. The new beam will be parallel to the existing beam, which is shown by the red line. The new beam will pass through the corner at (0, 10). What is an equation in slope-intercept form that represents the new beam?

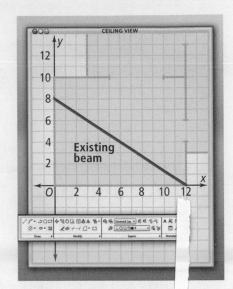

18. Use the slope formula to find the slope of the red line that represents the existing beam.

$$m = \frac{\boxed{} - \boxed{}}{\boxed{} - \boxed{}} = \boxed{}$$

19. In order for the new beam to be parallel to the existing beam, their slopes should be the same / opposite reciprocals .

20. Now find the equation of the line that will be parallel to the existing line and will pass through (0, 10).

Lesson Check • Do you UNDERSTAND?

Compare and Contrast How is determining if two lines are parallel similar to determining if they are perpendicular? How are the processes different?

21. To determine if two lines are parallel, what do you need to do?

22. To determine if two lines are perpendicular, what do you need to do?

23. How are the processes similar?

24. How are the processes different?

Math Success

Check off the vocabulary words that you understand.

☐ parallel lines ☐ perpendicular lines ☐ opposite reciprocals

Rate how well you can *write equations of parallel and perpendicular lines.*

Need to review 0 2 4 6 8 10 Now I get it!

Scatter Plots and Trend Lines

Vocabulary

● Review

A *scatter plot* is a graph that relates two sets of data. Plot each *ordered pair* on the graph at the right to make a scatter plot.

1. (2, 3)

2. (−1, −2)

3. (0, 2)

4. (−2, 0)

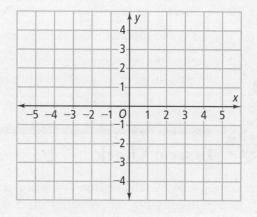

● Vocabulary Builder

correlation (noun) **kawr uh LAY shun**

Related Words: correlate (verb), relationship (noun), relate (verb), scatter plot (noun)

Definition: A **correlation** is a measure of the strength of a relationship between two quantities.

Example: The more a student studies, the higher the student's grades tend to be. So, there is a **correlation** between time spent studying and grades.

● Use Your Vocabulary

Label each scatter plot *positive correlation*, *negative correlation*, or *no correlation*.

5.

y increases as *x* increases

_____

6.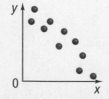

y decreases as *x* increases

_____

7.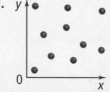

x and *y* are not related

_____

Got It? Make a scatter plot of the data in the table. What type of relationship does the scatter plot show?

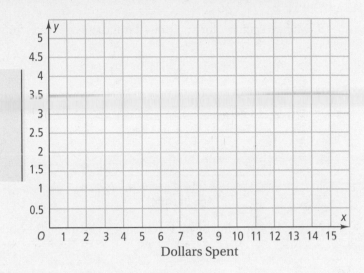

Gasoline Purchases							
Dollars Spent	10	11	9	10	13	5	8	4
Gallons Bought	2.5	2.8	2.3	2.6	3.3	1.3	2.2	1.1

8. Let x = dollars spent.

   Let y = _____.

9. Use the data to make a scatter plot.

10. Underline the correct word or words to complete each sentence.

    The number of gallons bought

    tends to increase / decrease

    as the number of dollars spent

    increases / decreases.

    The two sets of data have a

    positive / negative correlation.

Got It? Reasoning Consider the population of a city and the number of letters in the name of the city. Would you expect a *positive correlation*, a *negative correlation*, or *no correlation* between the two sets of data? Explain your reasoning.

11. As an example, think of the city or town that you live in. How many letters are in the name of your city and approximately how many people live there?

    _____

12. Now think of another city of a very different size than the one you chose for Exercise 11. How many letters are in the name of this city and approximately how many people live there?

    _____

13. Is the size of either city dependent on the number of letters in its name?   Yes / No

14. What kind of correlation would you expect between the two sets of data? Explain.

    _____

    _____

    _____

    _____

A **trend line** is a line on a scatter plot, drawn near the points, that shows a correlation. There should be about the same number of points above the line as below it.

Lesson 5-7

Problem 2 Writing an Equation of a Trend Line

Got It? Make a scatter plot of the data. Draw a trend line and write its equation. What is the approximate body length of a 7-month-old panda?

Body Length of a Panda								
Age (month)	1	2	3	4	5	6	8	9
Body Length (in.)	8.0	11.75	15.5	16.7	20.1	22.2	26.5	29.0

15. Make a scatter plot and draw a trend line.

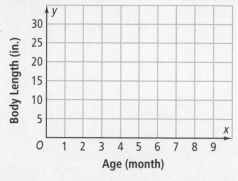

16. Write the equation of the trend line that you drew.

17. Use the equation of your trend line to estimate the body length of a 7-month-old panda.

18. A 7-month-old panda would be approximately ___ inches in length.

 Problem 3 Finding the Line of Best Fit

Got It? For data of tuition and fees charged at public four-year colleges, the equation of the line of best fit is $y = 409.43x - 815{,}446.71$, where $x =$ the year at the beginning of the academic year and $y =$ cost. Predict the cost of attending a public four-year college in the 2016–2017 academic year.

19. Let $x =$ ___ .

20. Complete the steps to find the estimated cost.

$$y = 409.43 \cdot \underline{} - 815{,}446.71$$

$$y = \underline{} - 815{,}446.71$$

$$y \approx \underline{}$$

21. The cost of attending a public four-year college in the 2016–2017 academic year will be about $ ___ .

Causation is when a change in one quantity causes a change in a second quantity. A correlation between quantities does not always imply causation.

Problem 4   Identifying Whether Relationships Are Causal

Got It? Consider the cost of a family's vacation and the size of their house. Is there likely to be a correlation? If so, does the correlation reflect a causal relationship? Explain.

22. Is there likely to be a correlation between the cost of a family's vacation and the size of their house? Explain.

23. If there is a correlation, does the correlation reflect a causal relationship? Explain.

Lesson Check • Do you UNDERSTAND?

Error Analysis Refer to the table below. A student says that the data have a negative correlation because as *x* decreases, *y* also decreases. What is the student's error?

x	10	7	5	4	1	0
y	1	0	−2	−4	−7	−9

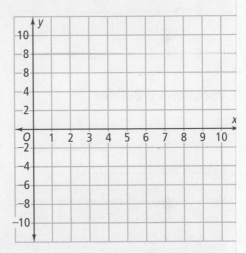

24. Make a scatter plot of the data.

25. The scatter plot shows a positive / negative correlation.

26. Explain the student's error.

Math Success

Check off the vocabulary words that you understand.

☐ scatter plot   ☐ correlation   ☐ trend line   ☐ causation

Rate how well you can *make a scatter plot and determine the type of correlation.*

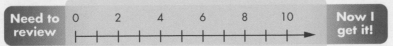

Lesson 5-7

Vocabulary

● Review

Compare the *absolute values*. Write <, >, or =.

1. $|3|$ ___ $|-3|$ **2.** $|-3|$ ___ $|-1|$ **3.** $|9|$ ___ $|-10|$ **4.** $|-9|$ ___ $|8|$

Write T for *true* or F for *false*.

____ **5.** The *absolute value* of a number is a measure of the distance from 0 to that number on the number line.

____ **6.** The *absolute value* of a number is always the opposite of that number.

● Vocabulary Builder

| translation (noun) **trans LAY shun**

Related Words: translate or slide (verb)

Math Usage: A **translation** (or a *slide*) is a shift of a graph (or shape) horizontally, vertically, or both. The graph (or shape) ends up being the same size and shape, but in a different place. This happens without rotation or reflection.

Word Origin: The word comes from the Latin word "translatum" or "transferre." **Trans** means "across"; **ferre** means "to carry."

● Use Your Vocabulary

Identify each pair of figures as a *translation* or *NOT a translation*.

7.

8.

9.

_____   _____   _____

Problem 1 Describing Translations

Got It? An absolute value function has a V-shaped graph that opens up or down. Below is the graph of $y = |x|$ and the graph of another absolute value function. How are the graphs related?

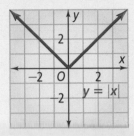

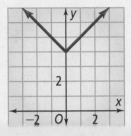

Underline the correct word to complete each sentence.

10. The two graphs have the same / different shape(s).

11. The second graph is translated up / down from $y = |x|$.

12. Complete the equation using the number of units the graph is translated.

$y = |x| \ +$ ▢

Got It? Reasoning What are the domain and range of each function above?

13. For $y = |x|$, are there any real numbers whose absolute value you could not find?   Yes / No

14. Multiple Choice What is the domain of $y = |x|$?

    Ⓐ all positive real numbers   Ⓒ all real numbers

    Ⓑ all positive integers   Ⓓ all integers

15. For $y = |x|$, will every y-value be positive or 0?   Yes / No

16. Multiple Choice What is the range of $y = |x|$?

    Ⓐ all nonnegative real numbers   Ⓒ all real numbers

    Ⓑ all nonnegative integers   Ⓓ all integers

Answer each question below about the function you wrote in Exercise 12.

17. The graph for this function was a vertical / horizontal translation of $y = |x|$.

So the domain / range of this function will change.

18. What is the domain of this function? Explain your reasoning.

_____

_____

19. What is the range of this function? Explain your reasoning.

_____

_____

Lesson 5-8

Problem 2 Graphing a Vertical Translation

Got It? What is the graph of $y = |x| - 7$?

20. Graph and label the equation $y = |x|$ on the coordinate plane at the right.

21. What does the -7 in $y = |x| - 7$ mean? Circle your answer.

| translate each | translate each |
| point 7 units up | point 7 units down |

22. Draw and label the graph of $y = |x| - 7$ on the coordinate plane at the right.

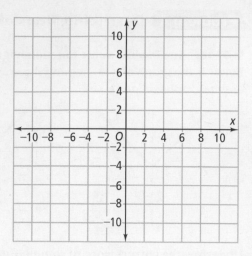

Problem 3 Writing Equations of Vertical Translations

Got It? What is an equation for a translation of $y = |x|$ eight units up?

23. A translation of $y = |x|$ eight units up is of the form ___?___. Circle your answer.

$y = |x| + k$, where k is positive $y = |x| - k$, where k is positive

24. Write an equation for a translation of $y = |x|$ eight units up.

Problem 4 Graphing a Horizontal Translation

Got It? What is the graph of $y = |x - 5|$?

25. Complete the table of values.

x	$y = x - 5$
0	$y = |0 - 5| =$
2	$y = |2 - 5| =$
5	$y = |5 - 5| =$
8	$y = |8 - 5| =$
10	$y = |10 - 5| =$

26. Use the table of values to plot five points. Connect the points to graph the absolute value function.

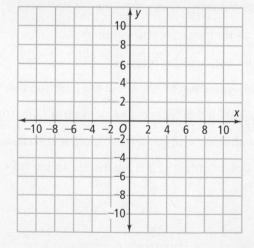

Problem 5 Writing Equations of Horizontal Translations

Got It? What is an equation for a translation of $y = |x|$ eight units right?

27. A translation of $y = |x|$ eight units right is of the form __?__. Circle your answer.

$y = |x + h|$, where h is positive $y = |x - h|$, where h is positive

28. Write an equation for a translation of $y = |x|$ eight units right.

Lesson Check • Do you UNDERSTAND?

Error Analysis A student is graphing the equation $y = |x - 10|$ and translates the graph of $y = |x|$ ten units left. Describe the student's error.

29. Complete the table to find values of the correct graph.

x	y = x − 10
0	$y = |0 - 10| = $ ☐
5	$y = |5 - 10| = $ ☐
10	$y = |10 - 10| = $ ☐
12	$y = |12 - 10| = $ ☐
−2	$y = |-2 - 10| = $ ☐

30. The graph below shows the student's incorrect translation. Now plot the points from the table and compare the graphs.

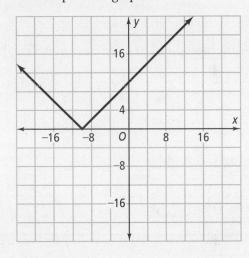

31. Describe the student's error.

_____

_____

_____

Math Success

Check off the vocabulary words that you understand.

☐ absolute value function   ☐ translation

Rate how well you can *graph absolute value functions*.

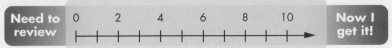

Need to review   0   2   4   6   8   10   Now I get it!

Lesson 5-8

Vocabulary

● Review

Write I if the amount described is *infinite*. Write F if the amount is *finite*.

_____ **1.** the rational numbers greater than 6   _____ **2.** the number of seats in a movie theater

_____ **3.** the number of grams in one kilogram   _____ **4.** the set of odd numbers

5. Give one example of an *infinite* amount. Explain why the amount is *infinite*.

_____

_____

● Vocabulary Builder

system (noun) sis **tum**

Other Word Forms: systematic (adjective), systematize (verb)

Main Idea: A **system** of linear equations has two or more linear equations. A solution to this **system** is an ordered pair that makes all of the equations true.

● Use Your Vocabulary

Complete each statement with the appropriate word from the list.

systematic   system   systematize

6. The librarian planned to __?__ the donated magazines.   _____

7. The American __?__ of government is based on the Constitution.   _____

8. Sam was __?__ in his approach to studying for his final exam.   _____

9. A __?__ of linear equations might consist of two equations.   _____

Problem 1 Solving a System of Equations by Graphing

Got It? What is the solution of the system? Use a graph. Check your answer.

$$y = 2x + 4$$
$$y = x + 2$$

10. Graph both lines on the coordinate plane at the right.

11. Circle the point of intersection of the two lines.

   (2, 0)   (0, 2)   (−2, 0)   (−2, 2)

12. Check that your answer to Exercise 11 makes both equations true.

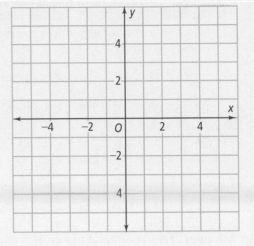

$$y = 2x + 4$$

$\square \overset{?}{=} 2 \cdot (\quad) + 4$

$\square \overset{?}{=} \square + 4$

$\square = \square$

$$y = x + 2$$

$\square \overset{?}{=} \square + 2$

$\square = \square$

13. The solution of the system is (,   ).

Problem 2 Writing a System of Equations

Got It? One satellite radio service charges $10 per month plus an activation fee of $20. A second service charges $11 per month plus an activation fee of $15. For what number of months is the cost of either service the same?

14. Complete the model below.

Relate   total cost   is   monthly charge   times   number of months   plus   activation fee

Define   Let $c =$ _____.

              Let $n =$ _____.

Write   Service 1: c = $10   · $\square$ + $20

             Service 2: $\square$ = $ $\square$ · n + $ $\square$

15. Which variable will you graph on the horizontal axis? _____

Which variable will you graph on the vertical axis? _____

16. What will the intersection of the graphs of the two linear equations tell you?

_____

_____

17. Graph the equations you wrote in Exercise 14 on the coordinate grid at the right.

18. Multiple Choice Which ordered pair gives the coordinates of the point of intersection of the two lines?

(A) $(0, 0)$ (C) $(5, 70)$

(B) $(1, 30)$ (D) $(70, 5)$

19. So, in month ☐ the total cost of either service is the same.

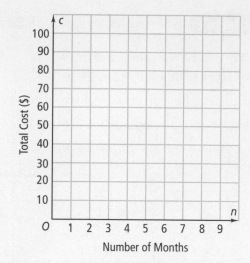

A system of equations that has at least one solution is **consistent.** A consistent system can be either *independent* or *dependent*.

A consistent system that is **independent** has exactly one solution. A consistent system that is **dependent** has infinitely many solutions.

A system of equations that has no solution is **inconsistent.**

Underline the correct word, words, or number to complete each sentence.

20. If two lines intersect at one point (have different slopes), the system of equations is *independent* and consistent / inconsistent . The system of equations has 0 / 1 / infinitely many solution(s).

21. If two lines are the same (have the same slope and y-intercept), the system of equations is *dependent* and consistent / inconsistent . The system of equations has 0 / 1 / infinitely many solution(s).

22. If two lines are parallel (have the same slope and different y-intercepts), the system of equations is consistent / inconsistent . The system of equations has 0 / 1 / infinitely many solution(s).

✓ **Problem 3** **Systems With Infinitely Many Solutions or No Solution**

Got It? What is the solution of the system? Use a graph. Describe the number of solutions.

$$y = -x - 3$$
$$y = -x + 5$$

23. Multiple Choice Which shows the solution of the two equations?

(A) 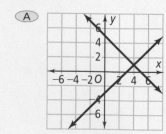   (B) 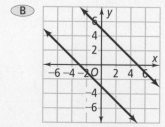   (C)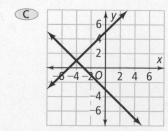

24. The lines are parallel / perpendicular . The system has no solution / one solution .

Lesson Check • Do you know HOW?

Solve the system by graphing.

$$y = \frac{1}{2}x + 6$$
$$y = x - 2$$

25. The slope of $y = \frac{1}{2}x + 6$ is ▢ .

    The y-intercept of $y = \frac{1}{2}x + 6$ is ▢ .

26. The slope of $y = x - 2$ is ▢ .

    The y-intercept of $y = x - 2$ is ▢ .

27. Graph each line in the system on the coordinate grid at the right.

28. The solution of the system

    is (▢ , ▢).

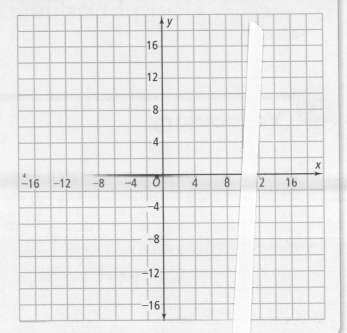

Lesson Check • Do you UNDERSTAND?

Vocabulary Draw a line from each type of system in Column A to the number of solutions the system has in Column B.

Column A	Column B
29. inconsistent	exactly one solution
30. consistent and dependent	infinitely many solutions
31. consistent and independent	no solution

Math Success

Check off the vocabulary words that you understand.

☐ system of linear equations   ☐ solution of a system of linear equations

☐ consistent   ☐ independent   ☐ dependent   ☐ inconsistent

Rate how well you can *solve a system of linear equations*.

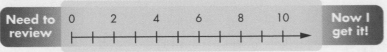

Lesson 6-1

Solving Systems Using Substitution

Vocabulary

● Review

1. Cross out the expression that does NOT include a *variable*.

| $y + 9$ | $a - b$ | $23 + 9$ | $3x + 4y + 12$ |

2. Circle the equation in which the *variable* is isolated.

| $8k = 16$ | $m + 3 = -2$ | $a = 7 - 3$ | $12 = z + 4$ |

● Vocabulary Builder

substitution (noun) **sub stuh TOO shun**

Related Words: substitute (verb or adjective)

Definition: A **substitution** is something taking the place of something else.

Example: A **substitution** of 4 for x and 8 for y in $x + y$ gives $4 + 8$, or 12.

● Use Your Vocabulary

Complete each statement with the appropriate form of the word *substitution*.

3. ADJECTIVE We had a _?_ teacher in social studies class today. _____

4. NOUN The coach made a _?_ of one player for another. _____

5. VERB To evaluate the expression $x + 6$, you can _?_ a number for x. _____

6. Write a combination of coins that you could *substitute* for each dollar amount.

| $1.00 | $2.00 | $5.00 |

You can solve linear systems by solving one of the equations for one of the variables. Then substitute the expression for the variable into the other equation. This is called the **substitution method.**

Problem 1 Using Substitution

Got It? What is the solution of the system? Use substitution. Check your answer.

$$y = 2x + 7$$
$$y = x - 1$$

7. Circle the equation that shows a substitution from one equation into the other.

$2x + 7 = x - 1$	$y = x - 1$	$y = 2x + 7$	$2y + 7 = y - 1$

8. Now find the value of x.

9. Use the value of x to find the value of y.

10. The solution is (,   ).

11. Check your answer by substituting the values for x and y in both equations.

$$y = 2x + 7$$

$$\boxed{} \overset{?}{=} 2 \cdot ( ) + 7$$

$$\boxed{} \overset{?}{=} \boxed{} + 7$$

$$\boxed{} = \boxed{}$$

$$y = x - 1$$

$$\boxed{} \overset{?}{=} \boxed{} - 1$$

$$\boxed{} = \boxed{}$$

Problem 2 Solving for a Variable and Using Substitution

Got It? What is the solution of the system? Use substitution.

$$6y + 5x = 8$$
$$x + 3y = -7$$

12. Complete the reasoning model below.

Think	Write
I need to solve one of the equations for one of the variables. Solving the second equation for x is quickest.	$x + 3y = -7$ $x = -7 - \boxed{}$
Next I substitute into the other equation. Then I solve the equation for y.	$6y + 5x = 8$ $6y + 5(\boxed{}) = 8$ $6y + \boxed{} = 8$ $\boxed{} = \boxed{}$ $\boxed{} \approx \boxed{}$
Now I substitute the y-value into either original equation and solve for x.	$x + 3y = -7$ $x + 3(\boxed{}) = -7$ $x \approx \boxed{}$

13. The solution is about (,   ).

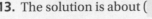

Got It? You pay $22 to rent 6 video games. The store charges $4 for new games and $2 for older games. How many new games did you rent?

14. Define the variables.

Let $x =$ the number of $4 games.

Let $y =$ _____.

15. Complete the models below.

Relate	total games	is	number of $4 games	plus	number of $2 games
Write	6	=	x	+	

Relate	total cost	is	cost of $4 games	plus	cost of $2 games
Write	22	=	4 ·	+	

16. Solve the first equation for y.

17. Substitute your answer from Exercise 16 to find the x-value.

18. The student rented ____ new ($4) games.

If you get an identity, such as $2 = 2$, when you solve a system of equations, then the system has infinitely many solutions. If you get a false statement, such as $8 = 2$, then the system has no solution.

Problem 4 Systems with Infinitely Ma

Got It? How many solutions does the system have?

19. Use substitution to solve the system of equations.

20. I obtained an identity / a false statement , so this sy

   infinitely many / no solutions .

Lesson Check • **Do you UNDERS**

For the system, tell which equation you would first us
the first step of the substitution method. Explain your

21. Each of the equations has been solved for a variable
   you would choose to solve for and why.

Equation 1

solved for *x*:	solved for *y*:	so
$x = \frac{1}{2} - \frac{1}{2}y$	$y = 2x - 1$	x

_____

_____

Math Success

Check off the vocabulary words that you understand.

☐ substitution   ☐ system of equation

Rate how well you can *solve systems using substitution.*

Need to review   0   2   4   6   8   10

Vocab

● **Review**

1. **Multiple Choic**

   Ⓐ a rule or

   Ⓑ a recipe

2. Circle the *form*

   $2(\ell + w)$

3. Cross out the pa

   $3y + 2x = 24;$

   $2m +$

● **Vocabulary B**

   elimination (no

   Other Word For

   Definition: Elim

   Example: A gar

   Math Usage: In
   equations to *el*

● **Use Your Voc**

Complete each ser

4. The city counc

5. The __?__ of the

6. The new floor

Solving Systems Using Elimination

∪lary

Which of the following does NOT describe a *formula*?

rinciple   **C**   a fixed method for doing something

r prescription   **D**   a constant

la you can use to find the volume of a rectangular prism.

$$\pi r^2 \qquad\qquad \ell hw \qquad\qquad s^2$$

irs of equations that are NOT *equivalent*.

$y = \frac{2}{3}x + 8$ $4a + b = 17; b = 17 - 4a$

$6n = 10; m + 3n = 5$ $j + k = 11; j = k + 11$

ilder

∪n)   **ee LIM in ay shun**

as: eliminate (verb), eliminated (verb), eliminating (verb)

ınation is the act of removing something.

ener works toward the **elimination** of weeds from a garden.

elimination, you use properties of equality to add or subtract
ninate a variable in a system.

bulary

ence with the word *elimination* or one of its other word forms.

will not __?__ funding for the public library.   _____

lance portion of the contest was disappointing.   _____

leaner is great for __?__ dirt.   _____

Got It? What is the solution of the system? Use elimination. $5x - 6y = -32$
$3x + 6y = 48$

7. **Reasoning** Why should your first step be to eliminate y?

Place a ✓ in the box if the response is correct. Place an ✗ if it is incorrect.

☐ I can't eliminate x.

☐ If I eliminate x, I can't add the expressions that contain y.

☐ The expressions $6y$ and $-6y$ are additive inverses.

8. Circle the equation you get after you eliminate y.

$$-2x = -16 \qquad\qquad 2x = 16 \qquad\qquad 8x = 16 \qquad\qquad -8x = 16$$

9. Solve the equation for x. Use that value to solve for y.

Solve the equation for x.

☐ $\cdot x = $ ☐

$\dfrac{\boxed{}}{\boxed{}} \cdot x = \dfrac{\boxed{}}{\boxed{}}$

$x = $ ☐

Use the x-value to solve for y.

$$3x + 6y = 48$$
$$3 \cdot \boxed{} + 6y = 48$$
$$6y = 48 - \boxed{}$$
$$\dfrac{6y}{6} = \dfrac{\boxed{}}{6}$$
$$y = \boxed{}$$

10. The solution of the system is (☐ , ☐).

Got It? Washing 2 cars and 3 trucks takes 130 min. Washing 2 cars and 5 trucks takes 190 min. How long does it take to wash each type of vehicle?

11. Use the equations at the right for this system. $2c + 3t = 130$
$2c + 5t = 190$

Let $c = $ _____.

Let $t = $ _____.

12. Eliminate the variable c. Then solve for t.

$2c + 3t = 130$

$\underline{2c + 5t = 190}$ To subtract the second row from the first, change to opposite signs and add down.

$$2c + 3t = 130$$
$$\underline{-2c + \boxed{} \cdot t = -190}$$
$$0 + \boxed{} \cdot t = -60$$
$$t = \boxed{}$$

Lesson 6-3

13. Use the value of t to solve one of the original equations for c.

14. Circle the correct value of c.

| $c = 10$ | $c = 20$ | $c = 30$ |

15. It takes ▢ min to wash a truck and ▢ min to wash a car.

Problem 4 Solving a System by Multiplying Both Equations

Got It? What is the solution of the system? Use elimination.
$$4x + 3y = -19$$
$$3x - 2y = -10$$

16. You want to eliminate x. Complete the boxes to solve for y.

$4x + 3y = -19$ Multiply by 3. ⟶ ▢ $\cdot x + 9y = $ ▢

$3x - 2y = -10$ Multiply by -4. ⟶ $\underline{\quad -12x + 8y = \text{▢}}$

$\qquad\qquad\qquad\qquad 0 + \text{▢} \cdot y = \text{▢}$ Add the two equations.

$\qquad\qquad\qquad\qquad\qquad y = \text{▢}$ Solve for y.

17. Now complete the steps to find the value of x. Write a justification for each step.

$4x + 3y = -19$ Write one of the original equations.

$4x + 3 \cdot (-1) = -19$ _____

$4x = -19 + 3$ _____

$4x = -16$ _____

$x = -4$ Solve for x.

18. The solution is (▢ , ▢).

Problem 5 Finding the Number of Solutions

Got It? How many solutions does the system have?
$$-2x + 5y = 7$$
$$-2x + 5y = 12$$

19. Circle a step you will do to find the number of solutions for this system.

| Subtract the equations. | Multiply by 0. | Multiply by 1. | Divide by 1. |

20. Solve the system.

21. How many solutions does the system have? Explain.

_____

_____

_____

Lesson Check • Do you UNDERSTAND?

Vocabulary If you add two equations in two variables and the sum is an equation in one variable, what method are you using to solve the system? Explain.

22. Add each system of two linear equations together.

A $5x + 6y = 30$
$\underline{-2x - 6y = -12}$

B $3x + 7y = 21$
$\underline{-7x + 2y = -14}$

23. Which system of equations, A or B, has a sum that is an equation in one variable?

_____

24. How can you use the equation in one variable to solve the system of equations?

_____

_____

_____

25. When you use an equation in one variable to solve a system of equations, what method are you using to solve the system? Explain.

_____

_____

_____

Math Success

Check off the vocabulary words that you understand.

☐ elimination method   ☐ solution of a system of linear equations

Rate how well you can *find the solution of a system of linear equations by elimination*.

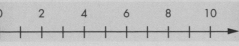

Lesson 6-3

6-4 Applications of Linear Systems

Review

1. **Multiple Choice** Which equation shows what happens when you use *substitution* to solve this system of equations?

$$3x - 4y = -14$$
$$y = 2x - 1$$

Ⓐ $2x - 1 - 4y = -14$

Ⓒ $3x - (2x - 1) = -14$

Ⓑ $3(2x - 1) - 4y = -14$

Ⓓ $3x - 4(2x - 1) = -14$

Vocabulary Builder

intersection (noun) ɪN **tur sek shun**

Definition: An **intersection** is where two or more lines or roads meet.

Math Usage: For two lines, the **point of intersection** is a point in common where they *intersect*, or meet.

> The **intersection** of $x + y = 3$ and $x - y = 1$ is (2, 1).

Use Your Vocabulary

2. The Ancient Spanish Monastery (shown by the red star on map) in North Miami Beach, Florida, is thought to be the oldest building in the western hemisphere. Name two streets that intersect at the Ancient Spanish Monastery.

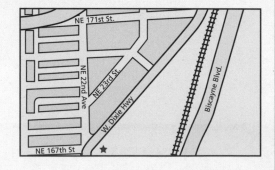

_____

Write the ordered pair for the point of *intersection*. If there is no point of intersection, write *none*.

3.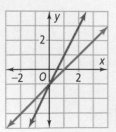

4.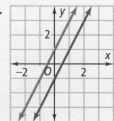

5.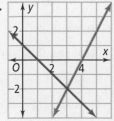

Problem 1 **Finding a Break-Even Point**

Got It? A puzzle expert wrote a new sudoku puzzle book. His initial costs are $864. Binding and packaging each book costs $.80. The price of the book is $2. How many copies must be sold to break even?

6. Complete the model below.

Relate expenses = $864 + $.80 · number of books sold   income = $2 · number of books sold

Define Let x = the number of books sold.

Let y = _____

Write y = [   ] y = [   ]

7. Use substitution to solve the system of equations.

y = [   ]   Start with the equation for expenses.

[   ] = [   ]   Substitute the income expression for y.

= [   ]   Subtract 0.8x from each side.

x = [   ]   Divide each side by 1.2.

8. The puzzle expert must sell [   ] books to break even.

 Problem 2 **Solving a Mixture Problem**

Got It? One antifreeze solution is 20% alcohol. Another antifreeze solution is 12% alcohol. How many liters of each solution should be combined to make 15 L of antifreeze solution that is 18% alcohol?

9. Let x equal the number of liters of 20% antifreeze and let y equal the number of liters of 12% antifreeze. Write a justification for each step.

$x + y = 15$
$0.2 \cdot x + 0.12 \cdot y = 0.18(15)$ Write a system of equations.

$y = 15 - x$ _____

$0.2 \cdot x + 0.12 \cdot (15 - x) = 0.18(15)$ _____

$0.20x + 1.8 - 0.12x = 2.7$ _____

$0.08x = 0.9$ _____

$x = 11.25$ _____

$11.25 + y = 15$ _____

10. Solve $11.25 + y = 15$ for y.

11. To make 15 L of 18% antifreeze, combine

[   ] L of 20% antifreeze and [   ] L of 12% antifreeze.

 Problem 3 **Solving a Wind or Current Problem**

Got It? You row upstream at a speed of 2 mi/h. You travel the same distance downstream at a speed of 5 mi/h. What would be your rowing speed in still water? What is the speed of the current?

12. Complete the model below.

Relate

| speed of boat in still water | + | speed of the current | = | downstream speed |

| speed of boat in still water | − | speed of the current | = | upstream speed |

Define   Let a = speed of the boat in still water.

Let c = _____.

Write $a + c$ =   [   ] $a - c$ =   [   ]

13. Circle the system of equations you will use to find the answer.

$a + c = 2$ $a + c = 5$ $c + a = 2$
$a - c = 5$ $a - c = 2$ $c - a = 5$

14. Now solve the system of equations.

15. Your rowing speed in still water is [   ] mi/h.

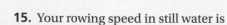 The speed of the current is [   ] mi/h.

Lesson Check • Do you UNDERSTAND?

Reasoning Which method would you use to solve the following system? Explain.

$$3x + 2y = 9$$
$$-2x + 3y = 5$$

16. Draw a line from each statement in Column A to the most appropriate method for solving a system of equations in Column B.

Column A

One equation is already solved for one of the variables.

A visual display of the equations is needed.

The coefficients of one variable are able to be made the same or opposite.

Column B

Substitution

Elimination

Graphing

17. Circle the method you would use to solve the given system.

Graphing	Elimination	Substitution

18. Explain why you chose that method.

_____

_____

_____

Math Success

Check off the vocabulary words that you understand.

☐ intersection   ☐ system of linear equations

   ☐ substitution   ☐ elimination

Rate how well you can *apply systems of equations*.

Lesson 6-4

Vocabulary

● Review

A *solution* is a value or values which, when substituted for a variable, make an equation true. Determine the *solution* of each inequality below. Circle your answer.

1. $x + 17 < 37$

$x > 20$ $x < 20$

2. $2m + 3 > 15$

$m > 6$ $m < 6$

3. Multiple Choice How many *solutions* does this system of equations have?

$x - 5y = 1$
$2x + 3y = 9$

(A) 0   (B) 1   (C) 2   (D) infinitely many

● Vocabulary Builder

linear inequality (noun) LIN **ee ur in ee** KWAL **uh tee**

linear inequality
$y \geq 2x - 9$

Definition: Replacing the equals sign in a linear equation with an inequality symbol makes a **linear inequality** in two variables.

Main Idea: A **linear inequality** in two variables has an infinite number of solutions, each an ordered pair that makes the inequality true.

Example: $y \geq 2x - 9$ is a **linear inequality** in two variables.

● Use Your Vocabulary

For Exercises 4–7, write an *inequality* using the symbol and the equation.

4. $>$ $6x = 18$ _____

5. $<$ $\frac{m}{2} = 55$ _____

6. $\geq$ $3y = x - 26$ _____

7. $\leq$ $y = 2x + 1$ _____

8. Circle the *linear inequalities* in two variables.

$6x > 3$ $y \leq 2x + 5$ $-x + y = 6$ $y = -7$ $2y > x$

Problem 1 Identifying Solutions of a Linear Inequality

Got It? Is (3, 6) a solution of $y \leq \frac{2}{3}x + 4$?

9. Complete the steps to determine whether (3, 6) is a solution.

$y \leq \frac{2}{3} \cdot x + 4$ Write the inequality.

$\boxed{} \leq \frac{2}{3} \cdot \boxed{} + 4$ Substitute.

$\boxed{} \leq \boxed{} + 4$ Multiply.

$\boxed{} \leq 6$ Simplify.

10. Is (3, 6) a solution?   Yes / No

For each inequality below, determine whether (3, 6) is a solution.

11. $y > x + 7$ 12. $y \leq 3x - 2$

Yes / No   Yes / No

Problem 2 Graphing an Inequality in Two Variables

Got It? What is the graph of $y \leq \frac{1}{2}x + 1$?

Underline the correct word to complete each sentence.

13. The symbol $\leq$ means greater / less than or equal to.

14. The boundary line will be dashed / solid .

15. Graph the boundary line on the grid.

16. The point (0, 0) is not on the line. Check to see whether that point is a solution of the inequality.

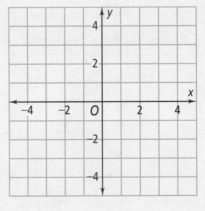

17. Circle the true statement. Then shade the graph.

The side of the line that contains (0, 0) should be shaded.

The side of the line that does NOT contain (0, 0) should be shaded.

Lesson 6-5

Got It? What is the graph of the inequality $x < -5$? Of $y \leq 2$?

18. Label each graph.

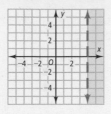 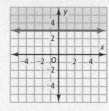 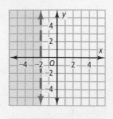 

type of
boundary line _____

equation of
boundary line

inequality

19. Describe the graph of each inequality. Use the words *boundary line, dashed* or *solid,* and *shade* or *shaded* in each description.

$x < -5$ _____

$y \leq 2$ _____

Problem 4 Rewriting to Graph an Inequality

Got It? For a party, you can spend no more than $12 on nuts. Peanuts cost $2/lb. Cashews cost $4/lb. What are three possible combinations of peanuts and cashews you can buy?

20. Let $x =$ the number of pounds of peanuts and let $y =$ _____.

21. Complete the steps to solve the inequality for y.

$2x + 4y \leq 12$ Write the inequality.

$2x - \boxed{} + 4y \leq \boxed{} + 12$ Subtract the same amount from both sides.

$\dfrac{4y}{\boxed{}} \leq \dfrac{-2x}{\boxed{}} + \dfrac{\boxed{}}{}$ Divide each side by the same amount.

$y \leq \boxed{} + \boxed{}$ Simplify.

22. Graph the inequality on the grid.

23. Write three possible combinations of peanuts and cashews that you can buy.

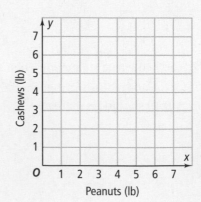

When a linear inequality is solved for *y*, the direction of the inequality symbol determines which side of the boundary line to shade. If the symbol is $<$ or $\leq$, shade below the boundary line. If the symbol is $>$ or $\geq$, shade above it.

 Problem 5 Writing an Inequality From a Graph

Got It? You are writing an inequality from a graph. The boundary line is dashed and has slope $\frac{1}{3}$ and *y*-intercept -2. The area above the line is shaded. What inequality should you write?

24. Write the equation of the boundary line in slope-intercept form.

25. Circle the symbol you will use in the inequality.

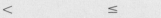

$<$ $\leq$ $>$ $\geq$

26. Now write the complete inequality.

 Lesson Check • **Do you UNDERSTAND?**

Writing To graph the inequality $y < \frac{3}{2}x + 3$, do you shade *above* or *below* the boundary line? Explain.

27. Describe how to determine which side of the boundary line should be shaded.

_____

_____

_____

28. Do you shade *above* or *below* the boundary line for $y < \frac{3}{2}x + 3$? Explain.

_____

_____

_____

 Math Success

Check off the vocabulary words that you understand.

☐ linear inequality   ☐ solution of an inequality

Rate how well you can *graph a linear inequality in two variables.*

| Need to review | 0 | 2 | 4 | 6 | 8 | 10 | Now I get it! |

Lesson 6-5

Systems of Linear Inequalities

Vocabulary

● **Review**

1. Circle the *system* of equations.

$3x + 2y = 20$ $3x - 2y = 12$ $3x + 2y = 12$ $7x + 2y < 10$
                                                    $4x + 4y = 20$

2. How can you tell if an ordered pair is a solution to a *system* of equations?

_____

_____

● **Vocabulary Builder**

boundary (noun) BOWN dree

Related Words: bounds (noun or verb), border (noun or verb), bounded (adjective)

Definition: A **boundary** is something that divides one item from another.

Math Usage: The graph of a linear inequality in two variables is a region bounded by a line. All points on one side of the **boundary line** are solutions.

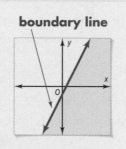

boundary line

● **Use Your Vocabulary**

3. Complete each sentence with *bounds, boundary,* or *border.*

The landscaper planted a __?__ of flowers along the sidewalk.   _____

The ball bounced out of __?__ .   _____

The __?__ line on the map between countries is shown in red.   _____

4. Circle the ordered pair that is on the *boundary* of $y + 2 \le x - 5$.

(9, 0)   (0, −6)   (6, −1)   (10, 5)   (5, −3)

Problem 1 · Graphing a System of Inequalities

Got It? What is the graph of the system? $y \geq -x + 5$
$-3x + y \leq -4$

5. The boundary line for $y \geq -x + 5$ will be solid / dashed .

The boundary line for $-3x + y \leq -4$ will be solid / dashed .

6. Write the inequality $-3x + y \leq -4$ in slope-intercept form.

$y \leq$ ⬜ $\cdot\, x - 4$

7. Graph the inequalities on the coordinate grid at the right.

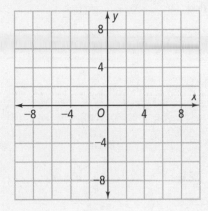

Problem 2 · Writing a System of Inequalities From a Graph

Got It? What system of inequalities is represented by the graph?

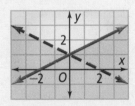

8. Find the inequality shown by the red line.

Determine the equation of the red line.

$y =$

The shaded region is above / below the

line. The boundary line is solid / dashed .

Circle the inequality symbol you should use to write the inequality for this graph.

$>$ $<$ $\leq$ $\geq$

9. Find the inequality shown by the blue line.

Determine the equation of the blue line.

$y =$

The shaded region is above / below the

line. The boundary line is solid / dashed .

Circle the inequality symbol you should use to write the inequality for this graph.

$>$ $<$ $\leq$ $\geq$

10. Write the system of inequalities represented by the graph.

Lesson 6-6

Got It? You want to build a fence for a rectangular dog run. You want the run to be at least 10 ft wide. The run can be at most 50 ft long. You have 126 ft of fencing. What is a graph showing the possible dimensions of the dog run?

Remember, a dog run must have fencing on all four sides.

11. Follow the steps to write a system of inequalities and graph it.

> **1**
> Define what each variable represents.
> Let x = the width of the dog run.
> Let y = _____.

> **2**
> Write a system of inequalities.
>
> $2x + 2y \leq$ [ ]   In slope-intercept form, this is $y \leq$ [ ].
>
> $x \geq$ [ ]
>
> $y \leq$ [ ]

> **3**
> Graph the system of inequalities.
>
>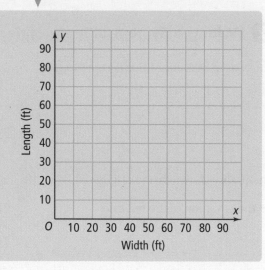

12. Why is the graph only in the first quadrant?

_____

_____

13. Use the graph to write possible dimensions of the dog run.

width (x): _____   width (x): _____   width (x): _____

length (y): _____   length (y): _____   length (y): _____

Lesson Check • Do you UNDERSTAND?

Reasoning Suppose you are graphing a system of two linear inequalities, and the boundary lines for the inequalities are parallel. Does that mean that the system has no solution? Explain.

14. Draw a line from each graph to the corresponding system of linear inequalities.

$y \leq -\frac{3}{4}x + 6$

$y \geq -\frac{3}{4}x + 3$

$y \geq -\frac{3}{4}x + 6$

$y \leq -\frac{3}{4}x + 3$

$y \geq -\frac{3}{4}x + 6$

$y \geq -\frac{3}{4}x + 3$

15. Which of the systems have solutions?

_____

_____

16. Would the system of $y \leq -\frac{3}{4}x + 6$ and $y \leq -\frac{3}{4}x + 3$ have a solution? If so, describe the solution.

_____

17. Is it possible for a system of two linear inequalities with parallel boundary lines to have a solution? Yes / No

18. Is it possible for a system of two linear inequalities with parallel boundary lines to have no solution? Yes / No

Math Success

Check off the vocabulary words that you understand.

☐ system of linear inequalities   ☐ solution of a system of linear inequalities

Rate how well you can *solve a system of linear inequalities.*

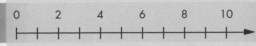

Need to review 0 2 4 6 8 10 Now I get it!

Lesson 6-6

Zero and Negative Exponents

Vocabulary

● Review

Circle the *exponent* in each equation.

1. $3^5 = 243$ **2.** $7^2 = 49$ **3.** $2^7 = 128$

Write an equivalent expression using an *exponent*.

4. $35 \cdot 35 \cdot 35 =$ ☐

5. $19 \cdot 19 \cdot 19 \cdot 19 \cdot 19 \cdot 19 \cdot 19 \cdot 19 \cdot 19 =$ ☐

6. In the expression 4^3, identify the *base* and the *exponent*.

base = ☐   exponent = ☐

● Vocabulary Builder

negative (adjective) NEG <u>**uh tiv**</u>

Definition: A **negative** quantity has a value less than zero.

Examples: $-3, -\frac{1}{2}$, and $-\pi$ are all **negative** numbers.

> The symbol for
> **negative**
> is
> $-$

● Use Your Vocabulary

7. Write a number to represent each situation.

The temperature is 4 degrees below zero.	You owe your brother eight dollars.	A worker's hourly pay increases by $.50.
☐	☐	☐

Draw a line from each *negative* number in Column A to its opposite in Column B.

Column A	Column B
8. $-\frac{1}{2}$	17
9. $-3\frac{3}{5}$	$\frac{1}{2}$
10. -17	$3\frac{3}{5}$

Properties Zero and Negative Exponents

11. Complete the table.

Exponent	Property	Examples
Zero	For every nonzero number a, $(a)^0 = 1$	$6^0 = 1$
		$(-24)^0 = \boxed{}$
Negative	For every nonzero number a and integer n, $(a)^{-n} = \dfrac{1}{a^n}$	$7^{-3} = \dfrac{1}{7^3} = \dfrac{1}{343}$
		$4^{-2} = \dfrac{1}{4^2} = \dfrac{1}{\boxed{}}$
		$(-3)^{-5} = \dfrac{1}{(-3)^5} = \dfrac{1}{\boxed{}}$

Write T for *true* or F for *false*.

____ **12.** $9^{-2} = \dfrac{1}{81}$ ____ **13.** $(-9)^0 = -1$ ____ **14.** $9^{-1} = -\dfrac{1}{9}$ ____ **15.** $9^{-3} = \dfrac{1}{27}$

 Problem 1 Simplifying Powers

Got It? What is the simplified form of 4^{-3}?

16. Complete each step to simplify 4^{-3}.

$4^{-3} = \dfrac{1}{4^{\boxed{}}}$ Move the power to the denominator and make the exponent positive.

$= \dfrac{1}{\boxed{}}$ Evaluate the power to simplify the expression.

 Problem 2 Simplifying Exponential Expressions

Got It? What is the simplified form of each expression?

x^{-9} $\dfrac{1}{n^{-3}}$ $4c^{-3}b$ $\dfrac{2}{a^{-3}}$ $\dfrac{n^{-5}}{m^2}$

Underline the correct word to complete each sentence.

17. To simplify a base in the numerator that has a negative exponent, move the base to the denominator and write a positive / negative exponent.

18. To simplify a base in the denominator that has a negative exponent, move the base to the numerator and write a positive / negative exponent.

Lesson 7-1

19. Simplify each expression.

$$x^{-9} = \dfrac{1}{x^{\boxed{}}}$$

$$\dfrac{1}{n^{-3}} = 1 \div n^{\boxed{}} = 1 \cdot \boxed{}$$

$$4c^{-3}b = \dfrac{4 \cdot \boxed{}}{\boxed{}}$$

$$\dfrac{2}{a^{-3}} = 2 \cdot \boxed{}$$

$$\dfrac{n^{-5}}{m^2} = \dfrac{\boxed{}}{\boxed{} \cdot \boxed{}}$$

Problem 3 Evaluating an Exponential Expression

Got It? What is the value of $n^{-4}w^0$ for $n = -2$ and $w = 5$?

Complete each method to solve the problem.

20. Method 1 Simplify first.

$$n^{-4}w^0 = \dfrac{w^0}{n^{\boxed{}}} \qquad \text{Use the definition of negative exponent.}$$

$$= \dfrac{\boxed{}^0}{(\boxed{})^4} \qquad \text{Substitute.}$$

$$= \dfrac{\boxed{}}{\boxed{}} \qquad \text{Simplify.}$$

21. Method 2 Substitute first.

$$n^{-4}w^0 = (-2)^{-4} \cdot \boxed{}^{\,0} \qquad \text{Substitute.}$$

$$= \dfrac{\boxed{}}{(-2)^{\boxed{}}} \qquad \text{Use the definition of negative exponent.}$$

$$= \dfrac{\boxed{}}{\boxed{}} \qquad \text{Simplify.}$$

Problem 4 Using an Exponential Expression

Got It? A population of insects triples every week. The number of insects is modeled by the expression $5400 \cdot 3^w$, where w is the number of weeks after the population was measured. Evaluate the expression for $w = -2$, $w = 0$, and $w = 1$. What does each value of the expression represent in the situation?

22. Use the information in the problem to complete the problem-solving model below.

Know	Need	Plan

23. Now solve the problem.

24. What does each value represent?

For $w = -2$, the value [ ] represents the number of insects ___?___.

For $w = 0$, the value [ ] represents the number of insects ___?___.

For $w = 1$, the value [ ] represents the number of insects ___?___.

✓ Lesson Check • Do you UNDERSTAND?

Error Analysis A student incorrectly simplified $\dfrac{x^n}{a^{-n}b^0}$ as shown at the right. Find and correct the student's error.

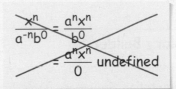

25. Did the student work correctly with —

base x? Yes / No   base a? Yes / No   base b? Yes / No

26. What error did the student make?

27. Now simplify the expression correctly.

✓ Math Success

Check off the vocabulary words that you understand.

☐ exponent   ☐ zero exponent   ☐ negative exponent

Rate how well you can *simplify zero and negative exponents*.

Need to review 0 2 4 6 8 10 Now I get it!

Lesson 7-1

Scientific Notation

Vocabulary

● Review

Write a *power* with the given base and exponent.

1. base 6; exponent 3

2. base 5; exponent −2

3. Multiple Choice Which of the following expresses 64 as a *power* of 2?

(A) 2^5 (B) 2^6 (C) 4^3 (D) 8^2

4. Multiple Choice Which of the following expresses $\frac{1}{9}$ as a *power* of 3?

(A) $\left(\frac{1}{3}\right)^2$ (B) 3^{-2} (C) 3^2 (D) 9^{-1}

● Vocabulary Builder

scientific notation
integer
$a \times 10^n$
$1 \le a < 10$

scientific notation (noun) sy un TIF ik noh TAY shun

Definition: A number in **scientific notation** is the product of two factors in the form $a \times 10^n$, where n is an integer and $1 \le a < 10$.

Main Idea: **Scientific notation** uses powers of 10 to make it easier to work with very large or very small numbers.

Examples: 5.16×10^7; 8.05×10^{-4}

Nonexamples: 32×10^9 (because 32 is not less than 10); 0.57×10^{-12} (because 0.57 is not greater than or equal to 1)

● Use Your Vocabulary

5. Write the most precise name for each expression. Use the words *power*, *power of 10*, or *scientific notation*.

10^2 1.2×10^2 2^{10}

Problem 1 Recognizing Scientific Notation

Got It? Is 53×10^4 written in scientific notation? If not, explain.

6. Use the words *an integer* and *scientific notation* and the compound inequality $1 \leq a < 10$ to complete the diagram at the right.

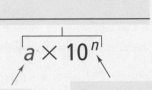

$$a \times 10^n$$

Underline the correct word(s) to complete each sentence.

7. In the expression 53×10^4, 53 is / is not greater than or equal to 1.

8. In the expression 53×10^4, 53 is / is not less than 10.

9. In the expression 53×10^4, 4 is / is not an integer.

10. Is the expression 53×10^4 written in scientific notation? If not, explain.

_____

11. Cross out the numbers that are NOT written in *scientific notation*.

9.103×10^{-5} 12×10^8 1.8×10^{25} 0.025×10^{-16}

Problem 2 Writing a Number in Scientific Notation

Got It? What is 678,000 written in scientific notation?

12. Circle the related number n such that $1 \leq n < 10$.

| 678,000 | 6,780 | 67.8 | 6.78 |

13. Circle the number of places you will move the decimal point in 678,000 to the left in order to get the answer to Exercise 12.

| 5 | 4 | 2 | 0 |

14. Use your answers to Exercises 12 and 13 to complete the equation.

$678,000 = \boxed{} \times 10$

15. **Reasoning** Which number, 6.78×10^5 or 6.78×10^{-5}, is greater? Explain.

_____

_____

_____

16. Write each number in scientific notation.

0.000032   51,400,000   0.0000007

$\boxed{} \times 10^{-\boxed{}}$ $\boxed{} \times 10$

Lesson 7-2

Problem 3 Writing a Number in Standard Notation

Got It? What is each number written in standard notation?

5.23×10^7 4.6×10^{-5}

Underline the correct word to complete each sentence about scientific notation.

17. A positive power of 10 means the decimal point moves to the left / right .

18. A negative power of 10 means the decimal point moves to the left / right .

19. Use the arrows to write 5.23×10^7 in standard notation. Insert zeros as needed.

So, $5.23 \times 10^7 =$.

20. Use the arrows to write 4.6×10^{-5} in standard notation. Insert zeros as needed.

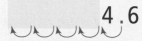

So, $4.6 \times 10^{-5} =$.

Write each number in standard notation.

21. $2.09 \times 10^{-4} =$

22. $3.8 \times 10^{12} =$

Problem 4 Comparing Numbers in Scientific Notation

Got It? What is the order of the following parts of an atom from least to greatest mass?

neutron: 1.675×10^{-24} g   electron: 9.109×10^{-28} g   proton: 1.673×10^{-24} g

23. Reasoning To compare, why do you first arrange the numbers by powers of 10?

24. Which of the numbers 1.675×10^{-24}, 9.109×10^{-28}, or 1.673×10^{-24} has the least value? How do you know?

25. The numbers 1.675×10^{-24} and 1.673×10^{-24} have the same exponent. How should you compare those two numbers?

26. Write the particles in order from least to greatest mass.

Got It? What is the order of 24.8×10^{-4}, 28×10^3, 0.025×10^4, and 258×10^{-5} from least to greatest?

27. Why are the above numbers, as written, difficult to compare?

28. Write each number in scientific notation.

$24.8 \times 10^{-4} = \boxed{} \times 10^{-3}$ $\qquad$ $28 \times 10^3 = 2.8 \times 10^{}$

$0.025 \times 10^4 = \boxed{} \times 10^{}$ $\qquad$ $258 \times 10^{-5} = \boxed{} \times 10^{}$

29. Write the numbers in scientific notation in order from least to greatest.

$\boxed{}$, $\boxed{}$, $\boxed{}$, $\boxed{}$

30. Now write the original numbers in order from least to greatest.

$\boxed{}$, $\boxed{}$, $\boxed{}$, $\boxed{}$

 Lesson Check • **Do you UNDERSTAND?**

Reasoning A student claims that 3.5×10^{11} is greater than 1.4×10^{13} because $3.5 > 1.4$. Is the student correct? Explain.

31. Write the numbers 3.5×10^{11} and 1.4×10^{13} in standard form. Then circle the number with the greater value.

$3.5 \times 10^{11} = \boxed{}$ $\qquad$ $1.4 \times 10^{13} = \boxed{}$

32. Did the student reason correctly when comparing 3.5×10^{11} and 1.4×10^{13}? Explain.

Math Success

Check off the vocabulary words that you understand.

☐ scientific notation ☐ power of 10 ☐ compare ☐ order

Rate how well you can *write and compare numbers in scientific notation.*

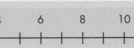

7-3 Multiplying Powers With the Same Base

Vocabulary

● Review

Circle the *base* in each expression.

1. 5^4

2. $(-3)^8$

3. n^{-5}

4. **Error Analysis** A student writes an expression with exponent 4 and *base* 3. Is the student's expression 4^3 correct? Explain.

_____

_____

● Vocabulary Builder

repeated multiplication (noun) rih PEET id mul tuh plih KAY shun

Related Words: factor, base, exponent, power

Main Idea: Repeated multiplication refers to the same number being used as a factor more than once.

Example: The expression $5 \cdot 5 \cdot 5 \cdot 5$ shows **repeated multiplication** because 5 is used as a factor more than once.

● Use Your Vocabulary

Write each *repeated multiplication* using a base and an exponent.

5. $7 \cdot 7 \cdot 7 =$

6. $(-4)(-4)(-4)(-4)(-4)(-4)(-4)(-4) =$

Write each expression as *repeated multiplication*.

7. $2^5 =$

8. $(-3)^2 =$

9. $\left(\frac{1}{2}\right)^3 =$

10. Cross out the expression(s) that you CANNOT write as *repeated multiplication*.

c^{17} $17c$ $27 + 3y$ $27y^3$

Property Multiplying Powers With the Same Base

Words To multiply powers with the same base, add the exponents.

Algebra $a^m \cdot a^n = a^{m+n}$, where $a \neq 0$ and m and n are integers.

Examples $4^3 \cdot 4^5 = 4^{3+5} = 4^8$ $\qquad$ $b^7 \cdot b^{-4} = b^{7+-4} = b^3$

Compare. Use <, > or =.

11. 6^5 ⬜ 6^{6-4} $\qquad$ **12.** 8^{2+9} ⬜ 8^{12-1} $\qquad$ **13.** 3^{7-6} ⬜ 3^0 $\qquad$ **14.** 1^{5+2} ⬜ 1^{7-7}

 Problem 1 Multiplying Powers

Got It? What is each expression written using each base only once?

$\qquad 8^3 \cdot 8^6$ $\qquad\qquad (0.5)^{-3}(0.5)^{-8}$ $\qquad\qquad 9^{-3} \cdot 9^2 \cdot 9^6$

15. When you multiply powers with the same base, you add / multiply the exponents.

Write each expression as a single power.

16. $8^3 \cdot 8^6 = 8^{3+\,\boxed{}}$

$\qquad\quad = 8^{\boxed{}}$

17. $(0.5)^{-3}(0.5)^{-8} = (0.5)^{\boxed{}\,+\,\boxed{}}$

$\qquad\qquad\qquad\quad = (0.5)^{\boxed{}}$

18. $9^{-3} \cdot 9^2 \cdot 9^6 = \boxed{}^{\,\boxed{}\,+\,\boxed{}\,+\,\boxed{}}$

$\qquad\qquad\qquad = \boxed{}^{\,\boxed{}}$

 Problem 2 Multiplying Powers in Algebraic Expressions

Got It? What is the simplified form of $5x^4 \cdot x^9 \cdot 3x$?

19. The expression is simplified below. Write a justification for each step.

$5x^4 \cdot x^9 \cdot 3x = 5x^4 \cdot 3x \cdot x^9$ $\qquad$ _____

$\qquad\qquad\quad = (5 \cdot 3)x^4 \cdot x \cdot x^9$ $\qquad$ _____

$\qquad\qquad\quad = 15x^4 \cdot x \cdot x^9$ $\qquad$ _____

$\qquad\qquad\quad = 15x^4 \cdot x^1 \cdot x^9$ $\qquad$ _____

$\qquad\qquad\quad = 15x^{(4+1+9)}$ $\qquad$ _____

$\qquad\qquad\quad = 15x^{14}$ $\qquad$ _____

Lesson 7-3

Problem 3 Multiplying Numbers in Scientific Notation

Got It? What is the simplified form of $(7 \times 10^8)(4 \times 10^5)$? Write your answer in scientific notation.

20. Use the Commutative and Associative Properties of Multiplication to write $(7 \times 10^8)(4 \times 10^5)$ as the product of a number and a power of 10.

$(7 \times 10^8)(4 \times 10^5) = (7 \cdot)(10^8 \times 10^{}) = () \times (10^{})$

21. Explain how to write the answer to Exercise 20 in scientific notation. Underline the correct word to complete each sentence.

The decimal point will move one place to the left / right .

The power of 10 will increase / decrease .

22. Write the number in scientific notation.

 Problem 4 Multiplying Numbers in Scientific Notation

Got It? At 20°C, one cubic meter of water has a mass of about 9.98×10^5 g. Each gram of water contains about 3.34×10^{22} molecules of water. About how many molecules of water are in a swimming pool that holds 200 m^3 of water? Write your answer in scientific notation.

23. Use the information in the problem to complete the model below.

Relate	number of molecules, m, of water in pool	is	number of cubic meters of water in pool	times	number of grams per cubic meter	times	number of molecules per gram
Write	☐	=	☐	·	9.98×10^5	·	$\dfrac{}{1}$
	☐	=	☐ $\times 10^{☐}$	·	☐ $\times 10^{☐}$	·	☐ $\times 10^{☐}$

24. Simplify the right side of the equation to find the number of water molecules m.

25. Circle the number of water molecules written in scientific notation.

3.33332×10^{26} 33.3332×10^{27} 66.6664×10^{29} 6.66664×10^{30}

26. Round the first factor to the nearest hundredth.

There are about [_____] molecules of water in the swimming pool.

Lesson Check • Do you know HOW?

What is the simplified form of $2n^3 \cdot 3n^{-2}$?

27. Use the Commutative and Associative Properties to rewrite the product.

$$2n^3 \cdot 3n^{-2} = (2 \cdot \boxed{})(n^{\boxed{} + \boxed{}}) = \boxed{}\, n^{\boxed{}}$$

Lesson Check • Do you UNDERSTAND?

Reasoning Suppose $a \times 10^m$ and $b \times 10^n$ are two numbers in scientific notation. Is their product $ab \times 10^{m+n}$ *always*, *sometimes*, or *never* a number in scientific notation? Justify your answer.

28. Suppose the value of a is 3. Complete each equation. Then place a ✓ in the box if the product is in scientific notation. Place an ✗ in the box if it is *not* in scientific notation.

[ ]   If $b = 1.1$, then $ab \times 10^{m+n} = \boxed{} \times 10^{m+n}$.

[ ]   If $b = 2$, then $ab \times 10^{m+n} = \boxed{} \times 10^{m+n}$.

[ ]   If $b = 4$, then $ab \times 10^{m+n} = \boxed{} \times 10^{m+n}$.

29. Underline the correct word to complete the sentence.

If $a \times 10^m$ and $b \times 10^n$ are in scientific notation, the product $ab \times 10^{m+n}$ is

always / sometimes / never in scientific notation.

Math Success

Check off the vocabulary words that you understand.

[ ] scientific notation   [ ] power   [ ] base

Rate how well you can *multiply powers with the same base*.

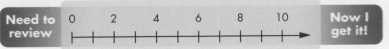

Lesson 7-3

More Multiplication Properties of Exponents

Vocabulary

● Review

1. Circle the equation that illustrates the *Commutative Property of Addition*.

   $3 + 5 = 5 + 3$ $(2 + 3) + 4 = 2 + (3 + 4)$ $7 + 0 = 7$

2. Circle the equation that illustrates the *Commutative Property of Multiplication*.

   $xyz = yxz$ $x \cdot 1 = x$ $a(bc) = (ab)c$

● Vocabulary Builder

> **simplify** (verb) SIM **pluh fy**
>
> **Related Words:** simple (adjective), simplified (adjective, verb)
>
> **Main Idea:** You **simplify** an expression to make it less complicated.
>
> **Definition:** To **simplify** an expression means to replace it with a simplified form.

● Use Your Vocabulary

3. Draw a line from each expression in Column A to its *simplified* form in Column B.

Column A	Column B
$x^3 \cdot x^5$	x^{15}
$x^6 \cdot x$	x^8
$x^4 \cdot x^{11}$	x^7

Complete each statement with the appropriate word from the list. Use each word only once.

    simplify   simplified   simplifying

4. The first step in __?__ the expression $10a \cdot (8 - 3)a^2$ is to subtract within parentheses.

5. The __?__ form of the expression $(17 - 14)h \cdot 6h^5$ is $18h^6$.

6. To __?__ the expression $z \cdot 2z^3 \cdot 6z^4$ means to replace it with $12z^8$.

Property Raising a Power to a Power

You can use repeated multiplication to simplify a power raised to a power.

$$(x^5)^2 = x^5 \cdot x^5 = x^{5+5} = x^{5 \cdot 2} = x^{10}$$

Words To raise a power to a power, multiply the exponents.

Algebra $(a^m)^n = a^{mn}$, where $a \neq 0$ and m and n are integers.

Simplify each power raised to a power.

7. $(4^2)^3 = 4^2 \cdot 4^2 \cdot \boxed{} = 4^{\boxed{}}$

8. $(5^4)^2 = 5^{4 \cdot \boxed{} \, 2} = 5^{\boxed{}}$

9. $(w^5)^2 = \boxed{} \cdot \boxed{} = w^{\boxed{}}$

10. $(m^3)^5 = m^{3 \cdot \boxed{} \, 5} = m^{\boxed{}}$

Problem 1 Simplifying a Power Raised to a Power

Got It? What is the simplified form of $(p^5)^4$?

11. Underline the correct word to complete the sentence.

To simplify $(p^5)^4$, you add / multiply the exponents.

12. Circle the expression that is equivalent to $(p^5)^4$.

$p^5 \cdot p^4$ $\qquad\qquad\qquad$ $p^5 \cdot p^5 \cdot p^5 \cdot p^5$ $\qquad\qquad\qquad$ $(p^5)^{20}$

13. The simplified form of $(p^5)^4$ is $p^{\boxed{}}$

Compare. Use $<$, $>$, or $=$.

14. $(4^2)^3$ $\boxed{}$ $(4^3)^2$

15. $(4^3)^0$ $\boxed{}$ $(3^0)^4$

16. $(4^{-2})^3$ $\boxed{}$ $(4^{-3})^{-2}$

17. $(4^3)^{-1}$ $\boxed{}$ $(4^{-2})^2$

Problem 2 Simplifying an Expression With Powers

Got It? What is the simplified form of $x^2(x^6)^{-4}$?

18. Complete the reasoning model below to simplify the expression.

Think	Write
First I multiply the exponents of the power raised to a power.	$x^2(x^6)^{-4} = x^2 \cdot x^{\boxed{}}$
Then I add the exponents of powers that have the same base.	$x^{\boxed{}}$
Now, I need to simplify the answer so that it has all positive exponents.	$\boxed{}$

Lesson 7-4

Property Raising a Product to a Power

Words   To raise a product to a power, raise each factor to the power and multiply.

Algebra $(ab)^n = a^n b^n$, where $a \neq 0$, $b \neq 0$, and n is an integer.

Example $(3x)^4 = 3^4 x^4 = 81x^4$

Problem 3 Simplifying a Product Raised to a Power

Got It? What is the simplified form of $(7m^9)^3$?

19. Complete each step to simplify $(7m^9)^3$.

$$(7m^9)^3 = 7^{\boxed{}} \cdot (m^9)^{\boxed{}}$$

$$= 7^{\boxed{}} \cdot m^{\boxed{}}$$

$$= \boxed{} \cdot m^{\boxed{}}$$

$$= \boxed{}$$

Problem 4 Simplifying an Expression With Products

Got It? What is the simplified form of $(x^{-2})^2 (3xy^5)^4$?

20. Use the diagram at the right. Circle the base being raised to the second power. Underline the base being raised to the fourth power.

$$(x^{-2})^2 (3xy^5)^4$$

21. Complete.

$$(x^{-2})^2 \cdot (3xy^5)^4 = x^{\boxed{}} \cdot 3^{\boxed{}} \cdot x^{\boxed{}} \cdot y^{\boxed{}}$$

$$= 3^{\boxed{}} \cdot x^{\boxed{}} \cdot y^{\boxed{}}$$

$$= \boxed{}$$

22. The simplified form of $(x^{-2})^2 (3xy^5)^4$ is $\boxed{}$.

Problem 5 Raising a Number in Scientific Notation to a Power

Got It? The expression $\frac{1}{2}mv^2$ gives the kinetic energy, in joules, of an object with a mass of m kg traveling at a speed of v meters per second. What is the kinetic energy of an aircraft with a mass of 2.5×10^5 kg traveling at a speed of 3×10^2 m/s?

23. Use the information in the problem to complete the model below.

Relate	kinetic energy	is	$\frac{1}{2}$	of	$\boxed{}$	times	v^2
Define	kinetic energy	=	$\frac{1}{2}$	·	$\boxed{}$	·	$\left(\boxed{}\right)^2$

24. Complete each step to solve the problem.

$\frac{1}{2}mv^2 = \frac{1}{2} \cdot (2.5 \times \boxed{}) \cdot (3 \times \boxed{})^2$ Substitute the values into the equation.

$= \frac{1}{2} \cdot (2.5 \cdot \boxed{}) \cdot 3^{\boxed{}} \cdot (\boxed{})$ Raise each factor to the second power.

$= \frac{1}{2} \cdot (2.5 \cdot \boxed{}) \cdot 3^{\boxed{}} \cdot (\boxed{})$ Simplify the exponent of a power raised to a power.

$= \frac{1}{2} \cdot (2.5 \cdot 3^{\boxed{}}) \cdot (\boxed{} \cdot \boxed{})$ Use the Commutative and Associative Properties.

$= \frac{1}{2} \cdot (2.5 \cdot 3^{\boxed{}}) \cdot \boxed{}$ Add exponents of powers with the same base.

$= \boxed{} \cdot \boxed{}$ Multiply the factors that are not base 10.

$= \boxed{} \cdot \boxed{}$ Simplify. Write in scientific notation.

25. The aircraft has about $\boxed{}$ joules of kinetic energy.

Lesson Check • Do you UNDERSTAND?

Error Analysis One student simplified $x^5 + x^5$ to x^{10}. A second student simplified $x^5 + x^5$ to $2x^5$. Which student is correct? Explain.

26. Draw a line from each expression in Column A to the method you would use to simplify it in Column B.

Column A	Column B
$x^4 \cdot x^4$	Multiply exponents.
$(x^4)^4$	Combine like terms.
$x^4 + x^4$	Add exponents.

27. Which student is correct? Explain.

_____

Math Success

Check off the vocabulary words that you understand.

☐ power   ☐ scientific notation

Rate how well you can *apply multiplication properties of exponents.*

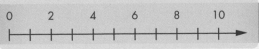

Need to review 0 2 4 6 8 10 Now I get it!

Lesson 7-4

Vocabulary

● Review

1. Circle the expressions that show a *quotient*.

$$3 + 6 \qquad \frac{3}{6} \qquad 3 - 6 \qquad 3 \cdot 6 \qquad 3 \div 6$$

Complete each sentence with *positive* or *negative*.

2. The *quotient* of two negative integers is always __?__ .

3. The *quotient* of two positive integers is always __?__ .

4. The *quotient* of a negative integer and a positive integer is always __?__ .

● Vocabulary Builder

property (noun) PRAHP **ur tee**

Main Idea: In mathematics, a **property** is a feature of a number, a set of numbers, an operation, or an equation.

Examples: Addition has the **properties** of commutativity and associativity.

● Use Your Vocabulary

5. Draw a line from each equation in Column A to the *property* it illustrates in Column B.

Column A	**Column B**
$(xy)z = x(yz)$	Raising a Power to a Power
$(x^{12})^3 = x^{36}$	Identity Property of Addition
$x + 0 = x$	Associative Property of Multiplication

Give an example of each *property*.

Sample: Associative Property of Addition

$(17 + c) + 3c = 17 + (c + 3c)$

6. Distributive Property

7. Commutative Property of Addition

8. Identity Property of Multiplication

Property Dividing Powers With the Same Base

Words   To divide powers with the same base, subtract the exponents.

Algebra $\frac{a^m}{a^n} = a^{m-n}$, where $a \neq 0$ and m and n are integers.

Problem 1 Dividing Algebraic Expressions

Got It? What is the simplified form of $\frac{y^5}{y^4}$?

9. To divide powers with the same base, you divide / subtract the exponents.

10. Identify the number of times y is used as a factor in each expression.

   y^5 y^4 $y^{5\ 4}$

   ▢ time(s)   ▢ time(s)   ▢ time(s)

11. The simplified form of $\frac{y^5}{y^4}$ is ▢.

Is each pair of expressions *always*, *sometimes*, or *never* equal? Assume no denominators are 0.

12. $\frac{d^3}{d^9}$ and d^6 13. $\frac{k^6 j^2}{kj^5}$ and $\frac{k^5}{j^3}$ 14. $\frac{a^{-3}b^7}{a^5 b^2}$ and $a^{-8}b^{-5}$ 15. $\frac{x^4 y^{-1} z^8}{x^4 y^{-5} z}$ and $y^4 z^7$

_____ _____ _____ _____

Problem 2 Dividing Numbers in Scientific Notation

Got It? Population density describes the number of people per unit area. During one year, Honduras had a population of 7.33×10^6 people. The area of Honduras is $4.33 \times 10^4 \text{mi}^2$. What was the population density of Honduras that year?

16. Complete each step to find the population density of Honduras for the year.

   $\dfrac{\text{population}}{\text{area}} = \dfrac{7.33 \times 10^6}{\boxed{}}$ Write the expression.

   $= \dfrac{7.33}{\boxed{}} \times 10^{\boxed{}-}$ Separate the powers of 10 from the other factors.

   $= \dfrac{7.33}{\boxed{}} \times 10^{\boxed{}}$ Simplify the exponent.

   $\approx \boxed{} \times 10^{\boxed{}}$ Divide. Round to the nearest thousandth.

   $\approx \boxed{}$ Write in standard notation.

17. The population density was about ▢ people per square mile.

Lesson 7-5

Property   Raising a Quotient to a Power

To raise a quotient to a power, raise the numerator and the denominator to the power and simplify.

$\left(\dfrac{a}{b}\right)^n = \dfrac{a^n}{b^n}$, where $a \neq 0$, $b \neq 0$, and n is an integer.

For all nonzero numbers a and b and positive integers n, $\left(\dfrac{a}{b}\right)^{-n} = \left(\dfrac{b}{a}\right)^n$.

Simplify each expression.

18. $\left(\dfrac{3}{10}\right)^4 = \dfrac{3^{\boxed{}}}{10^{\boxed{}}} = \dfrac{\boxed{}}{\boxed{}}$

19. $\left(\dfrac{3}{10}\right)^{-4} = \left(\dfrac{\boxed{}}{\boxed{}}\right)^4 = \dfrac{\boxed{}^4}{\boxed{}^4} = \dfrac{\boxed{}}{\boxed{}}$

Compare. Use $<$, $>$, or $=$.

20. $\left(\dfrac{1}{5}\right)^3 \boxed{}\ 5^{-3}$

21. $\left(\dfrac{1}{5}\right)^3 \boxed{}\ 5^3$

22. $\left(\dfrac{3}{4}\right)^2 \boxed{} \left(\dfrac{4}{3}\right)^2$

23. $\left(\dfrac{3}{4}\right)^2 \boxed{} \left(\dfrac{4}{3}\right)^{-2}$

24. $\left(\dfrac{1}{2}\right)^0 \boxed{} \left(\dfrac{1}{2}\right)^{-3}$

25. $\left(\dfrac{1}{2}\right)^0 \boxed{} \left(\dfrac{1}{2}\right)^3$

Problem 3   Raising a Quotient to a Power

Got It? What is the simplified form of $\left(\dfrac{4}{x^3}\right)^2$?

26. When raising a quotient to a power, what is raised to the power? Circle your answer.

| numerator | denominator | both numerator and denominator |

27. Simplify $\left(\dfrac{4}{x^3}\right)^2$.

$\left(\dfrac{4}{x^3}\right)^2 = \dfrac{\boxed{}^{\boxed{}}}{\boxed{}^{\boxed{}}} = \dfrac{\boxed{}}{\boxed{}}$

Problem 4   Simplifying an Exponential Expression

Got It? What is the simplified form of $\left(\dfrac{a}{5b}\right)^{-2}$?

28. Complete.

$\left(\dfrac{a}{b}\right)^{-n} = \dfrac{a^{\boxed{}}}{b^{\boxed{}}} = \dfrac{1}{\boxed{}^{\boxed{}}} \cdot \dfrac{\boxed{}^{\boxed{}}}{1} = \dfrac{\boxed{}}{\boxed{}}$

29. Use the result from Exercise 28 to simplify $\left(\dfrac{a}{5b}\right)^{-2}$.

Write T for *true* or F for *false*.

_____ **30.** $\left(\dfrac{1}{7}\right)^4 = 7^4$

_____ **31.** $\left(\dfrac{2}{7}\right)^{-3} = \dfrac{1}{8} \cdot 7^3$

_____ **32.** $\left(\dfrac{7}{2}\right)^{-2} = \dfrac{4}{7^2}$

_____ **33.** $\left(\dfrac{2}{7^4}\right)^{-5} = \left(\dfrac{2}{7^4}\right)^5$

Lesson Check • Do you UNDERSTAND?

Vocabulary How is the property for raising a quotient to a power similar to the property for raising a product to a power?

34. The property for raising a quotient to a power states that

$$\left(\dfrac{a}{b}\right)^n = \underline{\hphantom{xxx}}.$$

35. The property for raising a product to a power states that

$$(ab)^n = \underline{\hphantom{xxx}}.$$

36. How are the two properties similar?

_____

_____

_____

Math Success

Check off the vocabulary words that you understand.

☐ power ☐ quotient ☐ reciprocal

Rate how well you can *use the division properties of exponents.*

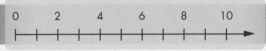

Lesson 7-5

Vocabulary

● Review

1. Circle each relation that is a *function*.

$\{(1, 3), (1, 5), (2, 7), (3, 9), (4, 11)\}$ $\{(0, 0), (-1, -1), (-2, -2), (-3, -3)\}$

$\{(5, 5), (5, 4), (5, 3), (5, 2)\}$ $\{(2, 5), (3, 5), (4, 5), (5, 5)\}$

2. Cross out the equations that are NOT linear *functions*.

$y = 3x + 2$ $y = \frac{3}{x}$ $y = -2$ $x = 4$ $y = x^2 + 5$

● Vocabulary Builder

exponential (adjective) **ek spoh NEN shul**

Related Word: exponent (noun)

Main Idea: You can use **exponential** notation to write a repeated multiplication (such as $8 \times 8 \times 8 \times 8$) using a base and an exponent (8^4). An **exponential** function has a variable as an exponent.

● Use Your Vocabulary

Underline the correct word to complete each sentence.

3. In the expression 5^3, the 3 is an exponential / exponent .

4. The expression 3^x is an exponent / exponential expression.

5. Draw a line from each *exponential* expression in Column A to an equivalent expression in Column B.

Column A	Column B
$(3n)^{-1}$	$\dfrac{1}{25n^2}$
$\left(\dfrac{1}{4}\right)^2$	$\dfrac{8}{n^3}$
$\left(\dfrac{2}{n}\right)^3$	4^{-2}
$(5n)^{-2}$	$\dfrac{1}{3n}$

Key Concept   Exponential Function

Definition An **exponential function** is a function of the form $y = a \cdot b^x$, where $a \neq 0$, $b > 0$, $b \neq 1$, and x is a real number.

Examples

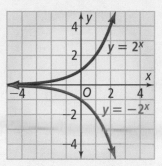
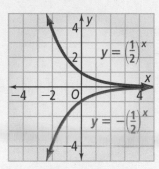

If all of the x-values in a table have a constant difference and all of the y-values have a constant ratio, then the table represents an exponential function.

 Problem 1 Identifying an Exponential Function

Got It? Does the table represent an exponential function? Explain.

For Exercises 6 and 7, use the table at the right.

6. Find the difference between each pair of consecutive x-values.

7. Find the ratio between each pair of consecutive y-values.

x	1	2	3	4
y	−1	1	3	5

8. Underline the correct word or words to complete each sentence.

There is / is not a constant difference between x-values.

There is / is not a constant ratio between y-values.

The table represents / does not represent an exponential function.

Got It? Does the rule $y = 3 \cdot 6^x$ represent an exponential function? Explain.

9. An exponential function has the form $y = a \cdot b^x$. In the rule $y = 3 \cdot 6^x$, identify a and b.

$a = $ ☐ $b = $ ☐

10. Does the rule $y = 3 \cdot 6^x$ meet the definition of an exponential function? Place a ✓ in the box if the statement is correct. Place an ✗ in the box if it is incorrect.

☐ $a \neq 0$ ☐ $b > 0$ ☐ $b \neq 1$

11. Is $y = 3 \cdot 6^x$ an exponential function? Explain.

Lesson 7-6

Problem 2 Evaluating an Exponential Function

Got It? An initial population of 20 rabbits triples every half year. The function $f(x) = 20 \cdot 3^x$ gives the population after x half-year periods. How many rabbits will there be after 3 years?

12. In 3 years, there are ⬚ half-year periods.

13. Complete the steps to evaluate the function.

$f(x) = 20 \cdot 3^x = 20 \cdot 3^{\boxed{}}$ Substitute the number of half-year periods.

$= 20 \cdot \boxed{}$ Evaluate the power.

$= \boxed{}$ Simplify.

14. There will be ⬚ rabbits after 3 years.

 Problem 3 Graphing an Exponential Function

Got It? What is the graph of $y = 0.5 \cdot 3^x$?

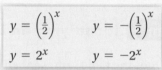

$$y = \left(\frac{1}{2}\right)^x \qquad y = -\left(\frac{1}{2}\right)^x$$
$$y = 2^x \qquad y = -2^x$$

15. Use one of the functions in the box to label each graph.

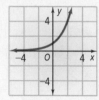   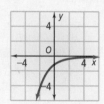   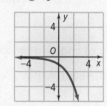   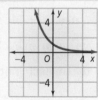

⬚   ⬚   ⬚   ⬚

16. Complete the table. Then graph each ordered pair and draw a smooth curve.

x	$y = 0.5 \cdot 3^x$	Ordered Pair (x, y)
-2	$0.5 \cdot 3^{-2} = \frac{1}{2} \cdot \frac{1}{9} = \frac{1}{\boxed{}}$	$\left(-2, \frac{1}{\boxed{}}\right)$
-1	$0.5 \cdot 3^{\boxed{}} = \frac{1}{2} \cdot \frac{1}{\boxed{}} = \frac{1}{\boxed{}}$	$\left(-1, \frac{}{\boxed{}}\right)$
0	$0.5 \cdot 3^{\boxed{}} = \frac{1}{2} \cdot \boxed{} = \frac{}{\boxed{}}$	$\left(0, \frac{}{\boxed{}}\right)$
1	$0.5 \cdot 3^{\boxed{}} = \frac{1}{2} \cdot \boxed{} = \frac{}{\boxed{}}$	$(1, \boxed{})$

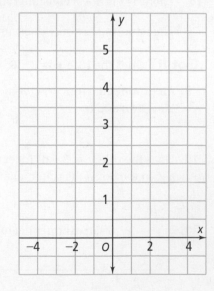

Problem 4 **Graphing an Exponential Model**

Got It? Computer mapping software allows you to zoom in or out on an area to view it in more detail. The function $f(x) = 100 \cdot 4^x$ models the percent of the original area the map shows after zooming out x times. Graph the function.

17. Complete the table of x and $f(x)$ values. Then use the values to make a graph and plot the points. Do not connect the points of the graph.

x	$f(x) = 100 \cdot 4^x$	$(x, f(x))$
0	$100 \cdot 4^0 = 100 \cdot 1 = \boxed{}$	$(0, \boxed{})$
1	$100 \cdot \boxed{}^{\boxed{}} = 100 \cdot \boxed{} = \boxed{}$	$(1, \boxed{})$
2	$100 \cdot \boxed{} = 100 \cdot \boxed{} = \boxed{}$	$(2, \boxed{})$
3	$100 \cdot \boxed{} = \boxed{} \cdot \boxed{} = \boxed{}$	
4	$100 \cdot \boxed{} = \boxed{} = \boxed{}$	

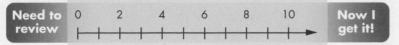 **Lesson Check** • **Do you UNDERSTAND?**

Reasoning Is $y = (-2)^x$ an exponential function? Justify your answer.

18. An exponential function has the form $y = a \cdot b^x$. What are the restrictions on b?

_____

19. Is $y = (-2)^x$ an exponential function? Justify your answer.

_____

Math Success

Check off the vocabulary words that you understand.

☐ exponent   ☐ exponential   ☐ exponential function

Rate how well you can *graph exponential functions.*

| Need to review | 0   2   4   6   8   10 | Now I get it! |

Lesson 7-6

Exponential Growth and Decay

Vocabulary

● Review

1. Match each situation in Column A with an equation that *models* it in Column B.

Column A	Column B
A person begins with $100 and earns $2 each day.	$y = 100 \cdot 2^x$
A person begins with $2 and earns $100 each day.	$y = 100 + 2x$
A person begins with $100. Each day the money doubles.	$y = 2 + 100x$

● Vocabulary Builder

compound interest (noun) KAHM **pownd** IN **trist**

Related Words: principal (noun), simple interest (noun), interest rate (noun)

Definition: Compound interest is interest earned on both the principal *and* on any interest the account has already earned that remains in the account.

● Use Your Vocabulary

Choose the correct word from the list to complete each sentence.

compound interest   simple interest   principal

2. The amount of money deposited in an account is the ⎯?⎯.

3. The amount of money earned on an investment only is ⎯?⎯.

4. Interest earned on both the principal and the interest left in the account is ⎯?⎯.

5. Use the situation below. Identify the *principal, interest rate, time in years,* and *balance.*

Suzanne deposits $1200 into a bank account paying 1.25% interest compounded annually for 5 years, at which point the account holds $1276.90.

principal: interest rate:

time in years: balance:

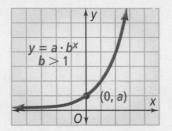

Key Concept Exponential Growth

The function $y = a \cdot b^x$, where $a > 0$ and $b > 1$, models **exponential growth**.

The base b is the **growth factor**.

Algebra initial amount (when $x = 0$)

$y = a \cdot b^x$ ← exponent

The base, which is *greater* than 1, is the growth factor.

$y = a \cdot b^x$
$b > 1$

$(0, a)$

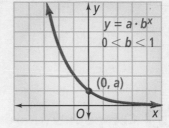

Key Concept Exponential Decay

The function $y = a \cdot b^x$, where $a > 0$ and $0 < b < 1$, models **exponential decay**.

The base b is the **decay factor**.

Algebra initial amount (when $x = 0$)

$y = a \cdot b^x$ ← exponent

The base, which is *less* than 1, is the decay factor.

$y = a \cdot b^x$
$0 < b < 1$

$(0, a)$

6. Circle the numbers that could be *growth factors*.

| 85% | 3 | $\frac{1}{2}$ | 1.05 | 0.93 |

7. Circle the numbers that could be *decay factors*.

| 85% | 3 | $\frac{1}{2}$ | 1.05 | 0.93 |

Problem 1 Modeling Exponential Growth

Got It? Suppose the population of a town was 25,000 people in 2000. If the population grows about 1.5% each year, what will the approximate population be in 2025?

8. Use the words *exponent, growth factor,* and *initial amount* to complete the diagram. Then find the value of the expression.

$$25{,}000 \cdot 1.015^{25} = \underline{\hspace{2cm}}$$

← value of the expression

new population

9. The population of the town in 2025 will be about _____ .

Lesson 7-7

The formula below gives the balance, A, in an account that earns compound interest. The formula is an *exponential function* with initial amount P and growth factor $\left(1 + \frac{r}{n}\right)^n$.

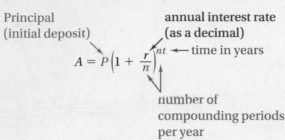

Principal
(initial deposit)

annual interest rate
(as a decimal)

$$A = P\left(1 + \frac{r}{n}\right)^{nt} \leftarrow \text{time in years}$$

number of
compounding periods
per year

Simplify each expression. Round your answers to the nearest tenth.

10. $1200\left(1 + \frac{0.045}{12}\right)^{12}$

11. $500\left(1 + \frac{0.015}{4}\right)^{4 \cdot 5}$

12. $15{,}000\left(1 + \frac{0.02}{6}\right)^{6 \cdot 10}$

Problem 2 Compound Interest

Got It? Suppose that when your friend was born, your friend's parents deposited $2000 in an account paying 4.5% interest compounded monthly. What will the account balance be after 18 yr?

13. Draw a line from each variable in Column A to its value from the problem in Column B.

Column A	Column B
P	18
r	0.045
n	2000
t	12

14. Substitute the values into the formula $A = P\left(1 + \frac{r}{n}\right)^{nt}$ to find the account balance.

15. The balance in the account after 18 yr will be $ _____ .

Problem 3 Modeling Exponential Decay

Got It? The kilopascal is a unit of measure for atmospheric pressure. The atmospheric pressure at sea level is about 101 kilopascals. For every 1000-m increase in altitude, the pressure decreases about 11.5%. What is the pressure at an altitude of 5000 m?

16. Between sea level and 5000 m, the atmospheric pressure will decrease

5000 ÷ ▢ , or ▢ times.

17. Write and simplify an equation to find the atmospheric pressure at 5000 m.

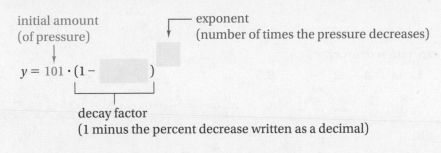

$y = 101 \cdot (1 - \boxed{} \boxed{})$

initial amount (of pressure)

exponent (number of times the pressure decreases)

decay factor (1 minus the percent decrease written as a decimal)

$= \boxed{}$

18. To the nearest whole unit, the pressure at 5000 m is about ▢ kilopascals.

Lesson Check • Do you UNDERSTAND?

Reasoning How can you simplify the compound interest formula when the interest is compounded annually? Explain.

19. When interest is compounded annually, the value of n in $P\left(1 + \dfrac{r}{n}\right)^{nt}$ is ▢ .

20. Now simplify the compound interest formula.

Math Success

Check off the vocabulary words that you understand.

☐ exponential growth   ☐ compound interest   ☐ exponential decay

Rate how well you can *model exponential growth and decay*.

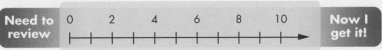

Lesson 7-7

8-1 Adding and Subtracting Polynomials

Vocabulary

● Review

Tell whether each is an *expression* or an *equation*.

1. $3x - 4$

2. $14 = 8 + 6b$

3. $\frac{r}{6}$

4. $0 = \frac{1}{3}x^2$

Write T for *true* or F for *false*.

_____ **5.** *Expressions* with only numbers are always like terms.

_____ **6.** An *expression* can have an equal sign.

_____ **7.** *Equations* can be true, false, or open.

● Vocabulary Builder

poly- (prefix) **PAHL ee**	**poly**nomial $3x^2 + 3xy - y^2$

Related Words: many, several, polynomial, polygon

Definition: The prefix **poly** means "many" or "several" and is used to make compound words such as polygon.

Main Idea: **Polynomials** may contain one or several monomials.

monomials
$3x^2, 3xy, -y^2$

● Use Your Vocabulary

Complete each statement with a word from the list. Use each word only once.

polygon   polygraph   polynomial

8. A monomial or a sum of monomials is a __?__ .

9. A __?__ test measures many tiny physical reactions of a person who is being questioned in order to determine whether that person is telling the truth.

10. A triangle is one example of a __?__ .

Problem 1 Finding the Degree of a Monomial

Got It? What is the degree of the monomial $8xy$?

11. Write the degree of each part of the monomial. Then find the degree of the monomial.

$$8xy = 8 \cdot x \cdot y$$

degree of each part $\boxed{}$ + $\boxed{}$ + $\boxed{}$ = $\boxed{}$ ← degree of monomial

12. The degree of the monomial $8xy$ is $\boxed{}$.

Got It? What are the degrees of the monomials $-7y^4z$ and 11?

13. Write the degree of each part of each monomial. Then find the degree of the monomial.

$-7y^4z$ 11

Problem 2 Adding and Subtracting Monomials

Got It? What is the sum $-6x^4 + 11x^4$? What is the difference $2x^2y^4 - 7x^2y^4$?

14. Circle the like terms and underline the coefficients.

$-6x^4 + 11x^4$ $2x^2y^4 - 7x^2y^4$

Simplify each expression.

15. $-6x^4 + 11x^4$ **16.** $2x^2y^4 - 7x^2y^4$

$= \left(\boxed{} + \boxed{} \right) x^4$ Use the Distributive Property. $= \left(\boxed{} + \boxed{} \right) x^2y^4$

$= \boxed{} \cdot x^4$ Simplify within parentheses. $= \boxed{} \cdot x^2y^4$

You can name a polynomial based on its degree or the number of monomials it contains.

Polynomial	Degree	Name Using Degree	Number of Terms	Name Using Number of Terms
6	0	Constant	1	Monomial
$5x + 9$	1	Linear	2	Binomial
$4x^2 + 7x + 3$	2	Quadratic	3	Trinomial
$2x^3$	3	Cubic	1	Monomial
$8x^4 - 2x^3 + 3x$	4	Fourth degree	3	Trinomial

Lesson 8-1

Got It? Write $2x - 3 + 8x^2$ in standard form. What is the name of the polynomial based on its degree and number of terms?

17. Complete the model to write the polynomial in standard form.

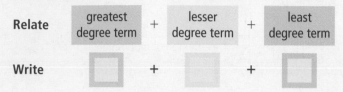

Relate | greatest degree term | + | lesser degree term | + | least degree term |

Write ☐ + ☐ + ☐

18. In standard form, the polynomial $2x - 3 + 8x^2$ is _____ .

19. Circle the best name for the polynomial based on its degree.

> constant   linear   quadratic   cubic   fourth degree

20. Circle the best name for the polynomial based on the number of terms.

> monomial   binomial   trinomial

21. Now write the combined name for the polynomial.

_____

Got It? A nutritionist studies the U.S. consumption of carrots and celery and of broccoli over a 6-yr period. The nutritionist modeled the results, in millions of pounds, with the following polynomials.

Carrots and celery: $-12x^3 + 106x^2 - 241x + 4477$

Broccoli: $14x^2 - 14x + 1545$

In each polynomial, $x = 0$ corresponds to the first year in the 6-yr period. What polynomial models the total number of pounds, in millions of carrots, celery, and broccoli consumed in the U. S. during the 6-yr period?

22. To add the polynomials, first group like terms. Then add or subtract the coefficients.

$(-12x^3 + 106x^2 - 241x + 4477) + (14x^2 - 14x + 1545)$

$= (-12x^3) + (\boxed{} + 14x^2) + (\boxed{} - 14x) + (\boxed{} + 1545)$

$= \boxed{} + \boxed{} - \boxed{} + \boxed{}$

23. The polynomial _____ models the number of

pounds, in millions, consumed in the U. S. during the 6-yr period.

Problem 5 **Subtracting Polynomials**

Got It? What is a simpler form of $(-4m^3 - m + 9) - (4m^2 + m - 12)$?

24. Subtract vertically.

$-4m^3 + \boxed{} m^2 - m + 9 \quad \longleftarrow$ 0 is the coefficient of each missing term.

$-(\boxed{} m^3 + \boxed{} m^2 + m - \boxed{}) \quad \longleftarrow$ Line up like terms.

$-4m^3 + \boxed{} m^2 - m + 9$

$- \boxed{} m^3 - m^2 - m + \boxed{} \quad \longleftarrow$ Rewrite the subtraction.

$-4m^3 + \boxed{} m^2 - \boxed{} m + \boxed{} \quad \longleftarrow$ Add each pair of terms.

25. Write the simplified form of $(-4m^3 - m + 9) - (4m^2 + m - 12)$.

 Lesson Check • **Do you UNDERSTAND?**

Vocabulary Name the polynomial $5x^2 + 2x + 1$ based on its degree and number of terms.

Underline the correct word(s) or number to complete each sentence.

26. The polynomial has two / three terms.

27. The greatest degree of a term is 0 / 1 / 2 .

28. Circle the best name for the polynomial.

cubic binomial   cubic trinomial   quadratic binomial   quadratic trinomial

---

Math Success

Check off the vocabulary words that you understand.

☐ standard form   ☐ classifying a polynomial   ☐ cubic   ☐ quadratic

Rate how well you can *add and subtract polynomials*.

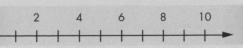

Lesson 8-1

Multiplying and Factoring

 ## Vocabulary

● **Review**

1. Place a ✓ if the number is a *multiple* of 10 and an ✗ if the number is NOT a *multiple* of 10.

☐ 250 ☐ 2 ☐ 50 ☐ 30

● **Vocabulary Builder**

factor (noun) FAK **tur**

Related Words: divide, factorable, factored form

Definition: A **factor** is a whole number or variable that divides another whole number with a remainder of 0.

The **factors** of $2x^2y$ include 2, x, and y.

● **Use Your Vocabulary**

2. Cross out the expression that does NOT have x^3 as a *factor*.

x^5 $12x^2$ x^2xy $(3x^2)^2$

3. Circle the *factor* tree that shows a prime factorization.

$6x^2$
/ \
6 x^2

$6x^2$
/ \
$6x$ x

$6x^2$
/ \
$2x$ $3x$

$6x^2$
/ | \ \
2 3 x x

Problem 1 **Multiplying a Monomial and a Trinomial**

Got It? What is a simpler form of $5n(3n^3 - n^2 + 8)$?

4. Distribute the $5n$. Use the arrows to help you.

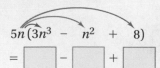

$5n\,(3n^3 - n^2 + 8)$

$= \boxed{} - \boxed{} + \boxed{}$

5. The simplified form of $5n(3n^3 - n^2 + 8)$

is 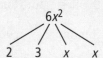 $\boxed{} - \boxed{} + \boxed{}$.

Finding the GCF of a pair of monomials is similar to finding the GCF of a pair of integers.

6. Circle the pair of numbers with a GCF of 4.

| 4 and 5 | 4 and 6 | 8 and 12 | 8 and 16 |

7. Circle the pair of monomials with a GCF of $4x$.

| $4x$ and $5x$ | $4x$ and $6x$ | $8x$ and $12x$ | $8x$ and $16x$ |

8. Cross out the pair(s) of numbers whose GCF is NOT 6.

| 15 and 16 | 16 and 18 | 24 and 36 | 30 and 36 |

9. Cross out the pair(s) of monomials whose GCF is NOT $6y^2$.

| $15y^2$ and $16y^2$ | $16y^2$ and $18y^2$ | $24y^2$ and $36y^2$ | $30y^2$ and $36y^2$ |

 Problem 2 **Finding the Greatest Common Factor**

Got It? What is the GCF of the terms of $3x^4 - 9x^2 - 12x$?

10. Circle the GCF of the numbers 3, 9, and 12.

| 1 | 2 | 3 | 6 | 9 | 12 |

11. Circle the GCF of x, x^2, and x^4.

| x^0 | x | x^2 | x^3 | x^4 |

12. The GCF of the terms of $3x^4 - 9x^2 - 12x$ is ____ .

 Problem 3 **Factoring Out a Monomial**

Got It? What is the factored form of $9x^6 + 15x^4 + 12x^2$?

13. Complete each factor tree.

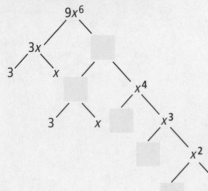
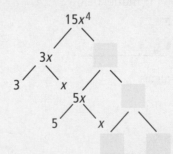
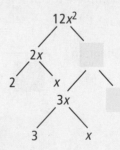

14. Use the factor trees in Exercise 13 to write each prime factorization.

$9x^6 = $ ____

$15x^4 = $ ____

$12x^2 = $ ____

Lesson 8-2

15. $9x^6$, $15x^4$, and $12x^2$ have

 common factors of 2   common factors of 3

common factors of 5   common factors of x

16. Multiply all common factors of $9x^6$, $15x^4$, and $12x^2$ to find the GCF.

17. Circle the next step to write $9x^6 + 15x^4 + 12x^2$ in factored form.

Add like terms.   Factor the GCF from each term.   Divide by $3x^6$.

18. The factored form of $9x^6 + 15x^4 + 12x^2$ is   (   ).

Problem 4 **Factoring a Polynomial Model**

Got It? A helicopter landing pad, or helipad, is sometimes marked with a circle inside a square so that it is visible from the air. What is the area of the orange-shaded region of the helipad at the right? Write your answer in factored form.

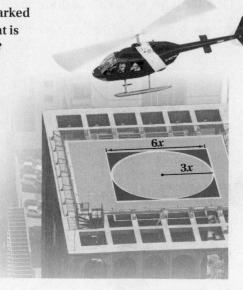

19. Write an algebraic expression for the area of the square.

Area of ▪ = (   )

20. Write an algebraic expression for the area of the circle.

Area of ● = π(   )

21. Complete the problem-solving model below.

Diagram

▪ minus ●

Relate

area of
the shaded region

area of
the square minus area of
the circle

Write

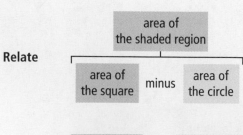

(   )   − π(   )

22. Use the justifications below to find the area of the shaded region.

$$\text{Area} = (\quad)^{\boxed{}} - \pi(\quad)^{\boxed{}} \qquad \text{Write the original equation.}$$

$$= \boxed{} - \boxed{}\pi \qquad\qquad \text{Simplify each power.}$$

$$= (\boxed{} - \boxed{}\pi)x^2 \qquad \text{Factor out } x^2.$$

$$= \boxed{}\,x^2(\boxed{} - \boxed{}) \qquad \text{Factor out the GCF of 36 and } 9\pi.$$

23. The factored form of the area of the shaded region is $\boxed{}$.

Lesson Check • Do you UNDERSTAND?

Find the GCF of each pair of monomials.

$$14n^2, 35n^4 \qquad\qquad 21n^3, 18n^2 \qquad\qquad 7n^2, 9$$

24. Factor each pair of monomials.

$$14n^2 = 2 \cdot \boxed{} \cdot \boxed{}^2 \quad \text{and} \quad 35n^4 = \boxed{} \cdot \boxed{} \cdot \boxed{}^4$$

$$21n^3 = 3 \cdot \boxed{} \cdot \boxed{}^3 \quad \text{and} \quad 18n^2 = \boxed{} \cdot \boxed{} \cdot \boxed{} \cdot \boxed{}^2$$

$$7n^2 = \boxed{} \cdot \boxed{}^2 \quad \text{and} \quad 9 = \boxed{} \cdot \boxed{}$$

Draw a line from each pair of monomials in Column A to the GCF of the monomials in Column B.

Column A	Column B
25. $14n^2, 35n^4$	1
26. $21n^3, 18n^2$	$7n^2$
27. $7n^2, 9$	$3n^2$

Math Success

Check off the vocabulary words that you understand.

☐ factor ☐ greatest common factor ☐ standard form ☐ factored form

Rate how well you can *multiply a monomial by a polynomial.*

Need to review 0 2 4 6 8 10 Now I get it!

Lesson 8-2

Vocabulary

● Review

1. Cross out the expressions that do NOT show a *product*.

| $7(-5)$ | $\frac{a}{3}$ | $12 \cdot (-1)$ | $8h$ | $10 + m$ |

2. Circle the integer that shows the *product* of 12 and 4.

| 3 | 8 | 16 | 48 |

3. Circle the *product* of the monomials 12 and x^2.

| $3x$ | $4x$ | $12x$ | $12 + x$ | $12x^2$ |

● Vocabulary Builder

acronym (noun) AK **ruh nim**

Main Idea: An **acronym** makes it easier to remember a group of words.

Definition: An **acronym** is an identifier formed from the first letters of a group of words.

Examples: GCF (greatest <u>c</u>ommon <u>f</u>actor), scuba (<u>s</u>elf-<u>c</u>ontained <u>u</u>nderwater <u>b</u>reathing <u>a</u>pparatus)

> The **acronym** RADAR stands for
>
> RAdio Detecting And Ranging

● Use Your Vocabulary

4. Draw a line from each word or phrase in Column A to its *acronym* in Column B.

Column A	Column B
identification	PIN
internet service provider	ID
as soon as possible	ATM
personal identification number	ASAP
for your information	ISP
automated teller machine	FYI

Problem 1 **Using the Distributive Property**

Got It? What is a simpler form of $(x - 6)(4x + 3)$?

5. Use the diagram at the right. Circle the second factor. Then underline each term of the first factor.

$$(x - 6)(4x + 3)$$

6. Use the diagram from Exercise 5 and the justifications below to simplify the expression.

$(x - 6)(4x + 3) = x() - 6()$ Distribute the second factor to each term of the first factor.

$= \boxed{} + \boxed{} - 6()$ Distribute x.

$= \boxed{} + \boxed{} - \boxed{} - \boxed{}$ Distribute -6.

$= \boxed{} - \boxed{} - \boxed{}$ Combine like terms.

7. A simpler form of the expression is \boxed{} .

8. **Reasoning** Would you get the same answer if you distributed the first factor instead of the second factor? Explain

_____

_____

 Problem 2 **Using a Table**

Got It? What is a simpler form of $(3x + 1)(x + 4)$? Use a table.

9. Circle the model that shows the product $(3x + 1)(x + 4)$.

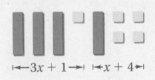

$\longleftarrow 3x + 1 \longrightarrow$ $\longleftarrow x + 4 \longrightarrow$

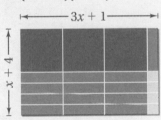

10. Complete the table to multiply $(3x + 1)$ and $(x + 4)$.

Factors	3x	1
x	$3x \cdot x = \boxed{}$	$1 \cdot x = \boxed{}$
4	$\boxed{} \cdot \boxed{} = \boxed{}$	$\boxed{} \cdot \boxed{} = \boxed{}$

11. Now write the simplified form of the expression.

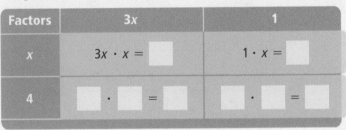

$\boxed{} + \boxed{} + \boxed{} + 4 = \boxed{} + \boxed{} + 4 \leftarrow$ Combine like terms.

Lesson 8-3

Problem 3 Multiplying Using FOIL

Got It? What is a simpler form of $(3x - 4)(x + 2)$? Use the FOIL method.

12. Use the arrows to multiply the binomials.

$$
\begin{array}{cccc}
\text{First} & \text{Outer} & \text{Inner} & \text{Last} \\
\end{array}
$$

$$(3x - 4)(x + 2) = 3x \cdot \boxed{} + 3x \cdot \boxed{} + (-4) \cdot \boxed{} + (-4) \cdot \boxed{}$$

$$= \boxed{} + \boxed{} - \boxed{} - \boxed{}$$

13. A simpler form of $(3x - 4)(x + 2)$ is $\boxed{}$.

14. Reasoning Without simplifying, explain how the simplified form of $(3x - 4)(x + 2)$ differs from the simplified form of $(3x + 4)(x + 2)$.

_____

_____

_____

Problem 4 Applying Multiplication of Binomials

Got It? What is the total surface area of a cylinder with radius $x + 2$ and height $x + 4$? Write your answer as a polynomial in standard form.

15. Use the information in the problem to label the diagram at the right.

16. The formula $S.A. = 2\pi r^2 + 2\pi rh$ gives the total surface area of a cylinder. Circle the correct substitution into the formula.

$$2\pi(x + 2)^2 + 2\pi(x + 2)(x + 4) \qquad 2\pi(x + 4)^2 + 2\pi(x + 4)(x + 2) \qquad 2\pi(x + 4)^2 + 2\pi(x)$$

17. The expression is simplified below. Write a justification for each step.

$$S.A. = 2\pi(x + 2)^2 + 2\pi(x + 2)(x + 4)$$

_____

$$= 2\pi(x + 2)(x + 2) + 2\pi(x + 2)(x + 4)$$

_____

$$= 2\pi(x^2 + 4x + 4) + 2\pi(x^2 + 6x + 8)$$

_____

$$= 2\pi(x^2 + 4x + 4 + x^2 + 6x + 8)$$

_____

$$= 2\pi(2x^2 + 10x + 12)$$

_____

$$= 4\pi x^2 + 20\pi x + 24\pi$$

_____

Problem 5 **Multiplying a Trinomial and a Binomial**

Got It? What is a simpler form of $(2x^2 - 3x + 1)(x - 3)$?

18. Complete the vertical multiplication.

$$
\begin{array}{rrrrr}
2x^2 & - & 3x & + & 1 \\
 & & x & - & 3 \\
\hline
-6x^2 & + & \square & + & (-3) \\
\square & + & \square & + & x \\
\hline
\square & - & \square & + & \square & - & 3
\end{array}
$$

← Multiply $(2x^2 - 3x + 1)$ by -3.

← Multiply $(2x^2 - 3x + 1)$ by x.

← Combine like terms.

19. A simpler form of $(2x^2 - 3x + 1)(x - 3)$ is _____.

✓ **Lesson Check** • **Do you UNDERSTAND?**

Compare and Contrast Simplify $(3x + 8)(x + 1)$ using a table, the Distributive Property, and the FOIL method. Which method is most efficient? Explain.

20. Use the boxes below to simplify the expression using the three methods.

21. Which method is most efficient? Explain.

_____

_____

✓ **Math Success**

Check off the vocabulary words that you understand.

☐ FOIL method   ☐ binomial   ☐ substitution   ☐ table of products

Rate how well you can *multiply binomials*.

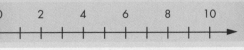

Lesson 8-3

Multiplying Special Cases

🔊 Vocabulary

● Review

1. Circle the *square* numbers below.

| 77 | 36 | 144 | $\frac{1}{4}$ | 1 | 6 |

Underline the correct word or words to complete each sentence.

2. The *square* of a nonzero number is sometimes / always / never positive.

3. The *square root* of a number is sometimes / always / never negative.

● Vocabulary Builder

binomial (noun) **by NOH mee ul**

Related Words: square of a binomial

Definition: A **binomial** is a polynomial with two terms.

> **binomials**
> $a^2 + b^2$, $xy - 3$,
> $7 + p^3$, $x + y$

● Use Your Vocabulary

4. Cross out the expression that is NOT a *binomial*.

| $y - 6$ | $z^3 + z - 1$ | $\frac{1}{7}r - t$ | $(x + 3)$ |

Write your own examples of *binomials*.

5. _____   **6.** _____

7. _____   **8.** _____

9. Use the words in the box at the right to complete the graphic organizer below. Then write your own examples of each type of polynomial.

> binomial
> polynomial
> trinomial

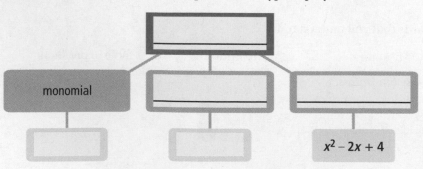

monomial

$x^2 - 2x + 4$

Key Concept The Square of a Binomial

Words The square of a binomial is the square of the first term plus twice the product of the two terms plus the square of the last term.

Algebra	**Examples**
$(a + b)^2 = a^2 + 2ab + b^2$	$(x + 4)^2 = x^2 + 8x + 16$
$(a - b)^2 = a^2 - 2ab + b^2$	$(x - 3)^2 = x^2 - 6x + 9$

10. Square each binomial.

$(x - 7)^2 = \boxed{}^2 - \boxed{}\ x + \boxed{}$ $(x + 9)^2 = \boxed{}^2 + \boxed{} + \boxed{}$

Problem 1 **Squaring a Binomial**

Got It? What is a simpler form of $(n - 7)^2$?

11. Circle the rule you would use to square the binomial.

$(a - b)^2 = a^2 - 2ab + b^2$ $(a + b)^2 = a^2 + b^2$ $(a + b)^2 = a^2 + 2ab + b^2$

12. Substitute n for a and 7 for b. Then simplify.

Problem 2 **Applying Squaring a Binomial**

Got It? A square outdoor patio is surrounded by a brick walkway as shown. Suppose the brick walkway is 4 ft wide. What is its area?

13. Use the information from the problem to complete the diagram.

14. Complete the problem-solving model below.

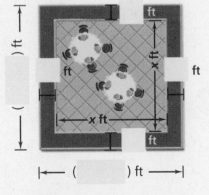

Relate	area of walkway	is	total area	minus	area of patio

Write   area of walkway $=$ $\boxed{}$ $-$ $\boxed{}$

15. Now solve the problem below.

Area of walkway $= \left(\boxed{}\right)^2 - \boxed{}^2$ Write the equation.

$= \left(\boxed{}^2 + \boxed{}\ x + \boxed{}\right) - \boxed{}^2$ Square the binomial.

$= \left(\boxed{}^2 - \boxed{}^2\right) + \boxed{}\ x + \boxed{}$ Group like terms.

$= \boxed{}$ Simplify.

16. The area of the walkway is $\left(\boxed{}\right)$ ft^2.

Lesson 8-4

Problem 3 Using Mental Math

Got It? What is 85^2? Use mental math.

In Exercises 17–19, circle each answer.

17. Choose a number close to 85 that you can square easily using mental math.

$$80 \,/\, 90$$

18. Write 85 as a binomial using the number you chose in Exercise 17.

$$(80 + 5) \,/\, (90 - 5)$$

19. Square the binomial.

$$(80 + 5)^2 \,/\, (90 - 5)^2$$

20. Now simplify the binomial.

---

take note

Key Concept The Product of a Sum and Difference

Words The product of the sum and difference of the same two terms is the difference of their squares.

Algebra

$$(a + b)(a - b) = a^2 - b^2$$

Example

$$(x + 2)(x - 2) = x^2 - 2^2 = x^2 - 4$$

21. Find the product $(r + 6)(r - 6)$.

$$(r + 6)(r - 6) = \boxed{} - \boxed{} + 6r - 36$$

$$= \boxed{} - 36$$

Problem 4 Finding the Product of a Sum and Difference

Got It? What is a simpler form of $(x + 9)(x - 9)$?

22. Circle the rule you use to simplify the expression.

$(a + b)^2$ $\qquad\qquad$ $(a - b)^2$ $\qquad\qquad$ $(a + b)(a - b)$

23. Substitute x for a and 9 for b. Then simplify.

Problem 5 **Using Mental Math**

Got It? What is 52 · 48? Use mental math.

24. Draw the point on the number line that is the same distance from 52 and 48.

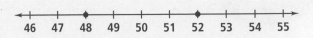

25. Circle the product that is equal to 52 · 48.

$(48 + 2)(48 - 2)$ $\qquad$ $(50 + 4)(50 - 4)$ $\qquad$ $(50 + 2)(50 - 2)$ $\qquad$ $(52 + 2)(52 - 2)$

26. Simplify the expression you circled in Exercise 25 to find the product.

 **Lesson Check** • **Do you UNDERSTAND?**

What rule would you use to find $(3x - 1)^2$? Why?

Underline the correct words or equation to complete each sentence.

27. The expression $(3x - 1)^2$ is the

square of a binomial / product of a sum and difference .

28. The rule I would use to simplify the expression is

$(a + b)^2 = a^2 + 2ab + b^2$ $\qquad$ $(a - b)^2 = a^2 - 2ab + b^2$ $\qquad$ $(a + b)(a - b) = a^2 - b^2$.

29. Simplify the expression.

Write the rule you would use to simplify each expression.

30. $(4x - 9)(4x + 9)$ $\qquad\qquad\qquad$ 31. $(7x + 2)(7x + 2)$

Math Success

Check off the vocabulary words that you understand.

☐ binomial $\qquad$ ☐ square of a binomial $\qquad$ ☐ product of a sum and difference

Rate how well you can *find products of binomials*.

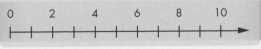

Lesson 8-4

Vocabulary

Review

1. Use the *Distributive Property*. Draw a line from each expression in Column A to an equivalent expression in Column B.

Column A	Column B
$y(y + 2)$	$y^3 + 3y^2 - 6y$
$(2y - 1)(y + 2)$	$-y - 2$
$y(y^2 + 3y - 6)$	$y^2 + 2y$
$-1(y + 2)$	$2y(y + 2) - 1(y + 2)$

2. Cross out the expressions that are NOT in *standard form*.

$x^2 + 4x + 3$	$(y - 5)(y + 2)$	$p(p + 1)$	$r^2 - 1$

Vocabulary Builder

	trinomial
	$x^2 + 3x - 1$

trinomial (verb) **try NOH mee ul**

Related Words: polynomial, monomial, binomial

Definition: A **trinomial** is a polynomial with three terms that are separated by plus or minus signs.

Use Your Vocabulary

3. Error Analysis Jay says that $x^3 + 5x^2 - 7x + 2$ is a *trinomial*. Explain why this is *not* true.

_____

_____

4. Circle the *trinomials*.

$h^3 - 2h + 4$	$d^3 - c^2$	$a^2 - b^2$
$r^2 + 3rs - 24s^2$	$g^2 + g + 1$	$x^3 + 7x^2y + 5xy^2 + y^3$

 **Problem 1** Factoring $x^2 + bx + c$ Where $b > 0$, $c > 0$

Got It? What is the factored form of $r^2 + 11r + 24$?

5. Complete the factor table. Then circle the pair of factors whose sum is 11.

Factors of 24	Sum of Factors
1, 24	$1 + \boxed{} = 25$
2, $\boxed{}$	$2 + \boxed{} = 14$
3, $\boxed{}$	$\boxed{} + \boxed{} = \boxed{}$
$\boxed{}$, $\boxed{}$	$\boxed{} + \boxed{} = \boxed{}$

6. Use the factors you circled in Exercise 5 to complete the factorization below.

$r^2 + 11r + 24 = (r + \boxed{})(r + \boxed{})$

7. Check your answer using FOIL.

 Problem 2 Factoring $x^2 + bx + c$ Where $b < 0$, $c > 0$

Got It? What is the factored form of $y^2 - 6y + 8$?

Underline the correct word(s) to complete each sentence.

8. I need to find factors that multiply / sum to -6 and multiply / sum to 8.

9. At least one of the factors that sum to -6 must be positive / negative .

10. The two factors that multiply to 8 must both be positive / negative .

11. Circle the factors of 8 that sum to -6.

1 and 8	-1 and -8	2 and 4	-2 and -4

12. Factor the expression.

$y^2 - 6y + 8 = (y - \boxed{})(y \boxed{})$

13. Check your answer using FOIL.

Lesson 8-5

Problem 3 Factoring $x^2 + bx + c$ Where $c < 0$

Got It? What is the factored form of $n^2 + 9n - 36$?

14. Reasoning You are looking for two factors of -36 that sum to 9. Which of the factors has the greater absolute value, the *negative factor* or the *positive factor*? How do you know?

_____

_____

_____

15. Circle the factors of -36 that sum to 9.

$(-4)(9)$ $(-9)(4)$ $(3)(-12)$ $(-3)(12)$ $(-6)(6)$

16. Write the factored form of the expression. Check your answer.

Problem 4 Applying Factoring Trinomials

Got It? A rectangle's area is $x^2 - x - 72$. What are possible dimensions of the rectangle? Use factoring.

17. Circle the number whose factors you want to find.

1   -1 2   72 -72

18. Circle the sum of the factors.

1   -1 2   72 -72

19. Reasoning Which of the factors has the greater absolute value, the *negative factor* or the *positive factor*? How do you know?

_____

_____

_____

20. Write pairs of factors of -72. Then circle the pair that sums to -1.

1,   2,   3,   4,   6,   8,

-1, -2,   ,   ,   ,   ,

21. Write the factored form of the expression.

$x^2 - x - 72 = ($ $)($ $)$

22. Possible dimensions of the rectangle are (   ) and (   ).

bulary

...entence with the correct form of the word *factor*.

factored   factoring

...ials $12x$, $3x^2$, and $6x^3$ have a common __?__ of $3x$

...trinomial, begin by looking for a factor common to all three terms.

..._ the expression $12x^3 - 6x^2$ into $6x^2(2x - 1)$.

Builder

...) **ree RYT**

...orm: rewritten

...ometimes you can **rewrite** trinomials in a different, but equivalent,
...them easier to factor.

...write means to write in another form.

cabulary

...ite the expression $23x + 14 + 3x^2$ in order to factor it. Cross out the
...ression that is NOT equivalent to the original expression.

$... + 14$ $3x^2 + 2x + 21x + 14$ $3x^2 + 20x + 2x + 14$

...rds that are similar in meaning to *rewrite*.

restate   compose   change

...om each trinomial in Column A to an equivalent and *rewritten*
... Column B.

Column B

$... b^2$ $a^2 + 6ab + b^2$

$... b^2$ $a^2 + ab + ab + b^2$

$... ab$ $a^2 + b^2 + 4ab$

Got It? What is the factored form of $m^2 + 6mn - 27n^2$?

23. Circle the factors of -27 that sum to 6.

1 and -27	-1 and 27	3 a

24. Circle the factored form of $m^2 + 6mn - 27n^2$.

$(m + n)(m - 27n)$	$(m - n)(m + 27n)$	$(m + 3n)$

25. Check your answer using FOIL.

 Lesson Check • **Do you UNDERSTAND**

Tell whether the sum of the factors of the constant term of s^2
positive or *negative* when you factor the trinomial.

26. Circle the constant term.

s^2	s	30

27. Circle the sum of the factors of the constant term.

1	-1	2	-2	30

28. The sum of the factors of the constant term is positive / n

 Math Success

Check off the vocabulary words that you understand.

☐ trinomial   ☐ factor   ☐ FOIL   ☐ star

Rate how well you can *factor trinomials of the form* $x^2 + bx$

| Need to review | 0 | 2 | 4 | 6 | 8 | 10 | N
ge |
|---|---|---|---|---|---|---|---|

VOCABULARY **Voc**

● **Review**

Complete each

factor

1. The monor

2. When __?__

3. A student _

● **Vocabulary**

| rewrite (ve

Other Word

Main Idea: S
way to make

Definition: R

● **Use Your V**

4. You can *reu*
rewritten ex

$3x^2 + 23x$

5. Circle the w

revise

6. Draw a line
expression i
   Column A

$a^2 + 2ab +$

$a^2 + 4ab +$

$b^2 + a^2 +$

Problem 5 **Factoring a Trinomial With Two Variables**

Got It? What is the factored form of $m^2 + 6mn - 27n^2$?

23. Circle the factors of -27 that sum to 6.

| 1 and -27 | -1 and 27 | 3 and -9 | -3 and 9 |

24. Circle the factored form of $m^2 + 6mn - 27n^2$.

| $(m + n)(m - 27n)$ | $(m - n)(m + 27n)$ | $(m + 3n)(m - 9n)$ | $(m - 3n)(m + 9n)$ |

25. Check your answer using FOIL.

Lesson Check • Do you UNDERSTAND?

Tell whether the sum of the factors of the constant term of $s^2 + s - 30$ should be *positive* or *negative* when you factor the trinomial.

26. Circle the constant term.

| s^2 | s | 30 | -30 |

27. Circle the sum of the factors of the constant term.

| 1 | -1 | 2 | -2 | 30 | -30 |

28. The sum of the factors of the constant term is positive / negative .

Math Success

Check off the vocabulary words that you understand.

☐ trinomial   ☐ factor   ☐ FOIL   ☐ standard form   ☐ Distributive Property

Rate how well you can *factor trinomials of the form $x^2 + bx + c$.*

Need to review 0 2 4 6 8 10 Now I get it!

Lesson 8-5

Vocabulary

● **Review**

Complete each sentence with the correct form of the word *factor*.

| factor | factored | factoring |

1. The monomials $12x$, $3x^2$, and $6x^3$ have a common __?__ of $3x$.

2. When __?__ a trinomial, begin by looking for a factor common to all three terms.

3. A student __?__ the expression $12x^3 - 6x^2$ into $6x^2(2x - 1)$.

● **Vocabulary Builder**

rewrite (verb) **ree RYT**

Other Word Form: rewritten

Main Idea: Sometimes you can **rewrite** trinomials in a different, but equivalent, way to make them easier to factor.

Definition: **Rewrite** means to write in another form.

● **Use Your Vocabulary**

4. You can *rewrite* the expression $23x + 14 + 3x^2$ in order to factor it. Cross out the rewritten expression that is NOT equivalent to the original expression.

| $3x^2 + 23x + 14$ | $3x^2 + 2x + 21x + 14$ | $3x^2 + 20x + 2x + 14$ |

5. Circle the words that are similar in meaning to *rewrite*.

| revise | restate | compose | change |

6. Draw a line from each trinomial in Column A to an equivalent and *rewritten* expression in Column B.

Column A	Column B
$a^2 + 2ab + b^2$	$a^2 + 6ab + b^2$
$a^2 + 4ab + b^2$	$a^2 + ab + ab + b^2$
$b^2 + a^2 + 6ab$	$a^2 + b^2 + 4ab$

Got It? What is the factored form of $6x^2 + 13x + 5$?

7. Complete the diagram below.

$$\underline{6}x^2 + 13x + \underline{5}$$

$$\boxed{} \cdot \boxed{} = 30$$

8. Circle the factors of 30 that sum to 13.

1 and 30	2 and 15	3 and 10	5 and 6
−1 and −30	−2 and −15	−3 and −10	−5 and −6

9. Reasoning Why is the pair −3 and 10 *not* one of the pairs listed in Exercise 8?

_____

10. Use your answer to Exercise 8 to complete the diagram below. Then rewrite the expression.

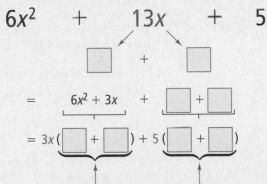

$$6x^2 \quad + \quad 13x \quad + \quad 5$$

$$\boxed{} + \boxed{}$$

$$= \quad \underbrace{6x^2 + 3x} \quad + \quad \boxed{} + \boxed{}$$

$$= 3x \left(\boxed{} + \boxed{} \right) + 5 \left(\boxed{} + \boxed{} \right)$$

The expressions inside the parentheses must be equal.

Use the Distributive Property to factor out the GCF, the part inside the parentheses.

$$= (3x + 5) \left(\boxed{} + \boxed{} \right)$$

11. Circle the factored form of $6x^2 + 13x + 5$.

$6x^2 + 13x + 5$	$6x^2 + 3x + 10x + 5$	$(6x^2 + 3x)(10x + 5)$	$(3x + 5)(2x + 1)$

12. Reasoning Suppose you rewrite the expression as $6x^2 + 10x + 3x + 5$. How would the GCF change? Explain.

_____

_____

_____

Lesson 8-6

✓ **Problem 2** Factoring When *ac* Is Negative

Got It? What is the factored form of $10x^2 + 31x - 14$?

13. Underline the correct word to complete each sentence.

The product *ac* is negative / positive .

The sum *b* of the factors of *ac* is negative / positive .

The factor of *ac* with the greater absolute value must be negative / positive .

The factor of *ac* with the lesser absolute value must be negative / positive .

14. Write the factor pairs of $ac = -140$. Then circle the factor pair that sums to 31.

15. Use the justifications at the right to factor the expression.

$10x^2 + 31x - 14 = \boxed{} x^2 - \boxed{} x + \boxed{} x - 14$ Rewrite *bx*.

$= \boxed{} (\boxed{} x - \boxed{}) + \boxed{} (\boxed{} x - \boxed{})$ Factor the GCF from each pair of terms.

$= (\boxed{} + \boxed{})(\boxed{} x - \boxed{})$ Use the Distributive Property.

16. Check your work.

✓ **Problem 3** Applying Trinomial Factoring

Got It? The area of a rectangle is $8x^2 + 22x + 15$. What are possible dimensions of the rectangle? Use factoring.

17. The factor pairs of *ac* are shown below. Circle the factor pair that sums to *b*.

1 and 120	2 and 60	3 and 40	4 and 30
5 and 24	6 and 20	8 and 15	10 and 12

18. Use the justifications below to factor the trinomial.

$8x^2 + \boxed{} x + \boxed{} x + 15$ Rewrite *bx*.

$\boxed{} (\boxed{}) + \boxed{} (\boxed{})$ Factor the GCF from each pair of terms.

$(\boxed{})(\boxed{})$ Use the Distributive Property.

19. Possible dimensions of the rectangle are $\boxed{}$ and $\boxed{}$.

Problem 4 **Factoring Out a Monomial First**

Got It? What is the factored form of $8x^2 - 36x - 20$?

20. Circle the first step in factoring the expression. Underline the second step.

| Factor out the GCF. | Find factors of the product ac. | Find the product ac. |

21. The polynomial is factored below. Write a justification for each step.

$8x^2 - 36x - 20 = 4(2x^2 - 9x - 5)$

$= 4(2x^2 - 10x + 1x - 5)$

$= 4[2x(x - 5) + 1(x - 5)]$

$= 4(2x + 1)(x - 5)$

 Lesson Check • **Do you UNDERSTAND?**

Reasoning Explain why you cannot factor the trinomial $2x^2 + 7x + 10$.

22. Consider the polynomial $2x^2 + 9x + 10$.

Can you factor out a monomial from the polynomial?   Yes / No

Can you rewrite 9 as the sum of two factors of 20?   Yes / No

Can you factor $2x^2 + 9x + 10$?   Yes / No

23. Now consider the polynomial $2x^2 + 7x + 10$.

Can you factor out a monomial from the polynomial?   Yes / No

Can you rewrite 7 as the sum of two factors of 20?   Yes / No

24. Complete. I cannot factor $2x^2 + 7x + 10$ because   ? .

 Math Success

Check off the vocabulary words that you understand.

☐ factoring   ☐ trinomial   ☐ standard form

Rate how well you can *factor trinomials of the form $ax^2 + bx + c$.*

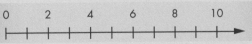

Lesson 8-6

Vocabulary

● Review

1. Circle the *operators* in each trinomial.

$$x^2 - 2 \cdot x - 3 \qquad k + 2 \cdot q - 7 \qquad a^3 - a^2 + 9a \qquad 4 \cdot w + d + 1$$

Write an algebraic expression for each *sum*.

2. *m* increased by 4

3. *c* more than 7

4. 16 greater than x^2

5. 8 added to $w^2 - 4w$

● Vocabulary Builder

> **case** (noun) **kays**
>
> **Related Words:** special case
>
> **Definition:** A **case** is a specific type of an event.
>
> **Examples:** A trinomial is one **case** of a polynomial. A perfect-square trinomial is a *special case* of a trinomial.

● Use Your Vocabulary

6. Draw a line from each event in Column A to a corresponding *special case* of the event in Column B.

Column A	Column B
a sport	math class
a meal	the Science Museum
a field trip	baseball
course	a term paper
homework	a biography
a book	dinner

Any trinomial of the form $a^2 + 2ab + b^2$ or $a^2 - 2ab + b^2$ is a **perfect-square trinomial** because it is the result of squaring a binomial.

take note

Key Concept   Factoring Perfect-Square Trinomials

Algebra   For every real number a and b,

$$a^2 + 2ab + b^2 = (a + b)(a + b) = (a + b)^2$$

$$a^2 - 2ab + b^2 = (a - b)(a - b) = (a - b)^2$$

Examples $x^2 + 8x + 16 = (x + 4)(x + 4) = (x + 4)^2$

$4n^2 - 12n + 9 = (2n - 3)(2n - 3) = (2n - 3)^2$

Complete.

7. $4^2 - 2(2)(4) + 2^2 = (4 - \boxed{})^2$ **8.** $25 + 30 + 9 = (5 + \boxed{})^2$

Problem 1   Factoring a Perfect-Square Trinomial

Got It? What is the factored form of $x^2 + 6x + 9$?

9. Circle the form your answer will have.

$(a + b)^2$ $(a - b)^2$

10. Use the justifications below to factor the expression.

$x^2 + \boxed{} \cdot x + \boxed{}$ Write the original expression.

$x^2 + \boxed{} \cdot x + \boxed{}^2$ Write the third term as a perfect square.

$x^2 + 2(\boxed{})(\boxed{})x + \boxed{}^2$ Write the middle term as $2(a)(b)x$.

$(x \boxed{} \boxed{})^2$ Write the expression as the square of a binomial.

Circle the factored form of each trinomial.

11. $64t^2 - 144t + 81$

$(64t - 9)^2$ $(32t - 9)^2$ $(8t + 9)^2$ $(8t - 9)^2$ $(4t - 3)^2$

12. $36h^2 + 60h + 25$

$(3h + 5)^2$ $(6h + 5)^2$ $(6h - 25)^2$ $(18h + 5)^2$ $(36h + 25)^2$

Problem 2   Factoring to Find a Length

Got It? You are building a square patio. The area of the patio is $16m^2 - 72m + 81$. What is the length of one side of the patio?

13. Use the information in the problem to complete the problem-solving model below.

Know	Need	Plan

14. Circle the form of the trinomial.

$a^2 + 2ab + b^2$ $\qquad\qquad$ $a^2 - 2ab + b^2$

15. Circle the form the factored expression will have.

$(a + b)^2$ $\qquad\qquad$ $(a - b)^2$

16. Write the first and last terms of the polynomial as squares.

$16m^2 - 72m + 81$

$(\ \square\ )^2 \qquad (\ \square\ )^2$

$\uparrow \qquad\qquad \uparrow$

$a \qquad\qquad\quad b$

17. Verify that $72m = 2ab$.

18. Now write the polynomial as the square of a binomial.

19. The length of one side of the patio is _____ .

---

take note

Key Concept Factoring a Difference of Two Squares

Algebra For all real numbers a and b,

$a^2 - b^2 = (a + b)(a - b)$

Examples $x^2 - 16 = (x + 4)(x - 4)$

$(5x)^2 - 16 = (5x + 4)(5x - 4)$

Problem 3 **Factoring a Difference of Two Squares**

Got It? What is the factored form of $v^2 - 100$?

20. Underline the correct word or words to complete each sentence.

The expression is a monomial / binomial / trinomial .

The expression is a difference / sum .

Both terms are / are not perfect squares.

I can use the perfect-square trinomial / difference of two squares rule.

21. Now factor $v^2 - 100$.

Problem 4 **Factoring a Difference of Two Squares**

Got It? What is the factored form of $25d^2 - 64$?

22. Is each term of the expression a perfect square? $\qquad$ Yes / No

23. Circle the expression that has both terms written as perfect squares.

| $5d - 8$ | $5d^2 - 8^2$ | $(5d)^2 - 8^2$ | $25d^2 - 8$ | $25d^2 - 64$ |

24. Circle the factored form of the expression.

| $(5d - 8)^2$ | $(5d + 8)^2$ | $(5d + 8)(5d - 8)$ | $(25d - 64)^2$ |

 Problem 5 **Factoring Out a Common Factor**

Got It? What is the factored form of $12t^2 - 48$?

25. Circle the GCF of 12 and 48.

| 3 | 4 | 6 | 12 | 48 |

26. Use the justifications at the right to factor the expression.

$12t^2 - 48$	Write the original expression.
▢ $(t^2 - $ ▢ $)$	Factor out the GCF.
▢ $(t^2 - $ ▢ $)$	Write the difference as $a^2 - b^2$.
▢ $(t + $ ▢ $)(t - $ ▢ $)$	Use the difference of two squares rule.

 Lesson Check • Do you UNDERSTAND?

Identify the rule you would use to factor $81r^2 - 90r + 25$.

27. Identify a, b, and $2ab$ in the expression.

$a = 9$ ▢ $\qquad b = $ ▢ $\qquad 2ab = $ ▢ r

28. Use your answers to Exercise 27 to rewrite the expression.

$81r^2 - 90r + 25 = (9$ ▢ $)^2 - $ ▢ $+ $ ▢ ^{2}

29. Circle the rule you would use to factor the expression.

| $a^2 + 2ab + b^2 = (a + b)^2$ | $a^2 - 2ab + b^2 = (a - b)^2$ | $a^2 - b^2 = (a + b)(a - b)$ |

 Math Success

Check off the vocabulary words that you understand.

☐ perfect square trinomial ☐ difference of two squares ☐ perfect square

Rate how well you can *factor perfect square trinomials and differences of two squares.*

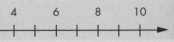

Need to review | 0 2 4 6 8 10 | Now I get it!

Factoring by Grouping

Vocabulary

● Review

1. Draw a line from each expression in Column A to the *GCF* of the terms of the expression in Column B.

Column A	Column B
$4x^2 + 6x$	$3x$
$7x^3 - 14x^2$	3
$3x^2 - 12x$	$2x + 1$
$18x^2 - 33x + 12$	$7x^2$
$5(2x + 1) + 2(2x + 1)$	$2x$

2. Explain why 4 is NOT the *GCF* of 12 and 24.

_____

_____

● Vocabulary Builder

cube (noun) **kyoob**

Related Words: cubic, perfect cube

Definition: For any number *a*, the **cube** of *a* is equal to $a \times a \times a$. A **cube** is a third power, such as 6^3 or $(2y - 4)^3$.

Examples: $5^3, 2x^3, (a + b)^3$

● Use Your Vocabulary

3. Circle each number that is the *cube* of an integer.

3	8	12	27	30

4. Cross out the expressions that are NOT *cubic* polynomials.

$3x^2$	$4x^3 + 1$	$2x^2 + 5x - 7$	$6x^3 - x^2 + 3x$

Problem 1 **Factoring a Cubic Polynomial**

Got It? What is the factored form of $8t^3 + 14t^2 + 20t + 35$?

5. Rewrite the polynomial by grouping the two terms with the highest degrees and grouping the other terms.

   ▢▢▢▢▢ + ▢▢▢▢

6. Factor the GCF from each pair of terms.

   ▢ $(4t + 7)$ + ▢ (▢ + 7)

7. Now factor $8t^3 + 14t^2 + 20t + 35$.

   (▢ + ▢)(▢ + ▢)

8. Check your answer using FOIL.

 Problem 2 **Factoring a Polynomial Completely**

Got It? What is the factored form of $6h^4 + 9h^3 + 12h^2 + 18h$? Factor completely.

9. Complete the flow chart.

$$6h^4 + 9h^3 + 12h^2 + 18h$$

The GCF of the terms is ▢ .

Factor out the GCF.

▢ (▢ + ▢ + ▢ + 6)

Group the terms with the greatest degrees.

▢ + ▢

Group the other terms.

▢ + ▢

Factor.

$2h^3 + 3h^2 = h^2(\ ▢\ +\ ▢\ )$

Factor.

$4h + 6 = 2(\ ▢\ +\ ▢\ )$

Write the three factors of the polynomial.

3 ▢ , $2h +$ ▢ , and $h^2 +$ ▢

Write the factored polynomial.

$6h^4 + 9h^3 + 12h^2 + 18h =$ ▢

Lesson 8-8

Got It? Geometry A rectangular prism has volume $60x^3 + 34x^2 + 4x$. What expressions can represent the dimensions of the prism? Use factoring.

10. Circle the GCF of the terms of the polynomial.

| x | $2x$ | x^2 |

11. Circle the expression with the GCF factored out.

| $x(60x^2 + 34x + 4)$ | $2x(30x^2 + 17x + 2)$ | $x^2(60x + 34 + 4)$ |

12. The expression ac for the trinomial factor in Exercise 11 is ____.

13. In order to rewrite bx so you can factor the trinomial, you must find the two numbers whose product is ____ and whose sum is ____.

14. Rewrite bx in the polynomial below.

$30x^2 + 12x + \boxed{} x + 2$

15. Factor the polynomial by grouping.

16. The expressions ____, ____, and ____ can represent the dimensions of the prism.

17. **Reasoning** Can the expressions x, $12x + 2$, and $5x + 2$ represent the dimensions of the prism? Explain.

_____

_____

_____

Summary   Factoring Polynomials

Vocabulary Complete each sentence with a word from the list below.

binomial factors   common factors   factor   group

18. _?_ out the greatest common factor (GCF).

19. If a polynomial has two or three terms, look for a difference of two squares, a perfect-square trinomial, or a pair of _?_ .

20. If the polynomial has four or more terms, _?_ terms to find common binomial factors.

21. As a final check, make sure there are no _?_ other than 1.

Lesson Check • Do you know HOW?

Factor the expression $20r^3 + 8r^2 + 15r + 6.$

22. I will use grouping / the perfect-square trinomial rule to factor the expression.

23. Now factor the polynomial.

Lesson Check • Do you UNDERSTAND?

Reasoning Can you factor the polynomial $6q^3 + 2q^2 + 12q - 3$ by grouping? Explain.

24. Group the two terms with the greatest degrees. Group the other two terms.

(⬚ + ⬚) + (⬚ − ⬚)

25. Factor out the GCF from each pair of terms.

⬚ (⬚ + 1) + ⬚ (⬚ − 1)

26. This time group the first and third terms of the polynomial. Group the other two terms.

(⬚ + ⬚) + (⬚ − ⬚)

27. Factor out the GCF from each pair of terms.

⬚ (⬚ + 2) + ⬚ (⬚ − 3)

28. Explain why you cannot factor the polynomial by grouping.

_____

Math Success

Check off the vocabulary words that you understand.

☐ cubic polynomial   ☐ factoring by grouping

Rate how well you can *factor cubic polynomials by grouping*.

Need to review | 0   2   4   6   8   10 | Now I get it!

Lesson 8-8

9-1 Quadratic Graphs and Their Properties

Vocabulary

● **Review**

1. **Multiple Choice** Which expression is a *quadratic* polynomial?

Ⓐ $-4x + 2$ Ⓑ $7x^4 + 3x^3 - 4x^2 + 2x - 4$ Ⓒ $x^3 - 8x^2 + 5$ Ⓓ $x^2 - 2x - 2$

● **Vocabulary Builder**

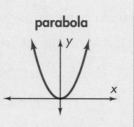

parabola

parabola (noun) puh RAB uh luh

Other Word Form: parabolic (adjective)

Definition: A **parabola** is a U-shaped curve that is the graph of a quadratic function.

● **Use Your Vocabulary**

Write T for *true* or F for *false*.

_____ **2.** A linear function has a *parabolic* graph.

_____ **3.** The path of a basketball free throw shot has a *parabolic* shape.

_____ **4.** A *parabola* that opens upward passes the vertical line test.

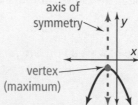

take note

Key Concept Standard Form of a Quadratic Function

A **quadratic function** is a function of the form $y = ax^2 + bx + c$, where $a \neq 0$. The graph of any quadratic function is a parabola.

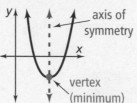

If $a > 0$ in $y = ax^2 + bx + c$, the parabola opens upward and the vertex is the *minimum* point.

axis of symmetry

vertex (minimum)

If $a < 0$ in $y = ax^2 + bx + c$, the parabola opens downward and the vertex is the *maximum* point.

axis of symmetry

vertex (maximum)

Problem 1 Identifying a Vertex

Got It? What is the vertex of the graph? Is it a *minimum* or a *maximum*?

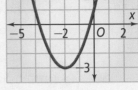

5. **Multiple Choice** What are the coordinates of the vertex of the graph?

Ⓐ (0, 3) Ⓑ (−2, 3) Ⓒ (−2, −3) Ⓓ (2, −3)

6. Underline the correct word to complete each sentence.

The vertex is at the lowest / highest point on the parabola.

So the vertex is the minimum / maximum point of the graph.

Problem 2 Graphing $y = ax^2$

Got It? Graph the function $y = -3x^2$. What are the domain and range?

7. Complete the table of values.

x	$y = -3x^2$	(x, y)
−2	$y = -3 \cdot (\ \ )^2 = \ \ $	(−2,)
−1	$y = -3 \cdot (\ \ )^2 = \ \ $	(−1,)
0	$y = -3 \cdot (\ \ )^2 = \ \ $	(0,)
$\frac{1}{2}$	$y = -3 \cdot (\ \ )^2 = \ \ $	($\frac{1}{2}$,)
1	$y = -3 \cdot (\ \ )^2 = \ \ $	(1,)
2	$y = -3 \cdot (\ \ )^2 = \ \ $	(2,)

8. Circle the graph of the function.

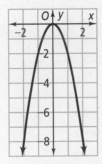 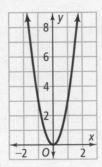 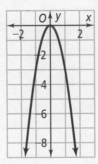

9. Circle the domain. Underline the range.

$y \leq 0$ $y \geq 0$ all real numbers   all integers

Lesson 9-1

Problem 4 Graphing $y = ax^2 + c$

Got It? Graph $y = x^2$ and $y = x^2 - 3$. How are the graphs related?

10. Complete the table of values.

x	$y = x^2$	$y = x^2 - 3$
−2		1
−1	1	
0		−3
1	1	
2		

11. Graph and label both functions on the coordinate grid.

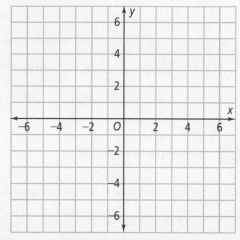

12. Explain how you can get the graph of $y = x^2 - 3$ from the graph of $y = x^2$.

_____

13. Reasoning In general, how can you get the graph of $y = ax^2 + c$ from the graph of $y = ax^2$?

_____

Problem 5 Using the Falling Object Model

Got It? An acorn drops from a tree branch 70 ft above the ground. The function $h = -16t^2 + 70$ gives the height h of the acorn (in feet) after t seconds. What is the graph of this function? At about what time does the acorn hit the ground?

14. Complete the table of values.

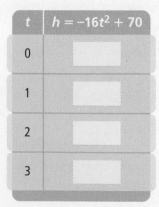

t	$h = -16t^2 + 70$
0	
1	
2	
3	

15. Why would you not calculate the heights for any negative values of t? Explain.

_____

_____

16. Circle the value of t that should not be graphed because it has a negative value for the height h.

| 0 | 1 | 2 | 3 |

17. Graph the function on the coordinate grid.

18. At what time does the acorn hit the ground? Explain.

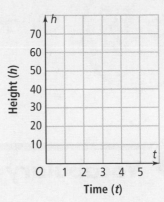

Vocabulary When is the vertex of a parabola the minimum point? When is it the maximum point?

19. Draw a line from each function in Column A to the description of its graph in Column B.

Column A	Column B
$y = -5x^2 + 1$	opens up
$y = x^2 - 2$	opens down

20. Make a conjecture about quadratic functions, the direction their graphs open and their maximum or minimum points. Explain.

Math Success

Check off the vocabulary words that you understand.

☐ quadratic function   ☐ parabola   ☐ vertex   ☐ axis of symmetry

Rate how well you can *graph a parabola*.

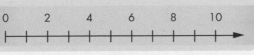

Lesson 9-1

9-2 Quadratic Functions

Vocabulary

● Review

Write the coordinates of the *vertex* of each graph.

1.

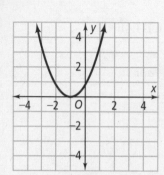

2.

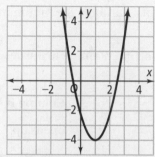

● Vocabulary Builder

symmetry (noun) <u>SIM</u> **uh tree**

Related Words: mirror image, symmetrical

Definition: A figure has **symmetry** if the figure can be reflected over a line so that the two halves match exactly.

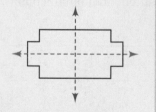

Math Usage: When a figure can be reflected over a line, the line is known as a line of **symmetry**. The line of **symmetry** for a parabola is called the *axis* of **symmetry**.

Example: The figure above has both horizontal and vertical lines of **symmetry**.

● Use Your Vocabulary

Draw all line(s) of *symmetry* on each figure. Then write the number of lines of *symmetry* you found.

3.

4.

5.

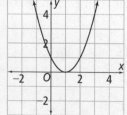

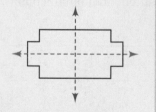

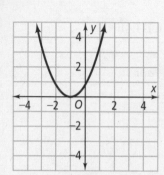

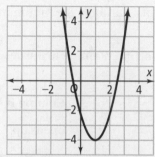

take note Property Graph of a Quadratic Function

The graph of $y = ax^2 + bx + c$, where $a \neq 0$, has the line $x = \dfrac{-b}{2a}$ as its axis of symmetry.

The x-coordinate of the vertex is $\dfrac{-b}{2a}$.

Identify a and b for each function. Then find the value of $\dfrac{-b}{2a}$.

6. $y = x^2 + 3x + 4$

$a = 1, b = \boxed{}$

$\dfrac{-b}{2a} = \dfrac{-\boxed{}}{2(\boxed{})} = \boxed{}$

7. $y = 2x^2 - 2x - 6$

$a = \boxed{}, b = \boxed{}$

$\dfrac{-b}{2a} = \dfrac{-\boxed{}}{2(\boxed{})} = \boxed{}$

8. $y = -2x^2 + 4x - 1$

$a = \boxed{}, b = \boxed{}$

$\dfrac{-b}{2a} = \dfrac{-\boxed{}}{2(\boxed{})} = \boxed{}$

When you substitute $x = 0$ into the equation $y = ax^2 + bx + c$, you get $y = c$. So the y-intercept of a quadratic function is c. You can use the axis of symmetry and the y-intercept to help you graph a quadratic function.

✓ Problem 1 Graphing $y = ax^2 + bx + c$

Got It? What is the graph of the function $y = -x^2 + 4x - 2$?

9. Circle the first step in graphing a quadratic function.

| Sketch the parabola. | Reflect a point across the axis of symmetry. | Find the axis of symmetry. |

10. Find the equation of the axis of symmetry.

11. Find the coordinates of the vertex of the parabola.

$y = -x^2 + 4x - 2$ Write the original equation.

$y = -(\boxed{})^2 + 4 \cdot \boxed{} - 2$ Substitute the x-value from axis of symmetry.

$y = \boxed{} + \boxed{} - 2$ Simplify powers and products.

$y = \boxed{}$ Simplify.

12. The vertex is ($\boxed{}$, $\boxed{}$).

259

Lesson 9-2

13. Complete the reasoning model below to determine two more points.

Think	Write
To find another point on the graph, I can use the *y*-intercept.	For the *y*-intercept, $x = 0$. $y = -x^2 + 4x - 2$ $y = -(\boxed{}) + 4 \cdot \boxed{} - 2$ $y = \boxed{}$ The *y*-intercept is $(0, \boxed{})$.
To determine another point on the graph, I can use $x = 1$.	$y = -x^2 + 4x - 2$ $y = -(\boxed{}) + 4 \cdot \boxed{} - 2$ $y = \boxed{}$ The point is $(1, \boxed{})$.

14. Plot the three points of the parabola that you have found.

15. Reflect the points across the axis of symmetry to get two more points of the parabola.

16. Finally, sketch the parabola through the five points on the graph.

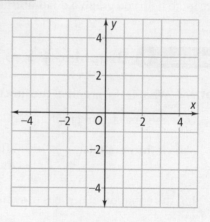

Problem 2 Using the Vertical Motion Model

Got It? From a height of 5 ft, a sling shot launches T-shirts at the crowd at a basketball game. The sling shot launches a T-shirt with an initial upward velocity of 64 ft/s. The T-shirt is caught 35 ft above the court. How long does it take the T-shirt to reach its maximum height? How far above court level is it at that point? What is the range of the function that models the height of the T-shirt?

17. The function $h = -16t^2 + 64t + 5$ gives the T-shirt's height *h* in feet after *t* seconds. Use the vertex formula to find the value of *t* at the T-shirt's maximum height. Then find *h*.

Find *t*: $t = \dfrac{-b}{2a}$

$t = \dfrac{-\boxed{}}{2 \cdot (\boxed{})}$

$t = \boxed{}$

Find *h*: $h = -16t^2 + 64t + 5$

$h = -16 \cdot (\boxed{})^2 + 64 \cdot \boxed{} + 5$

$h = \boxed{}$

18. The T-shirt will reach its maximum height of [ ] ft after [ ] s.

19. In order to determine the range of h, you need to know the minimum height of the T-shirt. The T-shirt was launched from a height of [ ] ft.

20. The height of the T-shirt at any time is between [ ] ft and [ ] ft, so the range of the function is [ ] $\le h \le$ [ ] .

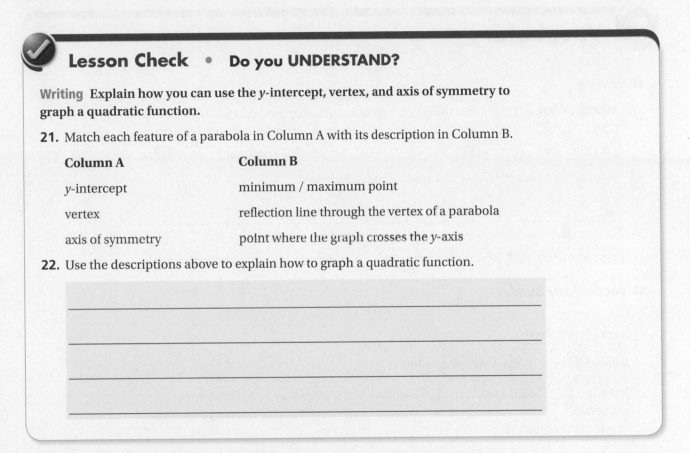

Lesson Check • Do you UNDERSTAND?

Writing Explain how you can use the y-intercept, vertex, and axis of symmetry to graph a quadratic function.

21. Match each feature of a parabola in Column A with its description in Column B.

Column A	Column B
y-intercept	minimum / maximum point
vertex	reflection line through the vertex of a parabola
axis of symmetry	point where the graph crosses the y-axis

22. Use the descriptions above to explain how to graph a quadratic function.

_____

_____

_____

_____

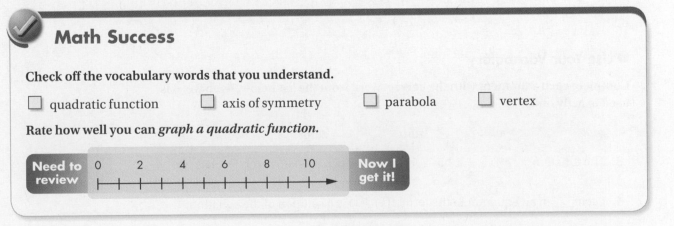

Math Success

Check off the vocabulary words that you understand.

☐ quadratic function   ☐ axis of symmetry   ☐ parabola   ☐ vertex

Rate how well you can *graph a quadratic function.*

Need to review   0   2   4   6   8   10   Now I get it!

Lesson 9-2

Solving Quadratic Equations

Vocabulary

● Review

1. **Multiple Choice** Toby wants to buy concert tickets. Each ticket costs $45.00. Circle the *function* rule Toby could use to find the cost c of any number of tickets t.

   Ⓐ $c = 45t$ Ⓑ $t = 45c$ Ⓒ $45 = ct$ Ⓓ $c = 45$

2. What is the difference between a relation and a function?

_____

_____

● Vocabulary Builder

> **root** (noun) **root**
>
> **Related Words:** x-intercept, zero, solution
>
> **Main Idea:** A **root** is a solution of an equation in the form $f(x) = 0$. The related function $y = f(x)$ has a *zero*, and the graph of $y = f(x)$ has an x-intercept, for each **root** of the equation.
>
> **Example:** The equation $x^2 - 1 = 0$ has two **roots**. So, the function $y = x^2 - 1$ has two *zeros*: -1 and 1.

● Use Your Vocabulary

Complete each statement with the correct word from the list below. Each word is used exactly once.

   root   *roots*   zero   zeros

3. The function $y = 4x^2 - 1$ has two zeros. The equation $0 = 4x^2 - 1$ has two _?_ .

4. Each _?_ of an equation in the form $f(x) = 0$ is a solution of the equation.

5. The function $y = 2x - 5$ has one _?_ .

6. One of the two _?_ of the function $y = x^2 - 4$ is 2.

Key Concept Standard Form of a Quadratic Equation

A **quadratic equation** is an equation that can be written in the form $ax^2 + bx + c = 0$, where $a \neq 0$. This form is called the **standard form of a quadratic equation.**

Examples $9x^2 + 81 = 0$ $x^2 + 4x + 16 = 0$

7. Cross out the quadratic equations that are NOT in standard form.

$x^2 - 81 = 0$ $12x^2 = 6x + 20$ $8x^2 - 10 = -5x$

8. Draw a line from each quadratic equation in Column A to an equivalent equation in Column B.

Column A

$x^2 + 3x + 18 = 5x + 11$

$3x^2 + x - x^2 - 1$

$(3x + 5)^2 = 0$

Column B

$2x^2 + x + 1 = 0$

$9x^2 + 30x + 25 = 0$

$x^2 - 2x + 7 = 0$

You can solve quadratic equations by a variety of methods. One way to solve a quadratic equation $ax^2 + bx + c = 0$ is to graph the related quadratic function $y = ax^2 + bx + c$. The solutions of the equation are the x-intercepts of the related function.

Problem 1 Solving by Graphing

Got It? What are the solutions of the equation $x^2 - 16 = 0$? Use a graph of the related function.

9. Graph the related function, $y = x^2 - 16$.

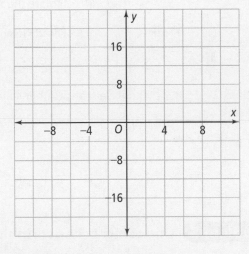

10. Which part of the graph gives you the solutions of the equation? Circle your answer.

vertex x-intercept(s) y-intercept(s)   axis of symmetry

11. Complete each sentence.

The equation has ▭ solutions.

The solutions are ▭ and ▭, or ± ▭ .

Lesson 9-3

Problem 2 Solving Using Square Roots

Got It? What are the solutions of $m^2 - 36 = 0$?

12. Follow the steps to find the solutions of $m^2 - 36 = 0$.

> **1** Write the original equation. [_____]
>
> ↓
>
> **2** Isolate m^2 on one side of the equation.
> $$m^2 = \boxed{}$$
>
> ↓
>
> **3** Find the square roots of each side and simplify.
> $$m = \pm\sqrt{\boxed{}} = \pm\boxed{}$$

Got It? What are the solutions of $3x^2 + 15 = 0$?

13. Complete the steps to find the solutions of $3x^2 + 15 = 0$.

$$3x^2 + 15 = 0 \qquad \text{Write the original equation.}$$

$$3x^2 = \boxed{} \qquad \text{Isolate the } x^2 \text{ term on one side.}$$

$$x^2 = \boxed{} \qquad \text{Divide each side by 3.}$$

$$x = \pm\sqrt{\boxed{}} \qquad \text{Find the square roots of each side.}$$

14. Does $3x^2 + 15 = 0$ have a real-number solution? Explain.

_____

_____

Problem 3 Choosing a Reasonable Solution

Got It? An aquarium is designing a new exhibit to showcase tropical fish. The exhibit will include a tank that is a rectangular prism with a length ℓ that is twice the width w. The height of the tank is 4 ft. The volume of the tank is 500 ft^3. What is the width of the tank to the nearest tenth of a foot?

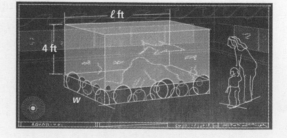

Chapter 9

264

15. Complete the reasoning model below.

Think	Write
I need to use the equation for the volume of a rectangular prism.	$V = \boxed{}$
I will substitute 500 for V, $2w$ for ℓ, and 4 for h.	$500 = (2w) \cdot \boxed{} \cdot \boxed{}$
I need to simplify.	$500 = \boxed{} \cdot w^2$
Finally, I need to isolate w and find the square roots of each side. I will use a calculator.	$\pm \sqrt{\dfrac{\boxed{}}{8}} = w$ $\pm \boxed{} \approx w$

16. The width of the tank is about $\boxed{}$ ft.

Lesson Check • Do you UNDERSTAND?

Compare and Contrast When is it easier to solve a quadratic equation of the form $ax^2 + c = 0$ using square roots than to solve it using a graph?

17. Solve each equation below using square roots.

$5x^2 - 50 = 0$　　　　　　　$5x^2 - 125 = 0$

$5x^2 = \boxed{}$　　　　　　$5x^2 = \boxed{}$

$x^2 = \boxed{}$　　　　　　　$x^2 = \boxed{}$

$x = \pm \boxed{}$　　　　　　$x = \pm \boxed{}$

18. The equation from Exercise 17 that is easy to solve using a graph is $\boxed{}$.

19. When is it easier to solve an equation of the form $ax^2 + c = 0$ using square roots?

_____

Math Success

Check off the vocabulary words that you understand.

☐ standard form of a quadratic equation　　☐ root of an equation　　☐ zero of a function

Rate how well you can *solve a quadratic equation*.

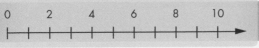

Need to review　0　2　4　6　8　10　Now I get it!

Lesson 9-3

9-4 Factoring to Solve Quadratic Equations

Vocabulary

Review

1. Circle the *product* of 8 and $x + 2$.

| $8x$ | $8x + 2$ | $8x + 16$ | $x + 10$ |

2. What is the *product* of $x + 3$ and $x - 4$?

Vocabulary Builder

factor (noun, verb) FAK **tur**

Definition (noun): A **factor** is a whole number that divides another whole number with a remainder of 0.

What It Means: Since $1 \cdot 8 = 8$ and $2 \cdot 4 = 8$, that means 1, 2, 4, and 8 are the **factors** of 8.

Definition (verb): To **factor** an expression is to write it as the product of two or more expressions.

Example: When you multiply $(x + 3)$ and $(x - 5)$, you get $x^2 - 2x - 15$. So when you **factor** the expression $x^2 - 2x - 15$, you get $(x + 3)(x - 5)$.

Use Your Vocabulary

3. Cross out the expression that does NOT have 6 as a *factor*.

| $6w^3$ | $12q$ | $3w^2$ | $18r^5$ |

4. Circle one *factor* of the expression $x^2 + 3x - 18$.

| $x + 6$ | $x + 3$ | $x - 6$ | $x + 4$ |

5. Multiple Choice *Factor* the expression $x^2 + 3x - 18$.

(A) $(x + 6)(x + 3)$

(B) $(x + 6)(x - 3)$

(C) $(x - 6)(x + 3)$

(D) $(x - 6)(x - 3)$

Property Zero-Product Property

For any real numbers a and b, if $ab = 0$, then $a = 0$ or $b = 0$.

Example If $(x + 3)(x + 2) = 0$, then $x + 3 = 0$ or $x + 2 = 0$.

Complete each statement.

6. If $(x + 7)(x - 2) = 0$, then

$x +$ ⬜ $= 0$ or $x -$ ⬜ $= 0$.

7. If $(x - 5)(x - 8) = 0$, then

$x -$ ⬜ $= 0$ or $x -$ ⬜ $= 0$.

✓ Problem 1 Using the Zero-Product Property

Got It? What are the solutions of $(x + 1)(x - 5) = 0$?

8. Underline the first step you will use to solve the equation $(x + 1)(x - 5) = 0$.

| Divide both sides by 2. | Set each factor equal to zero. | Multiply the factors together. |

9. Complete to solve $(x + 1)(x - 5) = 0$.

$x + 1 = 0$ or ⬜ $= 0$

$x =$ ⬜ or $x =$ ⬜

10. Solve each equation.

$(2x + 3)(x - 4) = 0$

$(7n - 2)(5n - 4) = 0$

✓ Problem 2 Solving by Factoring

Got It? What are the solutions of each equation?

$m^2 - 5m - 14 = 0$ $p^2 + p - 20 = 0$ $2a^2 - 15a + 18 = 0$

11. Write a justification for each step to solve $m^2 - 5m - 14 = 0$.

$m^2 - 5m - 14 = 0$ _____

$(m - 7)(m + 2) = 0$ _____

$m - 7 = 0$ or $m + 2 = 0$ _____

$m = 7$ or $m = -2$ _____

Lesson 9-4

12. Solve each equation.

$$p^2 + p - 20 = 0$$

$$2a^2 - 15a + 18 = 0$$

Problem 3 Writing in Standard Form First

Got It? What are the solutions of $x^2 + 14x = -49$?

13. Complete the reasoning model below.

Think	Write
I need to write the equation in standard form. So I need to add 49 to both sides.	$x^2 + 14x = -49$ $x^2 + 14x + \boxed{} = \boxed{}$
I should factor the equation and use the Zero-Product Property.	$(x + \boxed{})(x + \boxed{}) = 0$ $(x + \boxed{}) = 0 \quad \text{or} \quad (x + \boxed{}) = 0$ $x = \boxed{} \quad \text{or} \quad x = \boxed{}$
Finally, I need to write the solution(s).	The solution is $\boxed{}$.

Problem 4 Using Factoring to Solve a Real-World Problem

Got It? You are constructing a frame for the rectangular photo shown. You want the frame to be the same width all the way around and the total area of the frame and photo to be 391 in.^{2}. What should the outer dimensions of the frame be?

14. The length of the photo is 17 in., so the length of the frame will be $\boxed{} + 17$.

The width of the photo is 11 in., so the width of the frame will be $\boxed{} + 11$.

The total area of the frame and photo will be $(\boxed{} + 17)(\boxed{} + 11)$.

15. Complete the steps to solve the equation.

$(\quad\quad)(\quad\quad) = 391$ Write an equation for the total area.

$\quad + \quad + \quad = 391$ Multiply.

$\quad + \quad - \quad = 0$ Write the equation in standard form.

$4(x^2 + \quad - \quad) = 0$ Factor out 4.

$4(x + \quad)(x - \quad) = 0$ Factor the polynomial.

$\quad = 0$ or $\quad = 0$ Use the Zero-Product Property.

$x = \quad$ or $x = \quad$ Solve.

16. The dimensions must be positive, so the only reasonable solution is $x = \quad$.

17. The outer dimensions of the frame are $\quad$ in. by $\quad$ in.

Lesson Check • Do you know HOW?

Carpentry You are making a rectangular table. The area of the table should be 10 ft^2. You want the length of the table to be 1 ft shorter than twice its width. What should the dimensions of the table be?

18. If the width of the table is x ft, then the length of the table is $\quad$ ft.

19. Use these expressions to write and solve an equation for the area of the table.

20. The length of the table is $2 \cdot \quad$ 1, or $\quad$ ft.

21. The dimensions of the table should be $\quad$ ft by $\quad$ ft.

Math Success

Check off the vocabulary words that you understand.

☐ Zero-Product Property   ☐ quadratic equation   ☐ factor

Rate how well you can *solve quadratic equations by factoring.*

Need to review 0   2   4   6   8   10 Now I get it!

Lesson 9-4

 Vocabulary

● **Review**

Underline the correct word to complete each sentence about *square roots*.

1. Every positive number has one / two real *square roots*.

2. The *square root* symbol is also known as a radical / radicand .

3. The *square roots* of 121 are ___ and ___ .

● **Vocabulary Builder**

perfect square
49
because
$49 = 7^2$

perfect square (noun) PUR fikt skwehr

Definition: A **perfect square** is a number that can be written as the square of an integer.

Example: 16 is a **perfect square** because $16 = 4^2$. The expression $x^2 + 10x + 25$ is a **perfect square** trinomial because $x^2 + 10x + 25 = (x + 5)^2$.

Nonexample: 27 *is not* a **perfect square** because there is no integer that you can square to get 27.

● **Use Your Vocabulary**

Write each number as the square of another number. Then determine whether the original number is a *perfect square*.

Number	x^2	Perfect Square?
4. 144	$\square^2$	Yes / No
5. 49	$\square^2$	Yes / No
6. 8	$\left(\sqrt{\square}\right)^2$	Yes / No
7. 6	$\left(\sqrt{\square}\right)^2$	Yes / No
8. 4	$\square^2$	Yes / No

You can solve any quadratic equation by *completing the square*. This method turns every expression $x^2 + bx$ into a perfect-square trinomial. You *complete the square* by adding $\left(\frac{b}{2}\right)^2$ to $x^2 + bx$, where b is the coefficient of the x-term.

$$x^2 + bx + \left(\frac{b}{2}\right)^2 = \left(x + \frac{b}{2}\right)^2$$

 Problem 1 **Finding *c* to Complete the Square**

Got It? What is the value of c such that $x^2 + 20x + c$ is a perfect-square trinomial?

9. Use the justifications at the right to find the value of c.

$$c = \left(\frac{b}{2}\right)^2 = \left(\frac{}{2}\right)^2 \qquad \text{Substitute the value for } b.$$

$$= ()^2 \qquad \text{Simplify inside parentheses.}$$

$$= \qquad \text{Evaluate the power.}$$

10. Use your value of c to show that $x^2 + 20x + c$ is a perfect-square trinomial.

 Problem 2 **Solving $x^2 + bx = c$**

Got It? What are the solutions of the equation $t^2 - 6t = 247$?

11. In the expression $t^2 - 6t$, the value of b is $\boxed{}$.

12. Find the value of c.

$$c = \left(\frac{b}{2}\right)^2 = \left(\frac{}{2}\right)^2$$

$$= ()^2$$

$$= $$

13. Complete the square for $t^2 - 6t = 247$ by adding the value of c to both sides.

$$t^2 - 6t + \boxed{} = 247 + \boxed{}$$

14. Now complete the steps to find the solutions.

$(t - \boxed{})^2 = 256$ Factor the left side and simplify.

$t - \boxed{} = \pm\sqrt{256}$ Find the square roots of each side.

$t - \boxed{} = \pm\boxed{}$ Simplify.

$t - 3 = \boxed{}$ or $t - 3 = \boxed{}$ Write as two equations.

$t = \boxed{}$ or $t = \boxed{}$ Add 3 to both sides and simplify.

15. The solutions of $t^2 - 6t = 247$ are $\boxed{}$ and $\boxed{}$.

Lesson 9-5

Problem 3 Solving $x^2 + bx + c = 0$

Got It? What are the solutions of the equation $x^2 + 9x + 15 = 0$?

16. **Error Analysis** Jaime began to solve the equation by completing the square, but she noticed that she made an error. What error did she make? Explain.

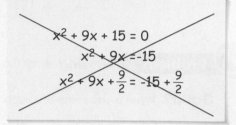

$$x^2 + 9x + 15 = 0$$
$$x^2 + 9x = -15$$
$$x^2 + 9x + \frac{9}{2} = -15 + \frac{9}{2}$$

_____

_____

_____

17. Correct Jaime's error. Find the solutions of $x^2 + 9x + 15 = 0$. Use a calculator.

The method of completing the square works when $a = 1$. To complete the square when $a \neq 1$, divide each side by a before completing the square.

Problem 4 Completing the Square When $a \neq 1$

Got It? You are planning a flower garden consisting of three square plots surrounded by a 1-ft border. The total area of the garden and the border is 150 ft². What is the side length x of each square plot? Round to the nearest hundredth.

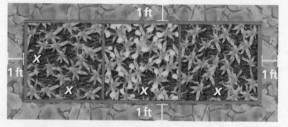

🌷 **Red tulips**   🌷 **Yellow tulips**

18. The width of the garden is the width of one square plot, x, plus two 1-ft borders.

So, the width of the garden is $x +$ ▢ .

The length of the garden is three times the length of one square plot, x, plus

two 1-ft borders. So, the length of the garden is ▢ + 2.

19. Substitute the expressions you wrote in Exercise 18 into the equation for area, $A = \ell w$.

▢ = 150

20. Multiply and simplify the left side of the equation you wrote in Exercise 19.

21. Now complete the following steps of solving the equation.

$3x^2 + \boxed{} \cdot x = \boxed{}$　　　　Subtract 4 from each side of the equation.

$x^2 + \dfrac{8 \cdot x}{\boxed{}} = \dfrac{146}{\boxed{}}$　　　　Divide each side by 3 to make $a = 1$.

$x^2 + \dfrac{8 \cdot x}{3} + \dfrac{16}{9} = \dfrac{146}{3} + \dfrac{16}{\boxed{}}$　　　Add $\left(\dfrac{4}{3}\right)^2$, or $\dfrac{16}{9}$, to each side.

$\left(x + \dfrac{4}{3}\right)^2 = \dfrac{\boxed{}}{}$　　　　Write left side as a square and right side as a fraction.

22. Solve the equation by finding the square roots of each side. Use a calculator.

23. A negative length does not make sense. So the side length is about $\boxed{}$ ft.

✓ Lesson Check • Do you UNDERSTAND?

Compare and Contrast How is solving a quadratic equation using square roots like completing the square? How is it different?

24. Explain how using square roots is similar to completing the square.

_____

25. Explain how using square roots is different from completing the square.

_____

_____

✓ Math Success

Check off the vocabulary words that you understand.

☐ completing the square　　　☐ quadratic equation

Rate how well you can *solve a quadratic equation by completing the square.*

Need to review　0　2　4　6　8　10　Now I get it!

Vocabulary

● Review

1. Writing What are some advantages to using a *formula* to express something like the area of a rectangle?

_____

_____

● Vocabulary Builder

discriminant
$b^2 - 4ac$

discriminant (noun) **dih SKRIM uh nunt**

Definition: The **discriminant** of the equation $ax^2 + bx + c = 0$ is the value of the related expression $b^2 - 4ac$.

Main Idea: The value of the **discriminant** tells how many real-number solutions a quadratic equation has.

Word Origin: The word **discriminant** comes from the Latin "discriminare," which means "to distinguish."

Discriminant $b^2 - 4ac$	positive	zero	negative
Number of Real-Number Solutions	2	1	0

● Use Your Vocabulary

Find the value of the *discriminant* of each equation. Then determine the number of real-number solutions the equation has.

2. $5x^2 + 3x - 9 = 0$

_____ solution(s)

3. $3x^2 - 2x + 7 = 0$

_____ solution(s)

4. $x^2 - 4x - 6 = 0$

_____ solution(s)

Key Concept Quadratic Formula

If $ax^2 + bx + c = 0$, and $a \neq 0$, then

$$x = \frac{-b \pm \sqrt{b^2 - 4ac}}{2a}$$

You can use the quadratic formula to solve any quadratic equation.

5. Suppose $5x^2 - 8x + 3 = 0$.
Write the values for a, b, and c
in the quadratic formula.

$$x = \frac{-() \pm \sqrt{()^2 - 4 \cdot \cdot }}{2 \cdot }$$

Problem 1 Using the Quadratic Formula

Got It? What are the solutions of $x^2 - 4x = 21$? Use the quadratic formula.

6. Write the equation $x^2 - 4x = 21$ in standard form and identify a, b, and c.

$$\boxed{} = 0$$

$a = \boxed{}$ $b = \boxed{}$ $c = \boxed{}$

7. Substitute the values from Exercise 6 into the quadratic formula.

$$x = \frac{-b \pm \sqrt{b^2 - 4ac}}{2a}$$ Use the quadratic formula.

$$x = \frac{-(-4) \pm \sqrt{()^2 - 4 \cdot \cdot }}{2 \cdot }$$ Substitute for a, b, and c.

$$x = \frac{4 \pm \sqrt{\boxed{} + \boxed{}}}{\boxed{}}$$ Simplify the power and the products.

$$x = \frac{4 \pm \sqrt{\boxed{}}}{\boxed{}}$$ Simplify the radicand.

$$x = \frac{4 + \boxed{}}{\boxed{}} \quad \text{or} \quad x = \frac{4 - \boxed{}}{\boxed{}}$$ Write as two equations.

$$x = \boxed{} \quad \text{or} \quad x = \boxed{}$$ Simplify.

Problem 2 Finding Approximate Solutions

Got It? A batter strikes a baseball. The equation $y = -0.005x^2 + 0.7x + 3.5$ models its path, where x is the horizontal distance, in feet, the ball travels and y is the height, in feet, of the ball. How far from the batter will the ball land? Round to the nearest tenth of a foot.

Lesson 9-6

8. The quadratic formula is used to solve for x below. Give a justification for each step.

$$x = \frac{-0.7 \pm \sqrt{(0.7)^2 - 4 \cdot (-0.005) \cdot (3.5)}}{2 \cdot (-0.005)}$$

_____
_____

$$x = \frac{-0.7 \pm \sqrt{0.56}}{-0.01}$$

_____
_____

$$x = \frac{-0.7 + \sqrt{0.56}}{-0.01} \quad \text{or} \quad x = \frac{-0.7 - \sqrt{0.56}}{-0.01}$$

_____
_____

$$x \approx -4.8 \quad \text{or} \quad x \approx 144.8$$

_____

9. The baseball will land about ⬚ feet from the batter.

There are many methods for solving a quadratic equation. You can always use the quadratic formula, but sometimes another method may be easier.

Method	When to Use
Graphing	Use if you have a graphing calculator handy.
Square Roots	Use if the equation has no x-term.
Factoring	Use if you can factor the equation easily.
Completing the Square	Use if the x^2 coefficient is 1, but you cannot easily factor the equation.
Quadratic Formula	Use if the equation cannot be factored easily or at all.

Problem 3 **Choosing an Appropriate Method**

Got It? Which method(s) would you choose to solve each equation? Justify your reasoning.

$$x^2 - 8x + 12 = 0 \qquad 169x^2 = 36 \qquad 5x^2 + 13x - 1 = 0$$

Draw a line from each equation in Column A to the most appropriate method for solving the equation in Column B.

Column A

10. $x^2 - 8x + 12 = 0$

11. $169x^2 = 36$

12. $5x^2 + 13x - 1 = 0$

Column B

square roots; there is no x-term

factoring; the equation is easily factorable

quadratic formula, graphing; the equation cannot be factored

Problem 4 **Using the Discriminant**

Got It? How many real-number solutions does $6x^2 - 5x = 7$ have?

13. Write the equation in standard form.

14. Evaluate the discriminant.

$$b^2 - 4ac = (\quad)^2 - 4 \cdot \quad \cdot \quad$$

$$= \quad + \quad$$

$$= \quad$$

15. Circle the number of real-number solutions $6x^2 - 5x = 7$ has.

| no solutions | 1 solution | 2 solutions | 7 solutions |

Lesson Check • Do you UNDERSTAND?

Reasoning What method would you use to solve the equation $x^2 + 9x + c = 0$ if $c = 14$? If $c = 7$? Explain.

16. Write the equation with $c = 14$.

17. Circle the method you would use to solve the equation.

graphing   square roots   factoring   completing the square   quadratic formula

18. Explain your choice in Exercise 17.

_____

_____

19. Write the equation with $c = 7$.

20. Circle the method you would use to solve the equation.

graphing   square roots   factoring   completing the square   quadratic formula

21. Explain your choice in Exercise 20.

_____

_____

Math Success

Check off the vocabulary words that you understand.

☐ quadratic formula   ☐ discriminant

Rate how well you can *use the quadratic formula*.

Need to review 0 2 4 6 8 10 Now I get it!

Lesson 9-6

9-7 Linear, Quadratic, and Exponential Models

Vocabulary

● Review

1. When should you use the *elimination* method to solve a system of equations? Place a ✓ in the box if the response is correct. Place an ✗ if it is incorrect.

☐ when the system has at least one equation that can be easily solved for a variable

☐ when you can use properties to add or subtract equations to remove a variable

2. Multiple Choice To solve this system of equations by *elimination*, by what number would you multiply the second equation?

$$3x - 6y = 12$$
$$5x - 3y = 13$$

Ⓐ 3 　　　　Ⓑ −1 　　　　Ⓒ −2 　　　　Ⓓ 5

● Vocabulary Builder

model (noun, verb) ᴍᴀʜ **dul**

Related Words: modeling (verb), modeled (verb), models (noun, verb)

Definition (noun): A **model** is a diagram, equation, graph, or object that can be used to represent a situation.

Definition (verb): To **model** a situation is to use a diagram, equation, graph, or object to describe it.

● Use Your Vocabulary

Complete each sentence with *model, modeling,* or *models.*

3. This graph best __?__ the data.

_____

4. You can use an equation to __?__ a situation.

_____

5. Alisha is __?__ the new winter wardrobe at the fashion show.

_____

Concept Summary Linear, Quadratic, and Exponential Functions

Linear	Quadratic	Exponential
$y = mx + b$ difference in y-values is constant	$y = ax^2 + bx + c$ difference of the difference in y-values is constant	$y = a \cdot b^x$ y-values have a common ratio

---

Problem 1 Choosing a Model by Graphing

Got It? Graph the set of points $(0, 0)$, $(1, 1)$, $(-1, -0.5)$, and $(2, 3)$. Which model is most appropriate for this set of points?

6. Graph the points.

7. Circle the most appropriate model.

linear   quadratic   exponential

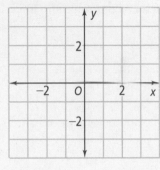

Problem 2 Choosing a Model Using Differences or Ratios

Got It? Which type of function best models the ordered pairs $(-1, 0.5)$, $(0, 1)$, $(1, 2)$, $(2, 4)$, and $(3, 8)$? Use differences or ratios.

Use the following exercises to help you find the best model.

8. Complete the table of ordered pairs.

9. The x-values are / are not evenly spaced.

10. Find the differences between consecutive y-values. The first is done for you.

11. The y-values have / do not have a common difference.

So a linear function does / does not model the data.

12. Complete the following to find the ratios of consecutive y-values.

$\dfrac{1}{0.5} = \boxed{}$ $\dfrac{2}{1} = \boxed{}$ $\dfrac{4}{2} = \boxed{}$ $\dfrac{8}{4} = \boxed{}$

13. The y-values do / do not have a common ratio.

So an exponential function does / does not model the data.

14. Circle the type of function that best models the ordered pairs.

linear   quadratic   exponential

x	y
-1	0.5

0.5

279

Lesson 9-7

Got It? Which type of function best models the data in the table? Write an equation to model the data.

x	−1	0	1	2	3
y	30	6	1.2	0.24	0.048

15. The data from the table are graphed on the coordinate plane at the right. An exponential function best models the data. Explain why linear and quadratic models are not appropriate for this set of data.

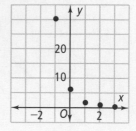

_____

_____

_____

_____

16. Test for a common ratio to verify that the data are exponential.

$\frac{6}{30} = $ ☐ $\frac{1.2}{6} = $ ☐ $\frac{0.24}{1.2} = $ ☐ $\frac{0.048}{0.24} = $ ☐

17. What is the y-value at $x = 0$?

$a = $ ☐

18. What is the decay factor? (*Hint:* common ratio)

$b = $ ☐

19. Use your answers from Exercises 17 and 18 to complete the equation $y = a \cdot b^x$.

$y = $ ☐ · ☐^{x}

20. To check your equation, test two points from the data set.

Test (1, 1.2)

$y = $ ☐ · ☐^{x}

$y = $ ☐ · ☐^{1}

$y = $ ☐

Test (3, 0.048)

$y = $ ☐ · ☐^{x}

$y = $ ☐ · ☐^{3}

$y = $ ☐

Write the equation.

Substitute the x-value.

Simplify.

Got It? The table shows the annual income of a small theater company. Which type of function best models the data? Write an equation to model the data.

21. Graph the data from the table on the coordinate grid at the right.

22. Multiple Choice Based on appearance, the data take the shape of which type of function?

- Ⓐ linear
- Ⓒ exponential
- Ⓑ quadratic
- Ⓓ circular

Theater Company

Year	Income ($)
0	18,254
1	18,730
2	19,215
3	19,695
4	20,175

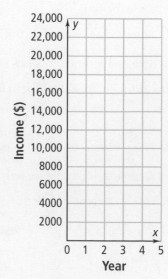

23. Write the general form of the equation for this type of model.

24. Determine the equation of the model.

25. Test two points in the model.

Lesson Check • Do you UNDERSTAND?

Writing Explain how to decide whether a *linear, exponential,* or *quadratic* function is the most appropriate model for a set of data.

26. Draw a line from each description in Column A to a corresponding model in Column B.

Column A	Column B
The *y*-values have a common difference.	Exponential
The *y*-values have a common ratio.	Quadratic
The *y*-values have a common second difference.	Linear

27. Explain how to decide the most appropriate model for a set of data.

_____

_____

_____

Math Success

Check off the vocabulary words that you understand.

☐ quadratic   ☐ exponential   ☐ linear   ☐ model

Rate how well you can *choose a linear, quadratic, or exponential model.*

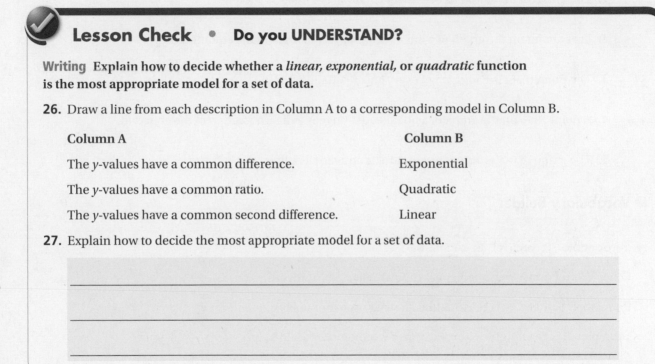

Need to review   0   2   4   6   8   10   Now I get it!

Systems of Linear and Quadratic Equations

Vocabulary

● Review

Each statement below is about the *solutions* of a linear equation.
Write T for *true* or F for *false*.

_____ **1.** The graph of the *solutions* of a linear equation is a line.

_____ **2.** Every point on the graph of a linear equation is a *solution* of the equation.

_____ **3.** The point (0, 0) is a *solution* of every linear equation.

_____ **4.** A point NOT on the graph of a linear equation may still be a *solution* of the equation.

_____ **5.** The graph of the *solutions* of a quadratic equation is a line.

● Vocabulary Builder

> **reasonable** (adjective) REE **zun uh bul**
>
> **Other Word Forms:** reasonableness (noun), reasonably (adverb)
>
> **Definition:** Something is **reasonable** if it makes sense or is sensible.
>
> **Example:** It is **reasonable** to expect warm weather in Orlando in July.
>
> **Opposite:** illogical, implausible, outrageous, unreasonable

● Use Your Vocabulary

6. Complete each statement with *reasonable*, *reasonably*, or *reasonableness*.

The student estimated a value to check the __?__ of her answer.

_____

A price of $1 is __?__ for a bottle of water.

_____

You can __?__ expect a movie to last an hour and a half.

_____

A system of linear and quadratic equations may have two solutions, one solution, or no solutions.

- If there are two points of intersection, there are two solutions.
- If there is one point of intersection, there is one solution.
- If there are no points of intersection, there are no solutions.

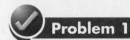 **Problem 1** Solving by Graphing

Got It? What are the solutions of the system? Solve by graphing.

$$y = 2x^2 + 1$$
$$y = -2x + 5$$

7. Complete the table of values for both equations.

x	$y = 2x^2 + 1$	$y = -2x + 5$
−2		
−1		
0		
1		
2		

8. Graph the points for $y = 2x^2 + 1$ in the coordinate plane. Draw a smooth curve through the points.

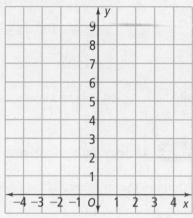

9. Now graph the points for $y = -2x + 5$ on the same coordinate plane. Draw the line through these points.

10. Circle the number of points of intersection.

0   1   2   3

11. Identify the points of intersection.

(   ) and (   )

 Problem 2 Using Elimination

Got It? Since opening day, attendance at Pool A has increased steadily, while the daily attendance at Pool B first rose and then fell. Equations modeling the attendance, y, at each pool are shown below, where x is the number of days since opening day. On what day(s) was the attendance the same at both pools? What was the attendance?

Pool A: $y = 32x + 74$ Pool B: $y = -x^2 + 39x + 64$

12. Subtract the second equation from the first to eliminate y.

$$
\begin{array}{rrrr}
y = & 32x & + 74 \\
-(y = -x^2 & + 39x & + 64) \\
\hline
0 = \quad\square & -\;\square & + 10 \\
\end{array}
$$

283

Lesson 9-8

13. Factor the trinomial. Then solve for x.

14. Find the corresponding y-values.

When $x =$ ☐ , $y = 32 \cdot$ ☐ $+ 74$ Substitute x into one of the equations.

$y =$ ☐ $+ 74$ Multiply.

$y =$ ☐   Simplify.

When $x =$ ☐ , $y = 32 \cdot$ ☐ $+ 74$ Substitute x into one of the equations.

$y =$ ☐ $+ 74$ Multiply.

$y =$ ☐   Simplify.

15. Each pool had ☐ people on Day ☐ and ☐ people on Day ☐ .

 Problem 3   **Using Substitution**

Got It?   **What are the solutions of the system?**

$$y - 30 = 12x$$
$$y = x^2 + 11x - 12$$

16. Substitute the expression for y in the second equation into the first equation.

☐ $- 30 = 12x$

17. Write the new equation in standard form. Then solve for x.

☐ $= 0$

$($ ☐ $-$ ☐ $)($ ☐ $+$ ☐ $) = 0$

☐   or   ☐

18. Find the corresponding y-value for each x-value.

19. The solutions are (☐ , ☐) and (☐ , ☐).

Use two different methods to solve the system $y = x$ and $y = 2x^2 + 10x + 9$.
Which method do you prefer? Explain.

20. Solve the system by graphing.

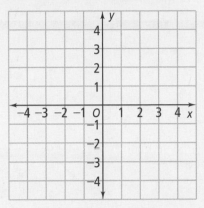

21. Solve the system using substitution.

22. The solutions are _____ and _____ .

23. Explain which method you prefer.

_____

_____

_____

_____

_____

Math Success

Check off the vocabulary words that you understand.

☐ quadratic equation   ☐ system of equations   ☐ linear equation   ☐ quadratic equation

Rate how well you can *solve a system of linear and quadratic equations.*

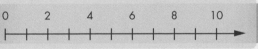

Lesson 9-8

10-1 The Pythagorean Theorem

Vocabulary

● Review

1. Circle each *right angle* below.

2. Underline the correct word or number to complete each sentence.

A *right angle* has a measure of 60 / 90 / 180 degrees.

Lines that meet at a *right angle* are parallel / perpendicular lines.

An angle that measures less than a *right angle* is called a(n) acute / obtuse angle.

● Vocabulary Builder

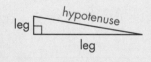

hypotenuse (noun) **hy PAH tuh noos**

Related Word: leg

Definition: In a right triangle, the longest side is the **hypotenuse**.

Main Idea: The *legs* of a right triangle form the right angle. The **hypotenuse** is across from, or opposite, the right angle.

● Use Your Vocabulary

Write T for *true* or F for *false*.

_____ **3.** The *hypotenuse* is the longest side in a right triangle.

_____ **4.** The *hypotenuse* of the triangle at the right has length 12 cm.

_____ **5.** The *legs* of a right triangle can be any two of the three sides.

_____ **6.** One *leg* of the triangle at the right has length 16 cm.

_____ **7.** The *hypotenuse* of the triangle at the right has length 20 cm.

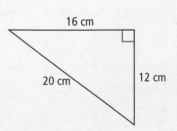

Theorem   The Pythagorean Theorem

Words

In any right triangle, the sum of the squares of the lengths of the legs is equal to the square of the length of the hypotenuse.

Diagram

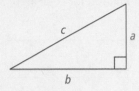

Algebra

$a^2 + b^2 = c^2$

8. The diagram at the right shows the sides of a right triangle with a square along each side. Count the number of square units in each region.

A [ ]   B [ ]   C [ ]

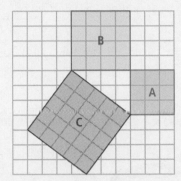

9. Write a sentence relating the number of square units in regions A and B to the number of square units in region C.

_____

_____

_____

Problem 1   **Finding the Length of a Hypotenuse**

Got It? What is the length of the hypotenuse of a right triangle with legs of lengths 9 cm and 12 cm?

10. Use the given information to label the sides of the triangle below.

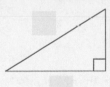

11. Complete each step to find the length of the hypotenuse.

$a^2 + b^2 = $ [ ]   Pythagorean Theorem

[ ]^2 + [ ]$^2 = c^2$ Substitute for a and b.

[ ] + 144 = c^2 Simplify.

[ ] = c^2 Add.

[ ] = c Find the principal square root of each side.

[ ] = c Simplify.

12. The length of the hypotenuse is [ ] cm.

Lesson 10-1

Problem 2 Finding the Length of a Leg

Got It? What is the side length *a* in the triangle at the right?

13. The equation is solved below. Write a justification for each step.

$$a^2 + b^2 = c^2$$

$$a^2 + 12^2 = 15^2$$

$$a^2 + 144 = 225$$

$$a^2 = 81$$

$$\sqrt{a^2} = \sqrt{81}$$

$$a = 9$$

take note

Property The Converse of the Pythagorean Theorem

If a triangle has sides of lengths *a, b,* and *c,* and $a^2 + b^2 = c^2$, then the triangle is a right triangle with hypotenuse of length *c.*

Underline the correct words to complete each sentence.

14. A triangle with side lengths 12, 16, and 20 is / is not a right triangle because

$12^2 + 16^2$ is equal / not equal to 20^2.

15. A triangle with side lengths 9, 11, and 14 is / is not a right triangle because

$9^2 + 11^2$ is equal / not equal to 14^2.

Problem 3 Identifying Right Triangles

Got It? Could the lengths 20 mm, 47 mm, and 52 mm be the side lengths of a right triangle? Explain.

16. Suppose the triangle is a *right* triangle. Circle the correctly labeled triangle.

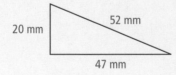

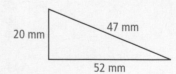

17. Circle the equation you will use to determine whether the triangle is a right triangle.

$$20^2 + 47^2 \stackrel{?}{=} 52^2 \qquad\qquad 52^2 + 47^2 \stackrel{?}{=} 20^2 \qquad\qquad 20^2 + 52^2 \stackrel{?}{=} 47^2$$

Chapter 10

288

Copyright © by Pearson Education, Inc. or its affiliates. All Rights Reserved.

18. Simplify your equation from Exercise 17.

19. Underline the correct words to complete the sentence.

The equation is true / false , so the triangle is / is not a right triangle.

Lesson Check • Do you UNDERSTAND?

Error Analysis A student found the length x in the triangle at the right by solving the equation $12^2 + 13^2 = x^2$. Describe and correct the student's error.

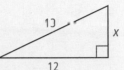

20. Circle the equation that correctly relates the sides of the triangle.

$$12^2 + 13^2 - x^2 \qquad\qquad 12^2 + x^2 = 13^2 \qquad\qquad x^2 + 13^2 = 12^2$$

21. Describe the student's error.

_____

_____

22. Find the length x.

Math Success

Check off the vocabulary words that you understand.

☐ hypotenuse   ☐ converse   ☐ leg   ☐ Pythagorean Theorem

Rate how well you can *use and apply the Pythagorean Theorem.*

Lesson 10-1

10-2 Simplifying Radicals

Vocabulary

● Review

Find each *square root*.

1. $\sqrt{36} =$

2. $\pm\sqrt{144} =$

3. $-\sqrt{\frac{100}{9}} =$

4. $\sqrt{\frac{36}{169}} =$

● Vocabulary Builder

| **radical** (noun, adjective) RAD **ih kul** |

Definition: A **radical** is the indicated root of a quantity, such as $\sqrt{7}$ or $\sqrt{x}$. The sign that indicates a root is to be taken is a **radical** sign.

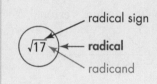

radical sign

radical

radicand

$\sqrt{17}$

Word Origin: from the Latin word "radix," which means "root"

Math Usage: A **radical** expression contains a radical. A **radical** expression is *simplified* if the following are true:
- The radicand has no perfect-square factors other than 1.
- The radicand contains no fractions.
- No radicals appear in the denominator of a fraction.

● Use Your Vocabulary

Write T for *true* or F for *false*.

_____ **5.** The expression $\sqrt{w + 2}$ is a *radical* expression.

_____ **6.** The *radical* expression $\sqrt{121}$ is in simplified form.

_____ **7.** The *radical* expression $5\sqrt{7}$ is in simplified form.

_____ **8.** The radicand in the *radical* expression $5\sqrt{7}$ is 5.

_____ **9.** The *radical* expression $\frac{5}{\sqrt{3}}$ is in simplified form.

Property Multiplication Property of Square Roots

Algebra

For $a \geq 0$ and $b \geq 0$, $\sqrt{ab} = \sqrt{a} \cdot \sqrt{b}$.

Example

$\sqrt{48} = \sqrt{16} \cdot \sqrt{3} = 4\sqrt{3}$

10. Cross out the equation below that is NOT true.

$$\sqrt{98} = \sqrt{49} \cdot \sqrt{2} \qquad \sqrt{200} = \sqrt{100} \cdot \sqrt{2} \qquad \sqrt{28} = 4\sqrt{7}$$

 Problem 2 Removing Variable Factors

Got It? What is the simplified form of $-m\sqrt{80m^9}$?

11. Circle the factor tree that shows the greatest perfect square factor of 80.

12. Circle the expression that should be used to simplify $-m\sqrt{80m^9}$.

$$-m\sqrt{40m^8} \cdot \sqrt{2m} \qquad -m\sqrt{16m^8} \cdot \sqrt{5m} \qquad -m\sqrt{16m^9} \cdot \sqrt{5}$$

13. Use your expression from Exercise 12 to simplify $-m\sqrt{80m^9}$.

Problem 3 Multiplying Two Radical Expressions

Got It? What is the simplified form of the expression $3\sqrt{6} \cdot \sqrt{18}$?

14. Complete the reasoning model below.

Think	Write
I need to multiply the radicals first.	$3\sqrt{6} \cdot \sqrt{18} = 3 \cdot \sqrt{}$
To simplify the radical, I need to think of the greatest perfect square factor of 108. Then I will use the Multiplication Property of Square Roots.	$3 \cdot \sqrt{} = 3 \cdot \sqrt{} \cdot \sqrt{}$ $= 3 \cdot \sqrt{} \cdot \sqrt{}$
Now I simplify the radicals.	$= 3 \cdot \cdot \sqrt{}$
Finally, I multiply the coefficients of the radicals.	$= \cdot \sqrt{}$

Copyright © by Pearson Education, Inc. or its affiliates. All Rights Reserved.

291

Lesson 10-2

Got It? A door's height is four times its width w. What is the maximum length of a painting that fits through the door?

15. When moving something tall through a doorway, how would you position the object to get the maximum amount of room for that object? Explain.

_____

_____

16. Based on your answer to Exercise 15, circle the measurement that you need to determine to fit a painting through a doorway.

width of doorway   height of doorway   diagonal length of doorway

17. Let w represent the width of the door. Circle the expression that represents the height of the door.

w $w + 4$ $4w$ $4w + 4$

18. Use the Pythagorean Theorem to find the length of the diagonal of the doorway.

19. The length of the diagonal of the doorway is equal to the width of the

doorway times [   ]. The maximum length of a painting that fits through

the door is $w \cdot$ [   ], or about [   ].

Property   **Division Property of Square Roots**

Algebra

For $a \geq 0$ and $b > 0$, $\sqrt{\dfrac{a}{b}} = \dfrac{\sqrt{a}}{\sqrt{b}}$.

Example

$\sqrt{\dfrac{36}{49}} = \dfrac{\sqrt{36}}{\sqrt{49}} = \dfrac{6}{7}$

Problem 5   **Simplifying Fractions Within Radicals**

Got It? What is the simplified form of the radical expression $\sqrt{\dfrac{144}{9}}$?

20. Write the justifications to simplify the radical expression.

$\sqrt{\dfrac{144}{9}} = \dfrac{\sqrt{144}}{\sqrt{9}}$ _____

$= \dfrac{12}{3}$ _____

$= 4$ _____

Problem 6 **Rationalizing Denominators**

Got It? What is the simplified form of the radical expression $\frac{\sqrt{2}}{\sqrt{3}}$?

21. Complete the steps to simplify the expression.

$$\frac{\sqrt{2}}{\sqrt{3}} = \frac{\sqrt{2}}{\sqrt{3}} \cdot \frac{\sqrt{}}{\sqrt{}}$$ Multiply the numerator and denominator by the radical you want to eliminate.

$$= \frac{\sqrt{}}{\sqrt{}}$$ Simplify your result.

$$= \frac{\sqrt{}}{}$$ Simplify completely.

 Lesson Check • **Do you UNDERSTAND?**

Compare and Contrast Simplify $\frac{3}{\sqrt{12}}$ two different ways. Which way do you prefer? Explain.

22. Simplify the expression. Then rationalize.

23. Rationalize the denominator. Then simplify.

24. Which way do you prefer to simplify rational expressions? Explain.

 Math Success

Check off the vocabulary words that you understand.

☐ radical expression   ☐ radical   ☐ radicand   ☐ rationalize the denominator

Rate how well you can *simplify radicals*.

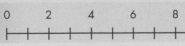

Lesson 10-2

Vocabulary

● Review

1. According to the __?__ Property, $a(b + c) = ab + ac$.

2. Multiple Choice Which equation illustrates the *Distributive Property*?

   Ⓐ $2x(x + 4) = 2x + 4$ Ⓒ $2x(x + 4) = 2x^2 + 8$

   Ⓑ $2x(x + 4) = 2x + 4x$ Ⓓ $2x(x + 4) = 2x^2 + 8x$

● Vocabulary Builder

conjugate (adjective) ᴋᴀʜɴ **jug gut**

Definition: **Conjugates** are the sum and difference of the same two terms, such as $\sqrt{6} + 3$ and $\sqrt{6} - 3$.

Main Idea: You can use **conjugates** to simplify a quotient whose denominator is a sum or difference of radicals.

Math Usage: The product of **conjugates** is a difference of squares.

Example: $(\sqrt{5} + 2)(\sqrt{5} - 2) = (\sqrt{5})^2 - 2(\sqrt{5}) + 2(\sqrt{5}) - (2)^2$

$$= (\sqrt{5})^2 - (2)^2 = 5 - 4 = 1$$

● Use Your Vocabulary

Draw a line from each expression in Column A to its *conjugate* in Column B.

Column A	Column B
3. $\sqrt{2} - 3$	$2 - \sqrt{3}$
4. $\sqrt{2} + \sqrt{3}$	$\sqrt{2} + 3$
5. $2 + \sqrt{3}$	$\sqrt{3} + 2$
6. $\sqrt{3} - 2$	$\sqrt{2} - \sqrt{3}$

Like radicals have the same radicand. **Unlike radicals** have different radicands.

like radicals	unlike radicals
$3\sqrt{5}$ and $7\sqrt{5}$	$4\sqrt{3}$ and $-2\sqrt{2}$
same radicand	different radicands

 Problem 1 Combining Like Radicals

Got It? What is the simplified form of $7\sqrt{2} - 8\sqrt{2}$?

7. Use the Distributive Property to help you combine like radicals.

$$7\sqrt{2} - 8\sqrt{2} = (7 - 8) \cdot \sqrt{\boxed{}}$$

8. Circle the correct simplification of $7\sqrt{2} - 8\sqrt{2}$.

| -1 | $-\sqrt{2}$ | $\sqrt{2}$ | $15\sqrt{2}$ |

 Problem 2 Simplifying to Combine Like Radicals

Got It? What is the simplified form of $4\sqrt{7} + 2\sqrt{28}$?

9. Complete the equation or write the correct justification to simplify the expression.

$$4\sqrt{7} + 2\sqrt{28} = 4\sqrt{7} + 2\sqrt{\boxed{} \cdot 7}$$ Factor out the greatest perfect square factor of 28.

$$= 4\sqrt{7} + 2 \cdot \sqrt{4} \cdot \sqrt{7}$$ _____

$$= 4\sqrt{7} + \boxed{} \cdot \sqrt{7}$$ Simplify $2 \cdot \sqrt{4}$.

$$= (4 + 4) \cdot \sqrt{7}$$ _____

$$= \boxed{} \cdot \sqrt{7}$$ Simplify.

Got It? What is the simplified form of $5\sqrt{32} - 4\sqrt{18}$?

10. Complete the steps to simplify $5\sqrt{32}$.

$$5\sqrt{32} = 5 \cdot \sqrt{\boxed{}} \cdot \sqrt{2}$$

$$= 5 \cdot \boxed{} \cdot \sqrt{2}$$

$$= \boxed{} \cdot \sqrt{2}$$

11. Complete the steps to simplify $4\sqrt{18}$.

$$4\sqrt{18} = 4 \cdot \sqrt{\boxed{}} \cdot \sqrt{2}$$

$$= 4 \cdot \boxed{} \cdot \sqrt{2}$$

$$= \boxed{} \cdot \sqrt{2}$$

12. Use your answers from Exercises 10 and 11 to simplify the original expression.

$$5\sqrt{32} - 4\sqrt{18} = \boxed{} \cdot \sqrt{2} - \boxed{} \cdot \sqrt{2}$$

$$= \boxed{} \cdot \sqrt{2}$$

Lesson 10-3

Problem 3 **Multiplying Radical Expressions**

Got It? What is the simplified form of $\sqrt{2}(\sqrt{6} + 5)$?

13. Circle the first step in simplifying $\sqrt{2}(\sqrt{6} + 5)$.

| Multiply by 2. | Use the Distributive Property. | Add $\sqrt{2}$. |

14. Complete the steps to simplify the expression.

$$\sqrt{2}(\sqrt{6} + 5) = (\boxed{} \cdot \sqrt{6}) + (\boxed{} \cdot 5)$$

$$= (\boxed{}) + 5\sqrt{2}$$

$$= \boxed{} + 5\sqrt{2}$$

Problem 4 **Rationalizing a Denominator Using Conjugates**

Got It? What is the simplified form of $\dfrac{-3}{\sqrt{10} + \sqrt{5}}$?

15. Circle the conjugate of the denominator.

| $\sqrt{10} - \sqrt{5}$ | $\sqrt{10} + \sqrt{5}$ | $(\sqrt{10} - \sqrt{5})(\sqrt{10} + \sqrt{5})$ |

16. Complete the equation or write the correct justification to simplify the expression.

$$\frac{-3}{\sqrt{10} + \sqrt{5}} = \frac{-3}{\sqrt{10} + \sqrt{5}} \cdot \frac{\boxed{} - \boxed{}}{\boxed{} - \boxed{}}$$

Multiply the numerator and denominator by the conjugate of the denominator.

$$= \frac{-3\left(\boxed{} - \boxed{}\right)}{\boxed{} - 5}$$

Multiply in the denominator.

$$= \frac{-3(\sqrt{10} - \sqrt{5})}{5}$$

_____

$$= \frac{-3\sqrt{10} + 3\sqrt{5}}{5}$$

_____

Problem 5 **Solving a Proportion Involving Radicals**

Got It? A golden rectangle is 12 in. long. What is the width of the rectangle? Write your answer in simplified radical form and rounded to the nearest tenth of an inch.

17. Multiple Choice Use the information in the rectangle at the right. Which proportion can you use to solve the problem?

> The ratio of the length to the width of a golden rectangle is
>
> $(1 + \sqrt{5}) : 2.$
>
> This rectangle is golden.

Ⓐ $\dfrac{12}{w} = \dfrac{\sqrt{5} + 1}{2}$ Ⓒ $\dfrac{w}{12} = \dfrac{\sqrt{5} + 1}{2}$

Ⓑ $\dfrac{12}{w} = \dfrac{2}{\sqrt{5} + 1}$ Ⓓ $\dfrac{w}{12} = \dfrac{\sqrt{5} - 1}{\sqrt{5} + 1}$

18. The proportion is solved below. Complete the missing steps and justifications.

$$\frac{\sqrt{5} + 1}{2} = \frac{12}{w}$$

Write the proportion.

$$w(\sqrt{5} + 1) = 24$$

_____

$$w = \frac{24}{\sqrt{5} + 1}$$

_____

$$w = \frac{24}{\sqrt{5} + 1} \cdot \frac{\sqrt{5} - 1}{}$$

Multiply the numerator and the denominator by by the conjugate of the denominator.

$$w = \frac{24\sqrt{5} - 24}{5 - 1}$$

_____

$$w = \frac{24\sqrt{5} - 24}{4}$$

_____

$$w = 6\sqrt{5} - $$

Simplify.

19. Use a calculator. To the nearest tenth, the width of the rectangle is ____ in.

Lesson Check • Do you UNDERSTAND?

Error Analysis A student simplified the expression at the right. Describe and correct the error.

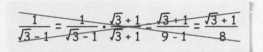

$$\frac{1}{\sqrt{3} - 1} = \frac{1}{\sqrt{3} - 1} \cdot \frac{\sqrt{3} + 1}{\sqrt{3} + 1} = \frac{\sqrt{3} + 1}{9 - 1} = \frac{\sqrt{3} + 1}{8}$$

20. The conjugate of $\sqrt{3} - 1$ is ____ .

21. Did the student use the correct conjugate?   Yes / No

22. Did the student correctly multiply the numerator and the denominator by the conjugate?   Yes / No

23. Describe and correct the error.

_____

_____

_____

Math Success

Check off the vocabulary words that you understand.

☐ conjugate   ☐ radical expression   ☐ like radicals   ☐ unlike radicals

Rate how well you can *perform operations on radicals.*

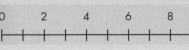

Lesson 10-3

Vocabulary

● Review

Draw a line from each equation in Column A to its *solution* in Column B.

Column A   Column B

1. $3x + 5 = -4$ $x = 3$

2. $4x^2 = 16$ $x = -2 \text{ or } x = 2$

3. $6x - 2 = 16$ $x = -3$

● Vocabulary Builder

> **extraneous** (adjective) **ek** STRAY **nee us**
>
> **Definition:** **Extraneous** means not essential or relevant to the situation or subject being considered.
>
> **Math Usage:** An **extraneous** solution is one that comes from the solving process but is not a valid solution of the original equation.
>
> **Main Idea:** A radical equation is an equation that has a variable in a radicand. When solving radical equations, it is possible to obtain **extraneous** solutions. You must check each solution in the original equation.

● Use Your Vocabulary

If you solve the equation $-\sqrt{x} = x$, you get two solutions: 0 and 1. The check for each solution is shown below.

Check $x = 0$.

$-\sqrt{x} = x$

$-\sqrt{0} \stackrel{?}{=} 0$

$0 = 0$

Check $x = 1$.

$-\sqrt{x} = x$

$-\sqrt{1} \stackrel{?}{=} 1$

$-1 \neq 1$

4. Which solution is *extraneous*? Explain.

_____

_____

Problem 1 · Solving by Isolating the Radical

Got It? What is the solution of $\sqrt{x} - 5 = -2$?

5. Circle the first step to solve the equation $\sqrt{x} - 5 = -2$. Underline the second step.

Add 5 to both sides.	Square both sides.	Subtract −2 from both sides.

6. Complete the steps to solve
$\sqrt{x} - 5 = -2$.

$$\boxed{} = 3$$

$$x = \boxed{}$$

7. Check your solution by substituting
for x in the original equation.

$$\sqrt{\boxed{}} - 5 \stackrel{?}{=} -2$$

$$\boxed{} - 5 \stackrel{?}{=} -2$$

$$\boxed{} \stackrel{?}{=} -2$$

8. The solution I found in Exercise 6 does / does not solve the equation.

Problem 2 · Using a Radical Equation

Got It? The time t in seconds it takes for a pendulum of a clock to complete a full swing is approximated by the equation $t = 2\sqrt{\dfrac{\ell}{3.3}}$, where ℓ is the length of the pendulum in feet. If the pendulum of a clock completes a full swing in 1 s, what is the length of the pendulum? Round to the nearest tenth of a foot.

9. Circle what you are trying to find to solve the problem.

length of the pendulum	time it takes for 1 swing	time it takes for 2 swings

10. Complete the reasoning model below to solve the equation.

Think	Write
First I substitute 1 for t in $t = 2\sqrt{\dfrac{\ell}{3.3}}$.	$\boxed{} = 2\sqrt{\dfrac{\ell}{3.3}}$
Then I divide each side by 2 to isolate the radical.	$\boxed{} = \sqrt{\dfrac{\ell}{3.3}}$
Now I square each side.	$\boxed{}^2 = \boxed{}$
Next I simplify.	$\boxed{} = \dfrac{\ell}{3.3}$
Finally, I multiply each side by 3.3.	$\boxed{} = \ell$

11. To the nearest tenth of a foot, the pendulum is $\boxed{}$ ft long.

Lesson 10-4

Problem 3 Solving With Radical Expressions on Both Sides

Got It? What is the solution of $\sqrt{7x - 4} = \sqrt{5x + 10}$?

12. The equation is solved below. Write a justification for each step.

$$\left(\sqrt{7x - 4}\right)^2 = \left(\sqrt{5x + 10}\right)^2$$

_____

$$7x - 4 = 5x + 10$$

_____

$$2x - 4 = 10$$

_____

$$2x = 14$$

_____

$$x = 7$$

_____

13. Check your solution.

When you solve an equation by squaring each side, you write a new equation. The new equation may have solutions that do not make the original equation true.

Original Equation	Square each side.	New Equation	Solutions of New Equation
$x = 3$	$x^2 = 3^2$	$x^2 = 9$	$3, -3$

In the example above, -3 is not a solution of the original equation. It is an *extraneous* solution.

Problem 4 Identifying Extraneous Solutions

Got It? What is the solution of $-y = \sqrt{y + 6}$?

14. Solve the equation.

$$y^2 = \boxed{} \qquad \text{Square each side.}$$

$$\boxed{} = 0 \qquad \text{Subtract } y + 6 \text{ from each side.}$$

$$(y - \boxed{})(y + \boxed{}) = 0 \qquad \text{Factor the quadratic equation.}$$

$$y - \boxed{} = 0 \quad \text{or} \quad y + \boxed{} = 0 \qquad \text{Use the Zero-Product Property.}$$

$$y = \boxed{} \quad \text{or} \qquad y = \boxed{} \qquad \text{Solve for } y.$$

15. Check to see whether each result satisfies the original equation.

$$-3 \stackrel{?}{=} \sqrt{\boxed{} + 6} \qquad\qquad 2 \stackrel{?}{=} \sqrt{\boxed{} + 6}$$

$$-3 \stackrel{?}{=} \sqrt{\boxed{}} \qquad\qquad\qquad 2 \stackrel{?}{=} \sqrt{\boxed{}}$$

$$-3 \neq \boxed{} \qquad\qquad\qquad 2 = \boxed{}$$

16. The only solution of the equation $-y = \sqrt{y + 6}$ is $\boxed{}$.

Problem 5 · Identifying Equations With No Solution

Got It? What is the solution of $6 - \sqrt{2x} = 10$?

17. Solve the equation.

18. Check the solution.

19. The equation does / does not have a solution.

Lesson Check • Do you UNDERSTAND?

Vocabulary Which is an extraneous solution of $s = \sqrt{s + 2}$?

(A) 2   (B) 0   (C) −1   (D) −2

20. Solve the equation to find possible solutions.

21. Circle the two possible solutions of the equation.

    2   0   −1   2

22. Check your solutions to find which is extraneous.

23. The extraneous solution is [ ]. The correct answer is C.

Math Success

Check off the vocabulary words that you understand.

☐ radical equation   ☐ solution   ☐ extraneous solution

Rate how well you can *solve radical equations.*

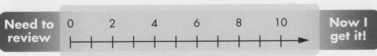

Need to review   0   2   4   6   8   10   Now I get it!

Lesson 10-4

Vocabulary

● Review

1. Cross out each mapping diagram or graph below that does NOT show a *function*.

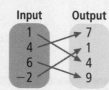

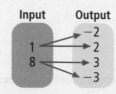

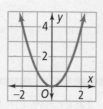

● Vocabulary Builder

Function	{(2, 3), (4, 5), (6, 7), (8, 9)}
Domain	{2, 4, 6, 8}
Range	{3, 5, 7, 9}

domain (noun) **doh** MAYN

Definition: The **domain** of a function is a set of values assigned to the independent variable.

Related Word: range

Math Usage: In a given function, the *x*-values (input) represent the **domain** and the *y*-values (output) represent the **range**.

Example: The example above shows the **domain** and the **range** for the given set of ordered pairs.

● Use Your Vocabulary

Consider the relation {(5.1, 3.2), (6, 4.7), (3, 1.5), (5.8, 3.2)}.

2. Use the words *domain* and *range* to complete the diagram.

3. Draw an arrow from each element in the *domain* to the corresponding element(s) in the *range*.

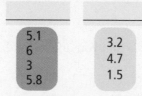

4. Is this relation a function?

Yes / No

Key Concept Square Root Functions

A *square root function* is a function that has the independent variable in the radicand. The parent square root function is $y = \sqrt{x}$.

For real numbers, the value of the radicand cannot be negative. So the domain of a *square root function* is limited to values of x for which the radicand is greater than or equal to 0.

Write T for *true* or F for *false*.

_____ **5.** $y = 3x$ is a square root function.

_____ **6.** $y = \sqrt{x} + 2$ is a square root function.

_____ **7.** The domain of $y = \sqrt{x - 3}$ includes the value 2.

Problem 1 Finding the Domain of a Square Root Function

Got It? What is the domain of $y = \sqrt{-2x + 5}$?

8. Complete the steps to find the domain.

$-2x + 5 \geq \boxed{}$ Set the radicand greater than or equal to 0.

$-2x \geq \boxed{}$ Use the Subtraction Property of Inequality.

$x \leq \boxed{}$ Solve for x using the Multiplication Property of Inequality.

9. The domain of the function is the set of numbers less than or equal to $\boxed{}$.

Problem 2 Graphing a Square Root Function

Got It? Graph the function $I = \frac{1}{5}\sqrt{P}$, which gives the current I in amperes for a certain circuit with P watts of power. When will the current exceed 1.5 amperes?

10. Complete the table of values.

P	$I = \frac{1}{5}\sqrt{P}$	
0	$\frac{1}{5} \cdot \boxed{}$	$= 0$
25	$\frac{1}{5} \cdot \boxed{}$	$= \boxed{}$
50	$\frac{1}{5} \cdot \boxed{}$	$\approx \boxed{}$
100	$\frac{1}{5} \cdot \boxed{}$	$= \boxed{}$

11. Plot the points from the table.

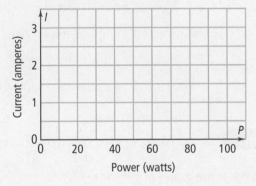

Lesson 10-5

12. Does the range of the function include 1.5?   Yes / No

13. Use your graph from Exercise 11. The *x*-coordinate of the point on the graph with

y-coordinate 1.5 is approximately _____ .

14. The current will exceed 1.5 amperes when the power is greater than

approximately _____ watts.

The graph of $y = \sqrt{x} + k$ is a translation of $y = \sqrt{x}$. If *k* is a positive number, then:

$y = \sqrt{x} + k$ translates the graph *up k* units

and

$y = \sqrt{x} - k$ translates the graph *down k* units.

Problem 3 **Graphing a Vertical Translation**

Got It? What is the graph of $y = \sqrt{x} - 3$?

15. What does the -3 in $y = \sqrt{x} - 3$ mean? Circle the correct answer.

Translate the graph of $y = \sqrt{x}$ up 3 units.   Translate the graph of $y = \sqrt{x}$ down 3 units.

16. Identify each graph below as $y = \sqrt{x}$, $y = \sqrt{x} + 3$, or $y = \sqrt{x} - 3$.

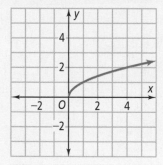   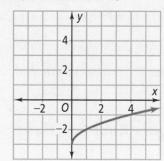   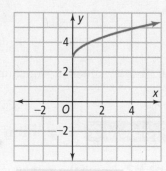

The graph of $y = \sqrt{x + h}$ is also a translation of $y = \sqrt{x}$. If *h* is a positive number, then:

$y = \sqrt{x + h}$ translates the graph to the *left h* units

and

$y = \sqrt{x - h}$ translates the graph to the *right h* units.

Problem 4 **Graphing a Horizontal Translation**

Got It? What is the graph of $y = \sqrt{x - 3}$?

17. Underline the correct word to complete the sentence.

The graph of $y = \sqrt{x - 3}$ is the graph of $y = \sqrt{x}$ translated 3 units to the left / right .

18. The graph of $y = \sqrt{x}$ is provided below. Use the graph of the parent square root function to draw and label the graph of $y = \sqrt{x - 3}$ on the same grid.

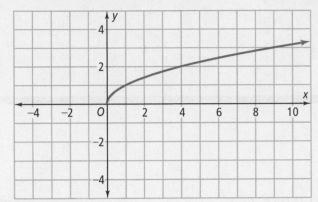

Lesson Check • Do you UNDERSTAND?

Reasoning Can the domain of a square root function include negative numbers? Explain.

19. Underline the correct words to complete the sentence.

In a square root function, the x-values must make the radicand

greater than / less than or equal to 0.

20. For each radicand below, are there negative values in the domain? Circle *Yes* or *No*. If *Yes*, write one negative value that is in the domain.

$\sqrt{x}$	$\sqrt{x + 2}$	$\sqrt{x - 2}$	$\sqrt{2 - x}$
Yes / No	Yes / No	Yes / No	Yes / No

21. Can the domain of a square root function include negative numbers? Explain.

_____

_____

Math Success

Check off the vocabulary words that you understand.

☐ square root function   ☐ translation

Rate how well you can *graph a square root function.*

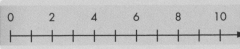

Lesson 10-5

Trigonometric Ratios

Vocabulary

● Review

Use the circles, triangles, and squares below. Write each *ratio*.

1. number of circles to number of squares = $\dfrac{5}{\quad}$

2. number of squares to number of circles = $\dfrac{\quad}{\quad}$

3. total number of shapes to number of triangles = $\dfrac{\quad}{4}$

● Vocabulary Builder

| elevation (noun) **el uh vay shun** |

Definition: An object's **elevation** is its height above a surface or other object.

Related Words: elevate (verb), elevator (noun), horizontal (adjective, noun)

Opposite: depression (noun)

Main Idea: The angle of *elevation* is the angle of a line of sight above the horizontal. The angle of *depression* is the angle of a line of sight below the horizontal.

● Use Your Vocabulary

Write *elevation* or *depression* to indicate the type of angle that is shown.

4.

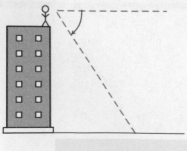

angle of _____

5.

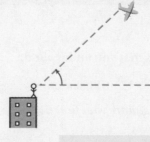

angle of _____

Key Concept Trigonometric Ratios

sine of ∠A	sin A	opposite leg / hypotenuse
cosine of ∠A	cos A	adjacent leg / hypotenuse
tangent of ∠A	tan A	opposite leg / adjacent leg

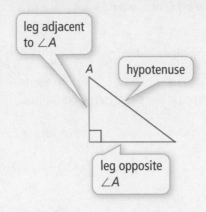

leg adjacent to ∠A

hypotenuse

leg opposite ∠A

For each triangle, label the *hypotenuse*, *opposite leg*, and *adjacent leg* for angle *C*.

6.

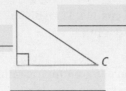

7.

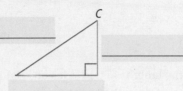

Problem 1   Finding Trigonometric Ratios

Got It? What are sin *E*, cos *E*, and tan *E* for the triangle at the right?

8. Underline the correct words to complete the sentence.

For angle *E*, the opposite leg is side $\overline{GE}$ / side $\overline{FG}$,

and the adjacent leg is side $\overline{GE}$ / side $\overline{EF}$.

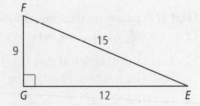

9. Complete each equation.

$$\sin E = \frac{\text{opposite leg}}{\text{hypotenuse}} \qquad \cos E = \frac{\text{adjacent leg}}{\text{hypotenuse}} \qquad \tan E = \frac{\text{opposite leg}}{\text{adjacent leg}}$$

$$= \frac{}{15} = \frac{}{5} \qquad = \frac{}{15} = \frac{}{5} \qquad = \frac{}{} = \frac{}{}$$

You can also use a calculator to find trigonometric ratios. In this chapter, use the degree mode when finding trigonometric ratios. That allows you to enter angles in degrees.

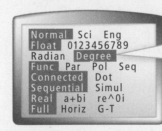

Set your calculator to Degree mode.

Lesson 10-6

Problem 3 Finding a Missing Side Length

Got It? To the nearest tenth, what is the value of x in the triangle at the right?

10. Circle the trigonometric equation that can be used to solve for x.

$$\sin 35° = \frac{\text{opposite leg}}{\text{hypotenuse}} \qquad \cos 35° = \frac{\text{adjacent leg}}{\text{hypotenuse}} \qquad \tan 35° = \frac{\text{opposite leg}}{\text{adjacent leg}}$$

11. Complete the steps below to solve the equation.

$$\boxed{} = \frac{\boxed{}}{x} \qquad \text{Substitute } x \text{ and } 1.575 \text{ from the diagram.}$$

$$\cos 35° \cdot x = \boxed{} \qquad \text{Multiply each side by } x.$$

$$x = \frac{\boxed{}}{\boxed{}} \qquad \text{Divide each side of the equation by } \cos 35°.$$

$$x \approx \boxed{} \qquad \text{Use a calculator to find } \cos 35°. \text{ Then divide and round to the nearest tenth.}$$

If you know the lengths of two sides of a right triangle, you can find a trigonometric ratio for each acute angle of the triangle. If you know a trigonometric ratio for an angle, you can use the inverse of that ratio to find the measure of the angle. Use the inverse trigonometric features $\sin^{-1}$, $\cos^{-1}$, and $\tan^{-1}$ on your calculator.

Problem 4 Finding the Measures of Angles

Got It? In a right triangle, the side opposite $\angle A$ is 8 mm long and the hypotenuse is 12 mm long. What is the measure of $\angle A$?

12. Label the diagram at the right to show which side is 8 mm long and which side is 12 mm long.

13. Circle the trigonometric function you can use to find the measure of angle A if you know the lengths of the opposite side and the hypotenuse.

$$\sin A \qquad\qquad \cos A \qquad\qquad \tan A$$

14. Circle the correct meaning for the trigonometric function $\sin^{-1}x$.

the angle whose sine is x \qquad\qquad the sine of x

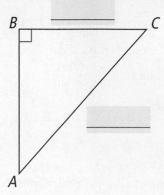

15. Complete the equation and solve.

$$\boxed{} = \frac{8}{\boxed{}} \qquad \text{Use a trigonometric definition.}$$

$$\sin A \approx \boxed{} \qquad \text{Divide.}$$

$$A \approx \boxed{} \qquad \text{Use the } \sin^{-1} \text{ function of a calculator.}$$

16. To the nearest degree, angle A measures $\boxed{}$.

Problem 5 **Using an Angle of Elevation or Depression**

Got It? Suppose that you are waiting in line for an amusement park ride. You see your friend at the top of the ride. The angle of elevation to the top of the ride is 50°. How far are you from the base of the ride?

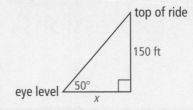

top of ride

150 ft

eye level
50°
x

17. Complete the steps to find the value of x.

$$\boxed{} = \frac{}{x} \qquad \text{Use the definition of tangent.}$$

$$\boxed{} \cdot x = 150 \qquad \text{Multiply each side by } x.$$

$$x = \frac{150}{\boxed{}} \qquad \text{Solve for } x.$$

$$x \approx \boxed{} \qquad \text{Use a calculator.}$$

18. To the nearest foot, you are $\boxed{}$ ft from the base of the ride.

 Lesson Check • **Do you UNDERSTAND?**

Vocabulary Describe the difference between finding the sine of an angle and the cosine of an angle.

19. Circle the ratio that is used to find the sine of an angle. Draw a line under the ratio that is used to find the cosine of an angle.

$$\frac{\text{adjacent leg}}{\text{hypotenuse}} \qquad\qquad \frac{\text{opposite leg}}{\text{adjacent leg}} \qquad\qquad \frac{\text{opposite leg}}{\text{hypotenuse}}$$

20. Describe how finding the sine of an angle differs from finding the cosine.

_____

_____

_____

Math Success

Check off the vocabulary words that you understand.

☐ trigonometric ratios ☐ angle of elevation ☐ angle of depression

Rate how well you can *work with trigonometric ratios.*

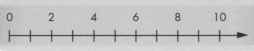

Need to review 0 2 4 6 8 10 Now I get it!

Lesson 10-6

Vocabulary

● Review

1. Circle the *greatest common factor* of 36 and 60.

| 3 | 6 | 12 | 18 |

2. Circle the *greatest common factor* of $4x^2yz^3$ and $2x^2yz$.

| $2x^2yz^3$ | $2x^2z^2$ | $2x^2yz$ | $4x^2yz^3$ |

3. Cross out the polynomial expressions that are NOT *common factors* of $4x^2 + 20x + 24$ and $2x + 6$.

| $2x + 6$ | $x + 2$ | $x + 3$ | $4x + 6$ |

● Vocabulary Builder

rational expression (noun) RASH **un ul ek** SPRESH **un**

Definition: An expression of the form $\dfrac{\text{polynomial}}{\text{polynomial}}$ is a **rational expression.**

Examples: $\dfrac{x^2 + 9}{3x^3 - 9x^2 + 11x - 15}$, $\dfrac{x - 3}{9x^2 - 5x - 10}$, $\dfrac{9t^3}{3y^5}$, $\dfrac{2}{3}$

Main Idea: A **rational expression** is in *simplified form* when the numerator and the denominator have no common factor except 1.

● Use Your Vocabulary

Is each expression a *rational expression*? Circle *Yes* or *No*. Explain your reasoning.

4. $\dfrac{\sqrt{2x - 9}}{x - 5}$

Yes / No

5. $\dfrac{1}{x - 5}$

Yes / No

6. 8

Yes / No

A rational expression is undefined when the denominator is 0. A value of a variable for which a rational expression is undefined is an *excluded value*.

 Problem 1 **Simplifying a Rational Expression**

Got It? What is the simplified form of $\frac{21a^2}{7a^3}$? State any excluded values.

7. Complete the reasoning model below.

Think	Write
First I find the greatest common factor so I can factor it out of the numerator and denominator.	$\dfrac{21a^2}{7a^3} = \dfrac{7a^2 \cdot \boxed{}}{7a^2 \cdot \boxed{}}$
Then I divide out common factors.	$= \dfrac{7a^2 \cdot \boxed{}}{7a^2 \cdot \boxed{}}$
Finally, I simplify.	$= \dfrac{3}{\boxed{}}$

8. Complete each sentence to find the restrictions on the variable.

Set the denominator of $\frac{21a^2}{7a^3}$ equal to $\boxed{}$.

$\frac{21a^2}{7a^3}$ is undefined when $a = \boxed{}$.

So the simplified form of $\frac{21a^2}{7a^3}$ is $\boxed{}$, $a \neq \boxed{}$.

 Problem 2 **Simplifying a Rational Expression Containing a Trinomial**

Got It? What is the simplified form of $\frac{2x - 8}{x^2 - 2x - 8}$? State any excluded values.

9. Complete the steps to simplify the rational expression.

$$\frac{2x - 8}{x^2 - 2x - 8} = \frac{2(x - 4)}{(\boxed{})(x - 4)} \qquad \text{Factor.}$$

$$= \frac{2(x - 4)}{(\boxed{})(x - 4)} \qquad \text{Divide out the common factor.}$$

$$= \frac{2}{\boxed{}} \qquad \text{Simplify.}$$

Lesson 11-1

10. The denominator of the original expression cannot equal 0. Complete the steps to find any restrictions on x.

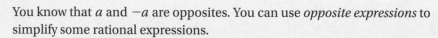

$$\boxed{} - 2x - \boxed{} \neq 0$$

$$(x - 4)(\boxed{}) \neq 0$$

$$x - 4 \neq 0 \qquad \text{and} \qquad \boxed{} \neq 0$$

$$x \neq \boxed{} \qquad \text{and} \qquad x \neq \boxed{}$$

11. The simplified form of the expression is $\boxed{}$, $x \neq \boxed{}$ and $x \neq \boxed{}$.

You know that a and $-a$ are opposites. You can use *opposite expressions* to simplify some rational expressions.

opposite expressions: $a + b$ and $-a - b$ $\qquad$ $x - 3$ and $3 - x$

12. To show that $x - 3$ and $3 - x$ are opposites, factor -1 from $3 - x$.

$$3 - x = -1(\boxed{} + x)$$

$$= -1(x - \boxed{})$$

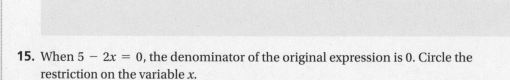

Problem 3 Recognizing Opposite Factors

Got It? What is the simplified form of $\frac{2x - 5}{5 - 2x}$? State any excluded values.

13. Multiple Choice Which expressions are opposites?

Ⓐ $2x - 5$ and $5 + 2x$ $\qquad$ Ⓒ $5 - 2x$ and $5 + 2x$

Ⓑ $5 - 2x$ and $2x - 5$ $\qquad$ Ⓓ $2x - 5$ and $-5 + 2x$

14. Now simplify $\frac{2x - 5}{5 - 2x}$.

15. When $5 - 2x = 0$, the denominator of the original expression is 0. Circle the restriction on the variable x.

$x \neq 5$ $\qquad\qquad\qquad$ $x \neq \frac{5}{2}$ $\qquad\qquad\qquad$ $x \neq -2$ $\qquad\qquad\qquad$ $x \neq -\frac{5}{2}$

Problem 4 Using a Rational Expression

Got It? A square has side length $6x + 2$. A rectangle with width $3x + 1$ has the same area as the square. What is the length of the rectangle?

16. The square has side length $6x + 2$. The area A of the square is

$(\boxed{}) \cdot (\boxed{})$.

17. Find the length ℓ of the rectangle. Complete the steps.

$$A = \ell w \qquad \text{Formula for area of a rectangle}$$

$$\frac{\boxed{}}{w} = \ell \qquad \text{Solve for } \ell.$$

$$\frac{(\boxed{})(\boxed{})}{3x + 1} = \ell \qquad \begin{array}{l}\text{Substitute the area of the square for } A.\\ \text{Substitute the width of the rectangle for } w.\end{array}$$

$$\frac{2(\boxed{}) \cdot 2(\boxed{})}{3x + 1} = \ell \qquad \text{Factor 2 from each term in the numerator.}$$

$$\frac{4(\boxed{})(\boxed{})}{3x + 1} = \ell \qquad \text{Divide out the common factor.}$$

$$\boxed{} = \ell \qquad \text{Simplify.}$$

18. The length of the rectangle is $\boxed{}$.

Lesson Check • Do you UNDERSTAND?

Writing When simplifying a rational expression, why may it be necessary to exclude values? Explain.

19. The simplified form of the expression $\dfrac{x^2 + x - 12}{x - 3}$ is $x + 4$.

Evaluate each expression below when $x = 3$.

$$\frac{x^2 + x - 12}{x - 3} = \boxed{} \qquad\qquad x + 4 = \boxed{}$$

20. Why might it be necessary to restrict the values of the variable when you simplify a rational expression?

_____

_____

_____

Math Success

Check off the vocabulary words that you understand.

☐ rational expression   ☐ simplified form   ☐ opposite expressions   ☐ excluded value

Rate how well you can *simplify a rational expression.*

Need to review   0   2   4   6   8   10   Now I get it!

Lesson 11-1

Vocabulary

● Review

Circle the *binomial factors* of each expression.

1. $2x^2 + 8x$

| 2 | 2x | x + 4 | x + 8 |

2. $x^2 + 4x + 3$

| x + 1 | x + 2 | x + 3 | x - 2 |

3. $3x^2 + 5x - 2$

| 3x + 1 | x + 2 | 3x - 1 | x - 2 |

● Vocabulary Builder

complex fraction (adjective) KAHM **pleks** FRAK **shun**

Main Idea: A **complex fraction** is a fraction that contains one or more fractions in its numerator, in its denominator, or both.

complex fraction

$$\dfrac{a \longleftarrow \text{numerator}}{\dfrac{b}{a+1} \Big\} \text{denominator}}$$

● Use Your Vocabulary

Write T for *true* or F for *false*.

_____ **4.** The fraction $\dfrac{\frac{1}{2}}{\frac{3}{4}}$ is a *complex fraction*.

_____ **5.** The fraction $\dfrac{x+1}{2y+3}$ is a *complex fraction*.

Circle the *complex fraction(s)*.

6. $\dfrac{a}{b+2}$ $\dfrac{c}{f+\frac{1}{2}}$ $\dfrac{h+2}{d}$

       $\dfrac{r+\frac{1}{2}}{t}$ $\dfrac{1}{2}\left(\dfrac{w}{v}\right)$ $\dfrac{j}{\frac{1}{k}}$

If a, b, c, and d represent polynomials (where $b \neq 0$ and $d \neq 0$), then $\frac{a}{b} \cdot \frac{c}{d} = \frac{ac}{bd}$.

 Problem 1 **Multiplying Rational Expressions**

Got It? What is the product $\frac{5}{y} \cdot \frac{3}{y^3}$? State any excluded values.

7. To find the product, multiply the numerators and multiply the denominators.

$$\frac{5}{y} \cdot \frac{3}{y^3} = \frac{5(3)}{y \cdot \boxed{}} = \frac{\boxed{}}{\boxed{}}$$

8. $\frac{5}{y} \cdot \frac{3}{y^3}$ is undefined when $y = \boxed{}$.

 Problem 2 **Using Factoring**

Got It? What is the product $\frac{3x^2}{x + 2} \cdot \frac{x^2 + 3x + 2}{x}$?

9. Complete the reasoning model below.

Think	Write
I need to factor the numerator.	$\dfrac{3x^2}{x+2} \cdot \dfrac{x^2 + 3x + 2}{x} = \dfrac{3x^2}{x+2} \cdot \dfrac{(x+2)(x+\boxed{})}{x}$
I can divide out common factors.	$= \dfrac{3x^2}{x+2} \cdot \dfrac{(x+2)(x+\boxed{})}{x}$
Now I can simplify.	$= 3x(x + \boxed{})$

 Problem 3 **Multiplying a Rational Expression by a Polynomial**

Got It? What is the product $\frac{2x - 14}{4x - 6} \cdot (6x^2 - 13x + 6)$?

10. Circle the first step in multiplying the rational expressions.

   Multiply the numerators.   Factor each expression.   Divide out common factors.

11. Complete the first step in multiplying the rational expressions.

$$\frac{2x - 14}{4x - 6} \cdot 6x^2 - 13x + 6 = \frac{2(x - \boxed{})}{2(2x - 3)} \cdot \frac{(2x - 3)(\boxed{})}{1}$$

12. What common factors can you divide out? $\boxed{}$ and $(\boxed{} - \boxed{})$

13. Divide out the common factors and simplify.

14. The product is $(\boxed{})(3x - 2)$.

Lesson 11-2

When you divide rational expressions, first rewrite the quotient as a product using the reciprocal *before* dividing out common factors.

 Problem 4 **Dividing Rational Expressions**

Got It? What is the quotient $\dfrac{x}{x+y} \div \dfrac{xy}{x+y}$?

15. Circle the reciprocal of $\dfrac{xy}{x+y}$.

| $\dfrac{xy}{x+y}$ | $\dfrac{xy}{x-y}$ | $\dfrac{x+y}{xy}$ | $\dfrac{x-y}{x+y}$ |

16. Write the justifications to divide the rational expressions.

$$\frac{x}{x+y} \div \frac{xy}{x+y} = \frac{x}{x+y} \cdot \frac{x+y}{xy}$$

$$= \frac{\cancel{x}}{\cancel{x+y}} \cdot \frac{\cancel{x+1}}{\cancel{x}y}$$

$$= \frac{1}{y}$$

_____

_____

_____

 Problem 5 **Dividing a Rational Expression by a Polynomial**

Got It? What is the quotient $\dfrac{z^2 - 2z + 1}{z^2 + 2} \div (z - 1)$?

17. Write the reciprocal of $z - 1$.

18. Complete the steps to divide the rational expressions.

$$\frac{z^2 - 2z + 1}{z^2 + 2} \div (z - 1) = \frac{z^2 - 2z + 1}{z^2 + 2} \cdot \boxed{}$$

$$= \frac{(\boxed{})(z - 1)}{z^2 + 2} \cdot \boxed{}$$

$$= \frac{\boxed{}}{z^2 + 2}$$

Any complex fraction of the form $\dfrac{\frac{a}{b}}{\frac{c}{d}}$ (where $b \neq 0$, $c \neq 0$, and $d \neq 0$) can be expressed as $\dfrac{a}{b} \div \dfrac{c}{d}$.

Write the complex fraction as division.

19. $\dfrac{\frac{2}{3}}{\frac{1}{3}} = \dfrac{2}{3} \div \boxed{}$

20. $\dfrac{\frac{1}{4}}{\frac{x}{2}} = \dfrac{1}{4} \div \boxed{}$

21. $\dfrac{\frac{w}{5}}{\frac{z}{y}} = \boxed{}$

Problem 6 Simplifying a Complex Fraction

Got It? What is the simplified form of $\dfrac{\frac{1}{q+4}}{\frac{2q^2}{2q+8}}$?

22. Complete the steps to simplify the complex fraction.

$$\dfrac{\frac{1}{q+4}}{\frac{2q^2}{2q+8}} = \frac{1}{q+4} \div \boxed{}$$ Write the complex fraction as division.

$$= \frac{1}{q+4} \cdot \boxed{}$$ Multiply by the reciprocal.

$$= \frac{1}{q+4} \cdot \boxed{}$$ Factor.

$$= \frac{1}{q+4} \cdot \boxed{}$$ Divide out common factors.

$$= \boxed{}$$ Simplify.

Lesson Check • Do you UNDERSTAND?

Reasoning Are the complex fractions $\dfrac{\frac{a}{b}}{c}$ and $\dfrac{a}{\frac{b}{c}}$ equivalent? Explain.

23. Complete the steps to simplify the complex fraction.

$$\dfrac{\frac{a}{b}}{c} = \frac{a}{b} \div \boxed{} = \frac{a}{b} \cdot \boxed{} = \boxed{}$$

24. Complete the steps to simplify the complex fraction.

$$\dfrac{a}{\frac{b}{c}} = a \div \boxed{} = a \cdot \boxed{} = \boxed{}$$

25. The complex fractions are / are not equivalent because the quotients you obtain

after simplifying are / are not the same.

Math Success

Check off the vocabulary words that you understand.

☐ complex fraction   ☐ rational expression

Rate how well you can *multiply and divide rational expressions.*

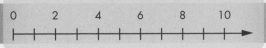

Lesson 11-2

Vocabulary

● **Review**

Write the *coefficient* of each term of $9x^3 - 11x^2 + 2$.

1. x^3-term: ⬚

2. x^2-term: ⬚

3. x-term: ⬚

4. Circle the *leading coefficient* of $-3x^2 - x + 2$.

| −3 | −1 | 1 | 2 | 3 |

5. Circle the *coefficient* of the x-term in $5x^2 - 7$ if the expression were written in standard form.

| −7 | 0 | 1 | 2 | 5 |

● **Vocabulary Builder**

quotient (noun) кwoн **shunt**

Definition: A **quotient** is the result of dividing one number or expression by another.

Origin: **Quotient** comes from the Middle English word "quocient," meaning *how many times.*

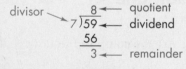

● **Use Your Vocabulary**

Complete each sentence with the correct word.

  dividend   quotient   divisor   remainder

6. In division, the number you divide by is the   ? .

7. The result of dividing one number by another number is the   ? .

8. After you divide, any number left over is the   ? .

9. The number that is divided by another number is the   ? .

Problem 1 Dividing by a Monomial

Got It? What is $(4a^3 + 10a^2 + 3a) \div 2a^2$?

10. Write the division problem as multiplication by the reciprocal.

$$(4a^3 + 10a^2 + 3a) \div 2a^2 = \frac{(4a^3 + 10a^2 + 3a)}{\boxed{}} \cdot \boxed{}$$

11. Use the Distributive Property and simplify each fraction to find the quotient.

$$= \frac{4a^3}{\boxed{}} + \frac{10a^2}{\boxed{}} + \frac{3a}{\boxed{}}$$

$$= \boxed{} + 5 + \boxed{}$$

The process of dividing a polynomial by a binomial is similar to long division of real numbers. When you subtract one polynomial from another, first change the sign of each term of the second polynomial to the opposite sign and then add the like terms together.

For example, $6x^2 + 3x - (2x^2 + 4x) = 6x^2 + 3x - 2x^2 - 4x = 4x^2 - x$.

 Problem 2 Dividing by a Binomial

Got It? What is $(2m^2 - m - 3) \div (m + 1)$?

12. Complete each step to divide $(2m^2 - m - 3)$ by $(m + 1)$.

Step 1 Begin by dividing the first term in the dividend by the first term in the divisor.

$$\begin{array}{r} \boxed{} \\ m + 1\overline{)2m^2 - m - 3} \\ -(2m^2 + \boxed{}) \\ \hline -3m\boxed{} \end{array}$$

— Write $2m$ above the term with the same degree, $-m$.

Divide: $2m^2 \div m = 2m$.

Multiply: $2m(m + 1) = 2m^2 + 2m$.

Subtract. Bring down -3.

Step 2 Divide the term $-3m$ by the first term in the divisor, m.

$$\begin{array}{r} 2m - \boxed{} \\ m + 1\overline{)2m^2 - m - 3} \\ -(2m^2 + 2m) \\ \hline -3m - 3 \\ -(\boxed{} -3) \\ \hline 0 \end{array}$$

— Write -3 above the constant term of the dividend.

Divide: $-3m \div m = -3$.

Multiply: $-3(m + 1) = -3m - 3$.

Subtract.

13. $(2m^2 - m - 3) \div (m + 1) = \boxed{}$.

When the dividend is in standard form and a term is missing, add the missing term with a coefficient of zero. For example, rewrite $6m^3 - 2m + 3$ as $6m^3 + 0m^2 - 2m + 3$.

Lesson 11-3

Problem 3 Dividing Polynomials With a Zero Coefficient

Got It? What is $(q^4 + q^2 + q - 3) \div (q - 1)$?

14. Multiple Choice Which of these expressions shows the missing term of $q^4 + q^2 + q - 3$ written with a coefficient of 0?

- Ⓐ $q^4 + q^2 + q - 3 + 0$
- Ⓒ $q^4 + q^2 + 0q^2 + q - 3$
- Ⓑ $q^4 + 0q^3 + q^2 + q - 3$
- Ⓓ $q^4 + q^2 + 0q + q - 3$

15. Use your answer to Exercise 14 as the dividend. Divide the polynomials.

16. $(q^4 + q^2 + q - 3) \div (q - 1) = $

Problem 4 Reordering Terms and Dividing Polynomials

Got It? What is $(-7 - 10y + 6y^2) \div (4 + 3y)$?

17. Circle the standard form of $-7 - 10y + 6y^2$.

| $-10y - 7 + 6y^2$ | $6y^2 - 10y - 7$ | $6y^2 - 7 - 10y$ |

18. Circle the standard form of $4 + 3y$.

| $4 + 3y$ | $4y + 3$ | $3y + 4$ |

19. Use the standard forms of each expression to divide $(-7 - 10y + 6y^2)$ by $(4 + 3y)$.

20. The remainder is ____. So, $(-7 - 10y + 6y^2) \div (4 + 3y) = $ ____ $\cdot y - $ ____ $+ \dfrac{}{3y + 4}$.

Concept Summary   Dividing a Polynomial by a Polynomial

Step 1 Arrange the terms of the dividend and divisor in standard form. If a term is missing from the dividend, add the term with a coefficient of 0.

Step 2 Divide the first term of the dividend by the first term of the divisor. This is the first term of the quotient.

Step 3 Multiply the first term of the quotient by the whole divisor and place the product under the dividend.

Step 4 Subtract this product from the dividend.

Step 5 Bring down the next term.

Repeat Steps 2–5 as necessary. Stop dividing when the degree of the remainder is less than the degree of the divisor. (Remember that the *degree of a polynomial* is the highest degree of the variable in the polynomial.)

Lesson Check • Do you UNDERSTAND?

Reasoning How would you rewrite $1 - x^4$ before dividing it by $x - 1$?

21. Is the polynomial $1 - x^4$ in standard form?   Yes / No

22. How do you arrange the terms of a polynomial so that it is in standard form?

_____

_____

23. Write $1 - x^4$ in standard form.

Math Success

Check off the vocabulary words that you understand.

☐ coefficient   ☐ quotient   ☐ dividend

Rate how well you can *divide polynomials*.

Need to review   0   2   4   6   8   10   Now I get it!

Adding and Subtracting Rational Expressions

 Vocabulary

● **Review**

Circle each number that could be used as a *like denominator* for each pair of fractions.

1. $\frac{7}{12}$ and $\frac{5}{6}$

| 6 | 9 | 12 | 24 | 72 |

2. $\frac{2}{15}$ and $\frac{1}{8}$

| 8 | 20 | 40 | 90 | 120 |

● **Vocabulary Builder**

unit analysis (noun) YOO **nit uh** NAL **uh sis**

Math Usage: When converting from one unit to another, such as hours to minutes, you must decide which conversion factor will produce the appropriate unit. This process is called **unit analysis.**

What It Means: You are given that 1 unit of a measure is equal to an amount of another measure (such as 1 h = 60 min). You can use that information to convert from one measure to another.

Example: You know that 1 h = 60 min, and 1 min = 60 s. To find the number of seconds in 4 hours, you can use **unit analysis.**

$$4\cancel{h} \times \frac{60\ \cancel{min}}{1\ \cancel{h}} \times \frac{60\ s}{1\ \cancel{min}} = 14,440\ s$$

● **Use Your Vocabulary**

3. Complete the *unit analysis* below to convert 21,600 seconds to hours.

$$21,600\ s \times \frac{1\ min}{60\ s} \times \frac{1\ h}{60\ min} = \boxed{}\ h$$

4. Complete the *unit analysis* below to convert 180 yards to inches.

$$180\ yd \times \frac{3\ ft}{1\ yd} \times \frac{12\ in.}{1\ ft} = \boxed{}\ in.$$

You can add rational expressions with like denominators. If a, b, and c represent polynomials (with $c \neq 0$), then $\frac{a}{c} + \frac{b}{c} = \frac{a+b}{c}$.

 Problem 1 Adding Expressions With Like Denominators

Got It? What is the sum $\frac{2a}{3a-4} + \frac{3a}{3a-4}$?

5. To add or subtract fractions with like denominators, you add or subtract the numerators and keep the denominator the same / add the denominators .

6. Complete the steps to add the expressions.

$$\frac{2a}{3a-4} + \frac{3a}{3a-4} = \frac{2a + \boxed{}}{3a-4} \qquad \text{Add the numerators.}$$

$$= \frac{\boxed{}}{3a-4} \qquad \text{Simplify the numerator.}$$

 Problem 2 Subtracting Expressions With Like Denominators

Got It? What is the difference $\frac{2}{z+3} - \frac{7}{z+3}$?

7. Complete the steps to find the difference.

$$\frac{2}{z+3} - \frac{7}{z+3} = \frac{2 - \boxed{}}{z+3} \qquad \text{Subtract the numerators.}$$

$$= \frac{\boxed{}}{z+3} \qquad \text{Simplify the numerator.}$$

Got It? What is the difference $\frac{9n-3}{10n-4} - \frac{3n+5}{10n-4}$?

8. Circle the simplified form of $-(3n+5)$.

$\qquad -3n+5 \qquad\qquad -15n \qquad\qquad -3n-5$

9. Now complete the steps to find the difference.

$$\frac{9n-3}{10n-4} - \frac{3n+5}{10n-4} = \frac{9n-3-(\boxed{})}{10n-4}$$

$$= \frac{9n-3-3n-\boxed{}}{10n-4}$$

$$= \frac{\boxed{}}{10n-4}$$

To find the least common denominator (LCD) of two rational expressions, first write each denominator as a product of prime factors. Then use each factor the greatest number of times it appears.

Lesson 11-4

Problem 3 Adding Expressions With Different Denominators

Got It? What is the sum $\frac{3}{7y^4} + \frac{2}{3y^2}$?

10. Complete to write each denominator as a product of prime factors.

$7y^4 = 7 \cdot y \cdot \boxed{} \cdot \boxed{} \cdot \boxed{}$ $\qquad\qquad$ $3y^2 = 3 \cdot \boxed{} \cdot \boxed{}$

11. Use each factor the greatest number of times it appears.

$7 \cdot \boxed{} \cdot y \cdot \boxed{} \cdot \boxed{} \cdot \boxed{} = \boxed{}$

12. Now complete the steps to add the expressions.

$$\frac{3}{7y^4} + \frac{2}{3y^2} = \frac{3 \cdot \boxed{}}{7y^4 \cdot \boxed{}} + \frac{2 \cdot \boxed{} \cdot \boxed{}}{3y^2 \cdot \boxed{} \cdot \boxed{}}$$ $\qquad$ Rewrite each fraction using the LCD.

$$= \frac{\boxed{}}{\boxed{} \cdot y^4} + \frac{\boxed{}}{\boxed{} \cdot y^4}$$ $\qquad$ Simplify numerators and denominators.

$$= \frac{\boxed{} + \boxed{}}{21y^4}$$ $\qquad$ Add the numerators.

13. The sum of $\frac{3}{7y^4}$ and $\frac{2}{3y^2}$ is $\boxed{}$.

Problem 4 Subtracting Expressions With Different Denominators

Got It? What is the difference $\frac{c}{3c-1} - \frac{4}{c-2}$?

14. Complete the reasoning model below.

Think	Write
I need to find the LCD of $\frac{c}{3c-1}$ and $\frac{4}{c-2}$.	There are no common factors so the LCD is $(3c-1)(c-2)$.
I can rewrite each fraction using the LCD.	$\dfrac{c}{3c-1} - \dfrac{4}{c-2} = \dfrac{c \cdot (c-2)}{(3c-1)(c-2)} - \dfrac{4 \cdot (\boxed{})}{(c-2)(\boxed{})}$
Then I simplify the numerators.	$= \dfrac{c^2 - 2c}{(3c-1)(c-2)} - \dfrac{\boxed{}}{(c-2)(\boxed{})}$
Now I subtract the numerators.	$= \dfrac{c^2 - 2c - \boxed{} + \boxed{}}{(3c-1)(c-2)}$
Finally, I simplify the numerators.	$= \dfrac{c^2 - 14c + \boxed{}}{(3c-1)(c-2)}$

Problem 5 Using Rational Expressions

Got It? A bicyclist rides 5 mi out and then rides back. His speed returning is reduced 20% because it is raining. Let r be his speed in miles per hour riding out. What is an expression that represents his total time in hours riding out and back?

15. Underline the correct expression to complete each sentence.

His rate during the return trip is 80% of the rate of the trip out, or $0.2r$ / $0.8r$.

His time for the trip out is the total ride time divided by his speed riding out, or $\frac{5}{r}$ / $\frac{5}{0.8r}$.

The time for his return trip is the total ride time divided by his speed on the return trip, or $\frac{5}{r}$ / $\frac{5}{0.8r}$.

16. Use your answers from Exercise 15 to write and simplify an expression that represents his total time in hours.

17. An expression that represents his total time in hours riding out and back is ____ .

Lesson Check • Do you UNDERSTAND?

Reasoning Your friend says she can always find a common denominator for two rational expressions by finding the product of the denominators. Is your friend correct? Will your friend's method always give you the LCD? Explain your answers.

18. The product of the denominators of $\frac{2}{3}$ and $\frac{5}{12}$ is ____ .

19. The LCD of the fractions $\frac{2}{3}$ and $\frac{5}{12}$ is ____ .

20. Is your friend correct? Will your friend's method always give the LCD? Explain.

_____

_____

Math Success

Check off the vocabulary words that you understand.

☐ rational expression   ☐ common denominator

Rate how well you can *add and subtract rational expressions*.

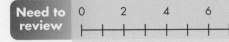

Need to review 0 2 4 6 8 10   Now I get it!

Solving Rational Equations

Vocabulary

● Review

1. What is on each side of an equal sign in a *proportion*? Explain.

2. Circle the property that you can use to solve any *proportion*.

Distributive Property   Associative Property   Cross Products Property

● Vocabulary Builder

rational equation (noun) RASH un ul ee KWAY zhun

Related Words: rational expression, rational function, extraneous solution

Definition: A **rational equation** is an equation that contains one or more rational expressions.

Examples: $\frac{3}{4} + \frac{1}{x^2} = \frac{1}{2x}$ and $\frac{x+5}{x-7} = \frac{3}{10}$

Nonexamples: $2x + y = 5$ and $f(x) = 3x^2 - 2x + 1$

● Use Your Vocabulary

Write T for *true* or F for *false*.

_____ **3.** The equation $\frac{3}{x} = \frac{x}{4}$ is a *rational equation*.

_____ **4.** The equation $\frac{1}{7} - \frac{1}{9} = \frac{1}{w}$ is a *rational equation*.

_____ **5.** The equation $y - \frac{1}{9} = 4$ is a *rational equation*.

You can solve a rational equation by first multiplying each side of the equation by the least common denominator (LCD).

Problem 1 Solving Equations With Rational Expressions

Got It? What is the solution of $\frac{1}{3} + \frac{3}{x} = \frac{2}{x}$? Check your solution.

6. The equation has been solved below. Write a justification for each step.

$$\frac{1}{3} + \frac{3}{x} = \frac{2}{x}$$

_____

$$3x \cdot \left(\frac{1}{3} + \frac{3}{x}\right) = 3x \cdot \left(\frac{2}{x}\right)$$

_____

$$\cancel{3}x \cdot \left(\frac{1}{\cancel{3}}\right) + 3\cancel{x} \cdot \left(\frac{3}{\cancel{x}}\right) = 3\cancel{x} \cdot \left(\frac{2}{\cancel{x}}\right)$$

_____

$$x + 9 = 6$$

_____

$$x = -3$$

_____

7. Check to see whether -3 makes the equation true.

$$\frac{1}{3} + \frac{3}{\boxed{}} \overset{?}{=} \frac{2}{\boxed{}}$$

$$\boxed{} = \boxed{}$$

 Problem 2 Solving by Factoring

Got It? What are the solutions of $\frac{5}{y} = \frac{6}{y^2} - 6$? Check your solutions.

8. Complete the steps to solve the equation.

$$\boxed{} \cdot \frac{5}{y} = \boxed{} \cdot \left(\frac{6}{y^2} - 6\right)$$ Multiply each side by the LCD, y^2.

$$\boxed{} \cdot \frac{5}{y} = \boxed{} \cdot \left(\frac{6}{y^2}\right) + \boxed{} \cdot (-6)$$ Distributive Property

$$\boxed{} = 6 - 6y^2$$ Simplify.

$$6y^2 + 5y - 6 = 0$$ Collect terms on one side.

$$(3y - \boxed{})(2y + \boxed{}) = 0$$ Factor the quadratic expression.

$$3y - \boxed{} = 0 \quad\text{or}\quad 2y + \boxed{} = 0$$ Zero-Product Property

$$y = \boxed{} \quad\text{or}\quad y = \boxed{}$$ Solve for x.

9. Check your solutions in the original equation.

Lesson 11-5

Problem 3 Solving a Work Problem

Got It? One hose can fill a pool in 12 h. Another hose can fill the same pool in 8 h. How long will it take for both hoses to fill the pool together?

10. Complete the model below to write an equation.

Relate | $\begin{array}{c}\text{fraction of pool}\\\text{first hose can fill}\\\text{in one hour}\end{array}$ + $\begin{array}{c}\text{fraction of pool}\\\text{second hose can fill}\\\text{in one hour}\end{array}$ = $\begin{array}{c}\text{fraction of pool}\\\text{both hoses can fill}\\\text{in one hour}\end{array}$

Define — Let t = the time (in hours) it takes both hoses to fill the pool.

Write — $\dfrac{1}{12}$ + $\dfrac{1}{\boxed{}}$ = $\boxed{}$

11. Solve the equation.

$$\frac{1}{12} + \frac{1}{\boxed{}} = \boxed{}$$

$$24t \cdot \left(\frac{1}{\boxed{}} + \frac{1}{\boxed{}}\right) = 24t \cdot \left(\frac{1}{t}\right) \qquad \text{Multiply each side by the LCD, } 24t.$$

$$\boxed{} + 3t = \boxed{} \qquad \text{Distributive Property}$$

$$\boxed{} = \boxed{} \qquad \text{Simplify.}$$

$$t = \boxed{} \qquad \text{Solve for } t.$$

12. It will take the two hoses about $\boxed{}$ hours working together to fill the pool.

Problem 4 Solving a Rational Proportion

Got It? Find the solution(s) of $\dfrac{3}{b+2} = \dfrac{5}{b-2}$. Check your solutions.

13. You can use the Cross Products Property.

$$\frac{3}{b+2} = \frac{5}{b-2}$$

$$\boxed{} \cdot (b-2) = \boxed{} \cdot (b+2)$$

14. Now, solve the equation for b.

Got It? What is the solution of $\frac{x-4}{x^2-4} = \frac{-2}{x-2}$? Check your solution.

15. Complete the steps for solving the equation or write a justification for a step.

$(x-4)(x-2) = -2(x^2-4)$ _____

$x^2 - \boxed{} + 8 = -2x^2 + \boxed{}$ Simplify each side of the equation.

$3x^2 - \boxed{} = 0$ Collect terms on one side.

$3x(x-2) = 0$ _____

$3x = 0$ or $\boxed{} = 0$ Zero-Product Property

$x = 0$ or $x = \boxed{}$ Solve for x.

16. Check your solutions in the original equation.

For $x = 0$: $\dfrac{-4}{0^2-4} \overset{?}{=} \dfrac{-2}{\boxed{}-2}$ For $x = \boxed{}$: $\dfrac{\boxed{}-4}{2^2-4} \overset{?}{=} \dfrac{-2}{\boxed{}-2}$

$\dfrac{4}{-4} \overset{?}{=} \dfrac{-2}{\boxed{}}$ $\dfrac{-2}{\boxed{}} \overset{?}{=} \dfrac{-2}{\boxed{}}$

17. The solution $\boxed{}$ is extraneous. The solution of the original equation is $\boxed{}$.

Lesson Check • Do you UNDERSTAND?

Error Analysis In the work shown at the right, what error did the student make in solving the rational equation?

18. Circle the first step for solving a rational equation with unlike denominators.

  Find the LCD.   Multiply the numerators.   Factor.

19. What error did the student make?

_____

_____

Math Success

Check off the vocabulary words that you understand.

☐ rational equation ☐ extraneous solution ☐ Cross Products Property ☐ factor

Rate how well you can *solve rational equations*.

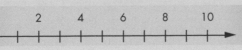

Need to review 0 2 4 6 8 10 Now I get it!

Vocabulary

● Review

1. Circle the *constant* term in each equation.

$$y = -5x + 7 \qquad\qquad x = 5 \qquad\qquad y = 4x^2 + 5x - 11$$

● Vocabulary Builder

---

inverse variation (noun) ɪɴ **vurs vehr ee** ᴀʏ **shun**

Definition: An **inverse variation** is a relationship between two quantities where one quantity increases as the other decreases.

Main Idea: "*y* varies inversely as *x*" means that when *x* increases, *y* decreases by the same factor.

Example: The amount of time a car travels increases as the car's speed decreases. This relationship between time and speed is an **inverse variation.**

Nonexample: One ticket to a play costs $10. The total cost of the tickets increases as the number of tickets bought increases. The relationship between total cost and number of tickets is a *direct variation*, not an **inverse variation.**

● Use Your Vocabulary

Consider each of the following situations. Then underline the correct word to complete each sentence.

2. A student downloads several songs at $2 each.

As the number of downloaded songs increases, the total cost of the downloads increases / decreases .

The relationship between the number of downloaded songs and the total cost of the downloads represents a(n) direct / inverse variation.

3. The job of building a patio is split evenly among several workers.

As the number of workers on the job increases, the workload of each person increases / decreases .

The relationship between the number of workers on the job and the workload of each person represents a(n) direct / inverse variation.

Key Concept Inverse Variation

An equation of the form $xy = k$ or $y = \frac{k}{x}$, where $k \neq 0$, is an **inverse variation.** The **constant of variation** is k, which is the product $x \cdot y$ for an ordered pair (x, y) that satisfies the inverse variation.

4. Cross out the equations that do NOT represent an inverse variation.

$y = 5$	$xy = 3$	$y = \frac{-6}{x}$	$x = 3y$

 Problem 1 Writing an Equation Given a Point

Got It? Suppose y varies inversely with x, and $y = 9$ when $x - 6$. What is an equation for the inverse variation?

5. Complete the reasoning model below.

Think	Write
First I write the general form of an inverse variation.	$xy = \boxed{}$
To find the value of k, I substitute 6 for x and 9 for y.	$\boxed{} \cdot \boxed{} = \boxed{}$
Then I simplify to find k.	$\boxed{} = k$

6. An equation for the inverse variation is $xy = \boxed{}$.

Problem 2 Using Inverse Variation

Got It? The weight needed to balance a lever varies inversely with the distance from the fulcrum to the weight. A 120-lb weight is placed on a lever, 5 ft from the fulcrum. How far from the fulcrum should an 80-lb weight be placed to balance the lever?

7. Let x be the distance of the 80-lb weight from the fulcrum. Complete the diagram.

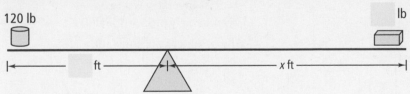

8. Circle the equation that models the inverse variation.

$\frac{120}{5} = \frac{80}{x}$	$5 + x = 120 + 80$	$120 \cdot 5 = 80 \cdot x$

Lesson 11-6

9. Complete the steps to solve the equation.

$120 \cdot \boxed{} = \boxed{} \cdot x$ Write the equation.

$ \boxed{} = \boxed{}$ Simplify.

$ \boxed{} = x$ Solve for x.

10. The 80-lb weight should be placed $\boxed{}$ ft from the fulcrum.

Problem 3   Graphing an Inverse Variation

Got It? What is the graph of $y = \frac{-8}{x}$?

11. Complete the table of values.

x	y
$\boxed{}$	2
-2	$\boxed{}$
-1	$\boxed{}$
0	undefined
1	$\boxed{}$
2	$\boxed{}$
4	$\boxed{}$

12. Plot the points from the table. Connect the points with smooth curves.

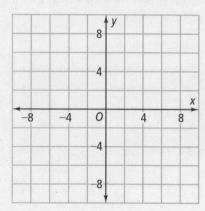

take note

Concept Summary   Direct and Inverse Variations

Direct Variation

y varies directly with x.

y is directly proportional to x.

The ratio $\frac{y}{x}$ is constant.

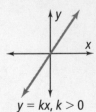

$y = kx, k > 0$

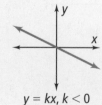

$y = kx, k < 0$

Inverse Variation

y varies inversely with x.

y is inversely proportional to x.

The product xy is constant.

$y = \frac{k}{x}, k > 0$

$y = \frac{k}{x}, k < 0$

Problem 4 **Determining Direct or Inverse Variation**

Got It? Do the data in the table represent a *direct variation* or an *inverse variation*? Write an equation to model the data.

x	y
4	−12
6	−18
8	−24

13. Find the value of each expression for the data.

xy	$\dfrac{y}{x}$
−48	
	−3

14. Circle the expression that is constant for this data.

xy $\qquad\qquad$ $\dfrac{y}{x}$

15. The data represent a(n) direct / inverse variation.

16. The equation _____ models the data.

 **Lesson Check** • **Do you UNDERSTAND?**

Does the graph of an inverse variation *always, sometimes,* or *never* pass through the origin? Explain.

17. At $x = 0$, what will the value of $\dfrac{y}{x}$ be? Explain.

_____

18. Does the graph of an inverse variation *always, sometimes,* or *never* pass through the origin? Explain.

_____

Math Success

Check off the vocabulary words that you understand.

☐ inverse variation $\qquad\qquad$ ☐ constant of variation

Rate how well you can *write and graph inverse variations*.

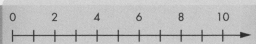

Lesson 11-6

11-7 Graphing Rational Functions

Vocabulary

● Review

1. Multiple Choice An expression is *undefined* when the value of its denominator is 0. Which expression is *undefined* when $x = -2$?

Ⓐ $\dfrac{x}{x^2 + 2}$ Ⓑ $\dfrac{5}{x - 2}$ Ⓒ $\dfrac{x + 2}{x - 1}$ Ⓓ $\dfrac{x + 1}{x + 2}$

● Vocabulary Builder

asymptotes

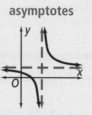

asymptote (noun) As im toht

Definition: A line is an **asymptote** of a graph if the graph gets closer to the line as x or y increases in absolute value.

Example: The graph shown at the right has a vertical **asymptote** and a horizontal **asymptote.**

● Use Your Vocabulary

Identify each dashed line as a *horizontal asymptote* or a *vertical asymptote*. Then write the equation for each *asymptote*.

2.

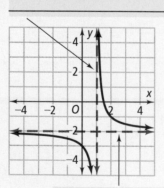

vertical asymptote: $x =$ ☐

horizontal asymptote: $y =$ ☐

3.

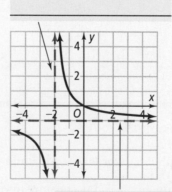

vertical asymptote: $x =$ ☐

horizontal asymptote: $y =$ ☐

Inverse variations are examples of *rational functions*. A **rational function** can be written in the form $f(x) = \dfrac{\text{polynomial}}{\text{polynomial}}$, where the denominator cannot be 0. Any value of x that makes the denominator of $f(x)$ equal 0 is an **excluded value.**

 Problem 1 **Identifying Excluded Values**

Got It? What is the excluded value for $y = \dfrac{3}{x + 7}$?

4. Determine where the function is undefined by setting the denominator equal to 0.

$$x + \boxed{} = 0$$
$$x = \boxed{}$$

5. The excluded value is $x = \boxed{}$.

 Problem 2 **Using a Vertical Asymptote**

Got It? What is the vertical asymptote of the graph of $h(x) = \dfrac{-3}{x - 6}$? Graph the function.

6. Circle the graph that shows the function $h(x) = \dfrac{-3}{x - 6}$.

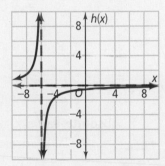 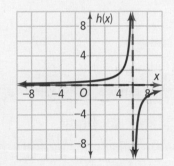 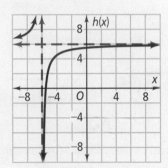

7. The vertical asymptote for the graph of $h(x)$ is $\boxed{}$.

take note

Concept Summary **Identifying Asymptotes**

Rational Function	Example
$y = \dfrac{a}{x - b} + c$	$y = \dfrac{2}{x - 1} + 3$
vertical asymptote: $x = b$	vertical asymptote: $x = 1$
horizontal asymptote: $y = c$	horizontal asymptote: $y = 3$

Write T for *true* or F for *false*.

_____ 8. The vertical asymptote of the graph of $y = \dfrac{1}{x - 5} + 2$ is $x = 2$.

_____ 9. The horizontal asymptote of the graph of $y = \dfrac{1}{x - 3} + 4$ is $y = 4$.

Lesson 11-7

Problem 3 Using Vertical and Horizontal Asymptotes

Got It? What are the asymptotes of the graph of $y = \dfrac{-1}{x+3} - 4$? Graph the function.

10. Circle the vertical asymptote and underline the horizontal asymptote.

$x = 3$ $\qquad\qquad$ $x = -3$ $\qquad\qquad$ $y = 4$ $\qquad\qquad$ $y = -4$

11. Complete the table of values.

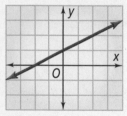

x	y
−8	
−6	
−4	
−2	
−1	
0	

12. Sketch the asymptotes and graph the function.

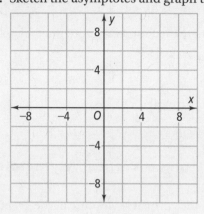

take note

Concept Summary   Families of Functions

Linear	Quadratic	Absolute Value
$y = mx + b$	$y = ax^2 + bx + c$	$y = |x - a| + b$

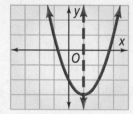

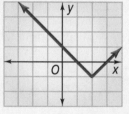

Linear

parent function: $f(x) = x$

slope $= m$

y-intercept $= b$

The greatest exponent is 1.

Quadratic

parent function: $f(x) = x^2$

parabola with axis of symmetry at $x = \dfrac{-b}{2a}$

The greatest exponent is 2.

Absolute Value

parent function: $f(x) = |x|$

Shift $y = |x|$ horizontally a units.

Shift $y = |x|$ vertically b units.

vertex at (a, b)

The greatest exponent is 1.

Identify the type of function as *linear*, *quadratic*, or *absolute value*.

13. $y = 3x^2 - 2x + 4$

14. $y = 6x + 2$

15. $y = |x - 1| - 2$

Chapter 11

336

Copyright © by Pearson Education, Inc. or its affiliates. All Rights Reserved.

Exponential	Square Root	Rational
$y = ab^x$	$y = \sqrt{x - b} + c$	$y = \dfrac{a}{x - b} + c$
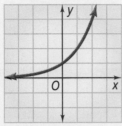	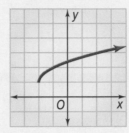	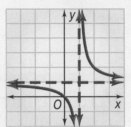
growth for $b > 1$ decay for $0 < b < 1$ The variable is the exponent.	Shift $y = \sqrt{x}$ horizontally b units. Shift $y = \sqrt{x}$ vertically c units. The variable is under the radical.	vertical asymptote at $x = b$ horizontal asymptote at $y = c$ The variable is in the denominator.

Identify the type of function as *exponential*, *square root*, or *rational*.

16. $y = \sqrt{x - 2}$

_____

17. $y = \dfrac{-2}{x - 1} + 3$

_____

18. $y = 0.25^x$

_____

Lesson Check • Do you UNDERSTAND?

Reasoning Write an example of a rational function with a vertical asymptote at $x = -2$ and a horizontal asymptote at $y = 4$.

19. Use the rational function at the right. Circle the variable that determines the vertical asymptote. Underline the variable that determines the horizontal asymptote.

$$y = \frac{a}{x - b} + c$$

20. If there is a vertical asymptote at $x = -2$, then $b = \boxed{}$.

If there is a horizontal asymptote at $y = 4$, then $c = \boxed{}$.

21. The rational function is $\boxed{}$.

Math Success

Check off the vocabulary words that you understand.

☐ rational function   ☐ excluded value   ☐ asymptote

Rate how well you can *graph rational functions*.

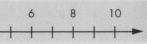

Need to review   0   2   4   6   8   10   Now I get it!

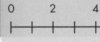

12-1 Organizing Data Using Matrices

Vocabulary

● Review

Use the multiplication *table* at the right for Exercises 1–3.

1. Write the number in the third row, second column.

2. Write the number in the fifth row, first column.

3. Name the row and column for the number 9.

_____

×	1	2	3	4	5
1	1	2	3	4	5
2	2	4	6	8	10
3	3	6	9	12	15
4	4	8	12	16	20
5	5	10	15	20	25
6	6	12	18	24	30

5 columns

6 rows

● Vocabulary Builder

> The plural of **matrix** is **matrices**, pronounced MAY-truh-seez.

matrix (noun) MAY **triks**

Related Words: row, column, element

Main Idea: A **matrix** is a rectangular arrangement of numbers positioned in rows and columns. **Matrices** can contain numbers, words, or variables. Each entry in a **matrix** is called an *element*.

Usage: **Matrices** are used in computer graphics, chemistry, calculus, probability and statistics, and many other fields.

● Use Your Vocabulary

Write the number of rows and columns for each *matrix*. Then write the element in the described location for each *matrix*.

4.
$$\begin{bmatrix} -2 & 1 & 0 & 0 \\ 5 & 1 & 3 & -8 \\ 2 & 1 & 6 & 0 \end{bmatrix}$$

5.
$$\begin{bmatrix} a & x \\ b & u \\ i & y \\ k & t \end{bmatrix}$$

rows: ___   columns: ___

row 2, column 3: ___

rows: ___   columns: ___

row 3, column 2: ___

You can add or subtract matrices that have the same number of rows and columns.
The sum is a matrix with the same number of rows and columns.

6. Write the number of rows and columns in each of the missing matrices.

$$\begin{bmatrix} 1 & 2 \\ 3 & 4 \end{bmatrix} + \blacksquare = \blacksquare \qquad \begin{bmatrix} l \\ m \\ n \end{bmatrix} + \blacksquare = \blacksquare \qquad \begin{bmatrix} 11 & 4 & -8 \\ -5 & 3 & 8 \end{bmatrix} + \blacksquare = \blacksquare$$

rows: ___   rows: ___   rows: ___

columns: ___   columns: ___   columns: ___

Problem 1 Adding and Subtracting Matrices

Got It? What is the sum $\begin{bmatrix} 5 \\ 3.2 \\ -4.9 \end{bmatrix} + \begin{bmatrix} -9 \\ -1.7 \\ -11.1 \end{bmatrix}$?

7. Add the corresponding elements to add the matrices. Fill in the missing numbers.

$$\begin{bmatrix} 5 \\ 3.2 \\ -4.9 \end{bmatrix} + \begin{bmatrix} -9 \\ -1.7 \\ -11.1 \end{bmatrix} = \begin{bmatrix} 5 + (-9) \\ \boxed{} + (-1.7) \\ -4.9 + \boxed{} \end{bmatrix}$$

$$= \begin{bmatrix} \\ \\ \end{bmatrix}$$

You can multiply a matrix by a real-number factor called a **scalar.** Multiplying a matrix by a scalar is called **scalar multiplication.** To use scalar multiplication, multiply each element in the matrix by the scalar.

Problem 2 Multiplying a Matrix by a Scalar

Got It? What is the product $-2\begin{bmatrix} -3 & 7.1 & 5 \end{bmatrix}$?

8. The number ___ is the scalar in the multiplication problem.

9. How is scalar multiplication similar to the Distributive Property?

_____

_____

_____

10. Complete the multiplication.

$$-2\begin{bmatrix} -3 & 7.1 & 5 \end{bmatrix} = \begin{bmatrix} ()(-3) & ()(7.1) & ()(5) \end{bmatrix}$$

$$= \begin{bmatrix} & & \end{bmatrix}$$

Lesson 12-1

Got It? Use the weather chart below. Which city has the greatest average number of cloudy days in a full year?

Average Number of Clear and Cloudy Days

September – February
Phoenix: 102 clear, 41 cloudy
Miami: 43 clear, 58 cloudy
Portland: 55 clear, 82 cloudy

March – August
Phoenix : 110 clear, 27 cloudy
Miami: 31 clear, 59 cloudy
Portland: 45 clear, 83 cloudy

Portland, ME

Phoenix, AZ

Miami, FL

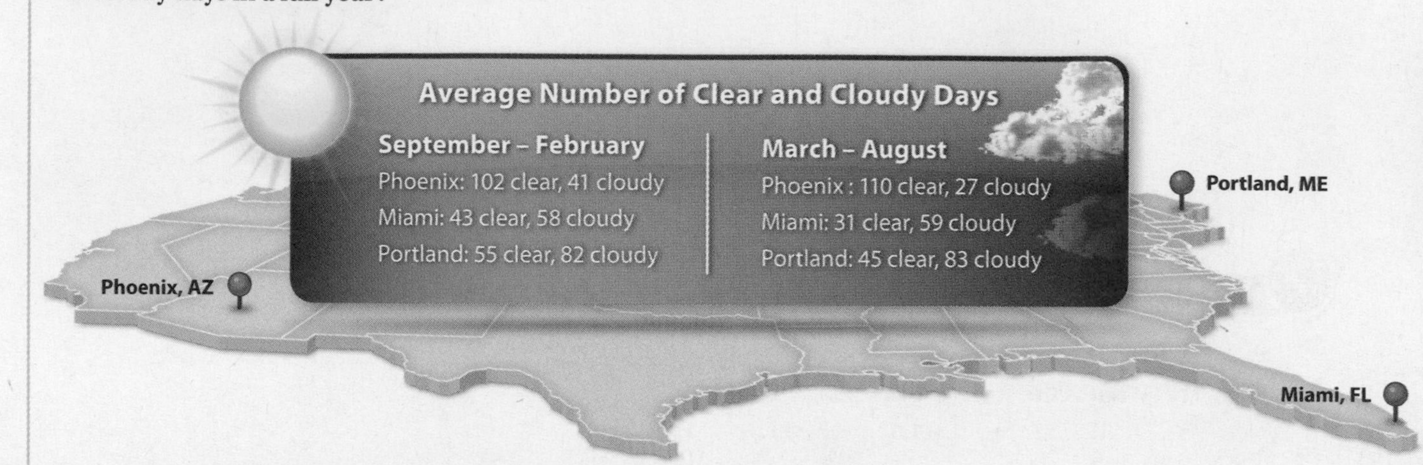

11. Write matrices to organize the information.

September–February

Clear   Cloudy

Phoenix [☐ ☐]
Miami   [☐ ☐]
Portland [☐ ☐]

March–August

Clear   Cloudy

Phoenix [☐ ☐]
Miami   [☐ ☐]
Portland [☐ ☐]

12. Underline the correct word to complete the sentence.

To find the average number of clear and cloudy days for a full year you must
add / subtract the matrices.

13. Use the matrices to write and simplify an expression to find the average number of clear and cloudy days in a full year.

14. Underline the correct word to complete each sentence.

The sum of the matrices represents the number of clear and cloudy days for a
month / year for each city.

The first / second column of the matrix represents the average number of cloudy days in a full year for each city.

Phoenix / Miami / Portland is the city with the greatest average number of cloudy days in a full year.

Error Analysis A student added two matrices as shown at the right. Describe and correct the mistake.

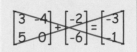

Complete the number sentences for Exercises 15 and 16.

15. $3 + (-4) + (-2) = $

16. $5 + 0 + (-6) = $

17. How do the number sentences in Exercises 15 and 16 relate to the numbers in the matrices added by the student?

_____

_____

_____

18. Circle the sentence(s) below that describe the student's error(s).

| The student added across all of the rows. | The student made an error when adding positive and negative integers. | The student added matrices of different dimensions. |

19. Circle the way(s) the student can correct the mistakes.

| Do not add matrices of different dimensions. | Add only corresponding elements of each matrix. | Add all elements in each column together. |

Math Success

Check off the vocabulary words that you understand.

☐ matrix   ☐ element   ☐ scalar   ☐ scalar multiplication

Rate how well you can *organize data in a matrix.*

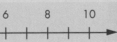

Need to review 0 2 4 6 8 10 Now I get it!

Vocabulary

Review

A researcher conducted a survey to determine the favorite colors of 130 people. Tally marks are used at the right to show the *data*.

Color	Number of Votes
Blue	|||| |||| |||| ||||
Pink	|||| |||| |||| |||| |||| |||| ||||
Yellow	|||| |||| ||||	
Green	|||| |||| |||| |||| |||| |||| |||| |||| ||
Purple	|||| |||
Red	|||| |||| |||| ||||	

1. The color ? received the most votes. _____

2. The color pink received [ ] votes.

3. [ ] more people voted for green than for pink.

4. Which two colors are closest in the number of votes they received?

   _____ and _____

Vocabulary Builder

frequency (noun) FREE **kwun see**

Related Words: frequent (adjective), frequents (verb), frequently (adverb)

Definition: The **frequency** of an event is the number of times the event occurs.

Example: If 39 people vote for pizza and 28 people vote for hamburgers, the **frequency** of pizza is 39. The **frequency** of hamburgers is 28.

Use Your Vocabulary

Complete each statement with the appropriate word from the list.

frequently   frequents   frequency

5. The tally chart shows how ? each color occurs. _____

6. During cold and flu season, the ? of student absences rises. _____

7. Use the data set below to complete each sentence.

   A   A   A   A   B   B   B   C   C   C   D   D

   The letter [ ] occurs with the greatest frequency. Its frequency is [ ].

A **frequency table** groups a set of data values into intervals and shows the frequency for each interval. Intervals in frequency tables do not overlap, do not have any gaps, and are usually of equal size.

 Problem 1 Making a Frequency Table

Got It? The numbers of home runs by the batters in a local home run derby are listed below. What is a frequency table that represents the data? Use intervals of 5.

7   17   14   2   7   9   5   12   3   10   4   12   7   15

8. Complete the boxes to show the end of each interval of 5. Then count the number of home-run data values in the interval and complete the blanks on the right.

1–5   There is/are [ ] data value(s) in this interval.

6–[ ]   There is/are [ ] data value(s) in this interval.

11–[ ]   There is/are [ ] data value(s) in this interval.

16–[ ]   There is/are [ ] data value(s) in this interval.

9. Use your findings to make a frequency table.

Interval	Frequency
1–5	[ ]
6–[ ]	[ ]
11–[ ]	[ ]
16–[ ]	[ ]

A **histogram** is a graph that can display data from a frequency table. A histogram has one bar for each interval. The height of each bar shows the frequency of the interval it represents. There are no gaps between bars. The bars are often of equal width.

 Problem 2 Making a Histogram

Got It? The finishing times, in seconds, for a race are shown below. What is a histogram that represents the data?

95   105   83   80   93   98   102   99   82   89   90   82   89

10. **Multiple Choice** Which of the following sets of intervals could be used for a frequency table to represent the data?

(A) 85–90
     91–96
     97–102
     103–108

(B) 80–85
     86–91
     92–97
     98–103
     104–109

(C) 80–85
     90–95
     96–101
     102–107

(D) 80–85
     85–90
     90–95
     95–100
     100–105

Lesson 12-2

11. Use your answer from Exercise 10 to make a frequency table.

Time (s)	Frequency
☐ – ☐	☐
☐ – ☐	☐
☐ – ☐	☐
☐ – ☐	☐
☐ – ☐	☐

12. Draw a histogram on the axes provided.

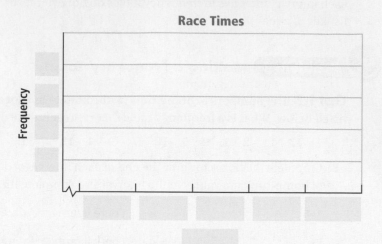

You can describe a histogram by its shape.

• If the bars are roughly the same height, the histogram has a *uniform* shape.

• If you can draw a vertical line that divides a histogram into two parts that are close to mirror images, then the histogram has a *symmetric* shape.

• If the histogram has one peak that is not in the center, the histogram has a *skewed* shape.

Problem 3 Interpreting Histograms

Got It? The following set of data shows the numbers of dollars Jay spent on lunch over the last two weeks. Make a histogram of the data. Is the histogram *uniform, symmetric,* or *skewed*?

17   1   4   11   14   14   5   16   6   5   9   10   13   9

13. Cross out the histograms that do NOT represent the data.

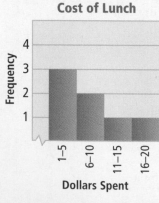

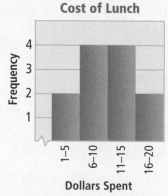

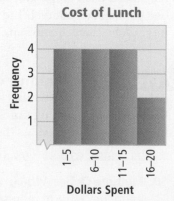

14. Circle the word that best describes the histogram you did not cross out in Exercise 13.

uniform   symmetric   skewed

Problem 4 **Making a Cumulative Frequency Table**

Got It? What is a cumulative frequency table that represents the data below?

12 13 15 1 5 7 10 9 2 2 7 11 2 1 0 15

15. Complete the cumulative frequency table.

Interval	Frequency	Cumulative Frequency
0–5		7
6–11	5	7 + 5, or
12–17		

✓ **Lesson Check** • **Do you UNDERSTAND?**

Compare and Contrast What is the difference between a symmetric histogram and a skewed histogram?

16. Underline the correct word to complete each sentence.

If you can draw a vertical line to make two parts of the histogram that

are mirror images, then the histogram is symmetric / skewed .

If the bars of the histogram are *not* roughly the same height AND they are not

symmetric, then the histogram is uniform / skewed .

17. How are skewed histograms and symmetric histograms different?

_____

_____

_____

✓ **Math Success**

Check off the vocabulary words that you understand.

☐ frequency   ☐ frequency table   ☐ histogram   ☐ cumulative frequency table

Rate how well you can *make and interpret frequency tables and histograms.*

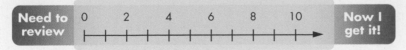

Lesson 12-2

Vocabulary

● Review

Use the set of test scores below for Exercises 1–2.

89   92   100   58   95   68

1. The *range* of a data set is the difference between the greatest and least data values.

greatest data value − least data value = range

[ ] − [ ] = [ ]

2. Suppose the score of 58 changes to 71. Write the new data set in order from the least data value to the greatest data value. Then describe how the *range* changes.

_____

_____

● Vocabulary Builder

outlier (noun) OWT **ly ur**

Related Word: outlying (adjective)

Definition: An **outlier** is a data value in a set that is much greater or less than the other values in the set.

Main Idea: An **outlier** disproportionately raises or lowers the mean.

Example: In the data set 5, 7, 8, 5, 109, 2, and 1, the data value 109 is an **outlier**.

● Use Your Vocabulary

3. Some people live in the city. Others live in the *outlying* suburbs. Circle all the words and phrases below that have the same meaning as *outlying*.

distant   centrally located   outside the boundary   remote

Circle the *outlier* in each data set.

4. 28   26   3   20   19   **5.** 599   702   586   1102   601

Key Concept   Mean, Median, and Mode

Measure	When to Use
The **mean** equals $\dfrac{\text{sum of the data values}}{\text{total number of data values}}$. The mean is often referred to as the *average*.	Use **mean** to describe the middle of a set of data that *does not* have an outlier.
The **median** is the middle value in a data set when the values are arranged in order. For a set containing an even number of data values, the median is the mean of the two middle data values.	Use **median** to describe the middle of a set of data that *does* have an outlier.
The **mode** is the data item that occurs the most times. A data set can have no mode, one mode, or more than one mode.	Use **mode** when the data are nonnumeric or when choosing the most popular item.

6. Draw a line from each term in Column A to its description in Column B.

Column A

median

mode

mean

Column B

often called the *average*

middle value when the data are ordered

item that occurs most frequently in a data set

One way to summarize a set of data is to use a *measure of central tendency*. Mean, median, and mode are all **measures of central tendency.**

 Problem 1 Finding Measures of Central Tendency

Got It? Consider the bowling scores 104, 117, 104, 136, 109, 113, and 104. What are the mean, median, and mode of the scores? Which measure of central tendency best describes the data?

7. List the data in order from least to greatest.

8. Find each measure of central tendency. Round the mean to the nearest tenth.

Mean

Median

Mode

9. Circle the measure of central tendency that best describes the data set.

mean   median   mode

Lesson 12-3

Problem 2 Finding a Data Value

Got It? Your grades on three exams are 80, 93, and 91. What grade do you need on the next exam to have an average of 88 on the four exams?

10. Let $x =$ the grade on the fourth exam. Solve the equation and complete the justifications below to find the value of x.

$$\frac{80 + 93 + 91 + \boxed{}}{\boxed{}} = 88 \qquad \text{Use the formula for the mean.}$$

$$\frac{\boxed{} + x}{\boxed{}} = 88 \qquad \text{Simplify the numerator.}$$

$$\boxed{} + x = 352 \qquad \text{Multiply each side by } \boxed{}.$$

$$x = \boxed{} \qquad \text{Subtract } \boxed{} \text{ from each side.}$$

11. You need a grade of $\boxed{}$ on the next exam to have an average of 88.

When you add the same amount to each item, the mean, median, and mode of the new data set increase by that number. The range stays the same.

Problem 4 Adding a Constant to Data Values

Got It? Several athletes spend the following times, in minutes, on a treadmill each day during the second week of training: 55, 25, 46, 25, 35, 25, and 55. In the third week of training, the athletes add 10 minutes to their training times from the second week. What are the mean, median, mode, and range of the athletes' training times for the third week?

12. Find the mean, median, mode, and range for the training times for the second week.

13. Add 10 to each measure of central tendency from the second week to find the mean, median, and mode for the third week.

mean for third week: median for third week: mode for third week:

$\boxed{} + 10 = \boxed{}$ $\boxed{} + 10 = \boxed{}$ $\boxed{} + 10 = \boxed{}$

14. The range does not change from the second to third week.

So, the range of the data for the third week is $\boxed{}$.

If you multiply each data value by the same amount, you can multiply the mean, median, mode, and range of the original data set by the same number to find the new mean, median, mode, and range.

Got It? A store sells seven models of televisions. The regular prices are $144, $479, $379, $1299, $171, $479, and $269. This week the store offers a 25% discount off the regular prices. What are the mean, median, mode, and range of the discounted prices?

15. Find the mean, median, mode, and range of the original prices.

16. A 25% discount means that you will pay 75% of the original amount. So, to find the discounted prices, you can multiply each original amount by 0.25 / 0.75 .

17. Multiply each measure of central tendency and the range by your answer to Exercise 16 to find the mean, median, mode, and range of the discounted prices.

 Lesson Check • **Do you UNDERSTAND?**

Reasoning How is the range of a data set affected by an outlier?

18. The range of the data set 7, 8, 12, 3, 6, and 9 is ___ .

19. Circle the value that would be an outlier if it were included in the data set in Exercise 18.

| 8 | 40 | 7 | 4 |

20. Suppose you include the outlier you circled in Exercise 19 in the data set. The range of the data set including the outlier is ___ .

21. How is the range of a data set affected by an outlier?

_____

 Math Success

Check off the vocabulary words that you understand.

☐ measure of central tendency ☐ outlier ☐ range

☐ mean ☐ median ☐ mode

Rate how well you can *find mean, median, mode, and range*.

| Need to review | 0   2   4   6   8   10 | Now I get it! |

Lesson 12-3

Vocabulary

● **Review**

Percent means parts per 100. *Percentiles* separate a data set into 100 equal parts.
Write *percent* or *percentile* to complete each sentence.

1. In a bag of coins, 20 of the 80 coins are pennies. So, 25 __?__ of the coins are pennies.

_____

2. A score at the 70th __?__ of a data set is greater than or equal to 70 __?__ of the scores.

_____   _____

● **Vocabulary Builder**

quartile (noun) KWAR tyl

Definition: A **quartile** is one of three values that divide a data set into four parts such that each part contains the same number of data values.

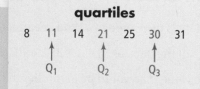

quartiles

8   11   14   21   25   30   31

Q_1 Q_2 Q_3

Math Usage: The median, or second **quartile**, separates the data into upper and lower halves. The first **quartile** is the median of the lower half of the data. The third **quartile** is the median of the upper half of the data.

Related Term: The **interquartile range** is the difference between the third and first quartiles. In the example above, the *interquartile range* is $30 - 11 = 19$.

● **Use Your Vocabulary**

Write T for *true* or F for *false*.

_____ **3.** The *quartiles* of a data set divide the data so that each part has the same range.

_____ **4.** The *quartiles* of a data set divide the data so that there is an equal number of scores in each part.

_____ **5.** The second *quartile* of a data set is greater than about 50% of the scores.

Find the second *quartile* for each set of data.

6. 8   15   19   21   25   25   29

second quartile = _____

7. 17   28   30   30   32   33   35   39

second quartile = _____

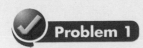 **Problem 1** Summarizing a Data Set

Got It? What are the minimum (least value), first quartile, median, third quartile, and maximum (greatest value) of the data set?

| 95 | 85 | 75 | 85 | 65 | 60 | 100 | 105 | 75 | 85 | 75 |

8. Arrange the data in order from least to greatest. Then circle the median.

60　　65　　75　　　　　　　　85　　85　　85　　95　　100

9. The minimum data value is ☐ .

The maximum data value is ☐ .

10. Write each data value from Exercise 8 in the correct box.

Values to the left of the median:

Values to the right of the median:

Complete the first sentence. Then underline the correct word to complete the second sentence.

11. The median of the numbers in the blue box is ☐ .

This is the first / third quartile.

12. The median of the numbers in the red box is ☐ .

This is the first / third quartile.

A **box-and-whisker plot** is a graph that summarizes a set of data by displaying it along a number line. It consists of three parts: a box and two whiskers.

Box-and-Whisker Plot

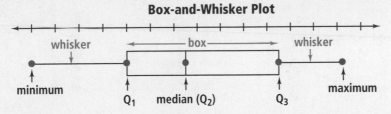

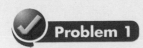 **Problem 2** Making a Box-and-Whisker Plot

Got It? What box-and-whisker plot represents the following monthly sales, in millions of dollars, of audio devices?

| 15 | 4 | 9 | 16 | 10 | 16 | 8 | 14 | 25 | 34 |

13. Order the data from least to greatest.

Lesson 12-4

14. Draw a line from the description in Column A to the value in Column B.

Column A	Column B
minimum value	9
maximum value	34
median	14.5
first quartile	16
third quartile	4

15. Use the number line and the box-and-whisker plot below. Label the minimum, maximum, and quartiles on the plot with the values from Exercise 14.

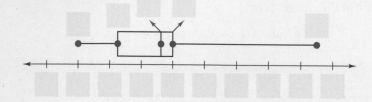

✓ **Problem 3** **Interpreting Box-and-Whisker Plots**

Got It? Use the box-and-whisker plots below. What do the medians tell you about the average monthly rainfalls for Miami and New Orleans?

Average Monthly Rainfall (in.)

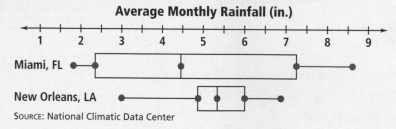

SOURCE: National Climatic Data Center

16. Circle the median of each box-and-whisker plot.

Miami					New Orleans				
7.1	4.5	1.75	8.6	2.25	3	6.9	6	5.3	4.8

17. What do the medians tell you about the average monthly rainfall for the two cities?

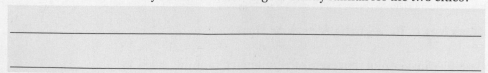

The **percentile rank** of a data value is the percentage of data values that are less than or equal to that value.

✓ **Problem 4** **Finding a Percentile Rank**

Got It? Of 25 test scores, there are 15 scores less than or equal to 85. What is the percentile rank of a test score of 85?

18. Complete the reasoning model below.

Think	Write
I should write a ratio to compare the number of scores less than or equal to 85 to the total number of test scores.	▢ ― ▢
Then I rewrite the fraction as a percent.	▢ ――― = ▢ % ▢

19. A test score of 85 in this group of test scores ranks at the ▢ percentile.

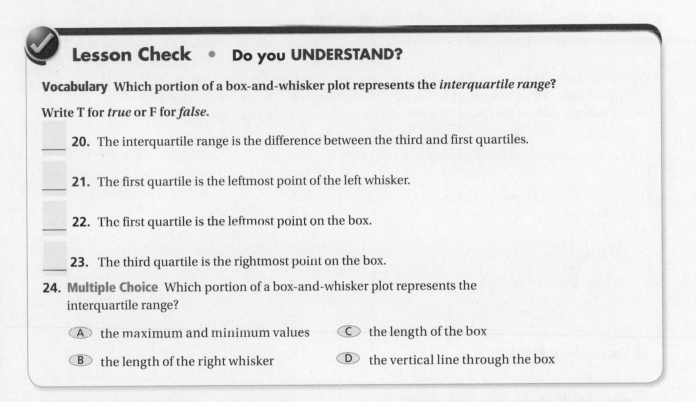

Lesson Check • Do you UNDERSTAND?

Vocabulary Which portion of a box-and-whisker plot represents the *interquartile range*?

Write T for *true* or F for *false*.

____ **20.** The interquartile range is the difference between the third and first quartiles.

____ **21.** The first quartile is the leftmost point of the left whisker.

____ **22.** The first quartile is the leftmost point on the box.

____ **23.** The third quartile is the rightmost point on the box.

24. Multiple Choice Which portion of a box-and-whisker plot represents the interquartile range?

(A) the maximum and minimum values   (C) the length of the box

(B) the length of the right whisker   (D) the vertical line through the box

Math Success

Check off the vocabulary words that you understand.

☐ quartile   ☐ interquartile range   ☐ box-and-whisker plot   ☐ percentile rank

Rate how well you can *make and interpret box-and-whisker plots.*

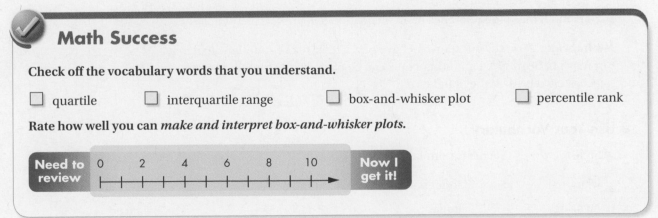

Lesson 12-4

12-5 Samples and Surveys

Vocabulary

● Review

1. Circle the statements that describe the *population* of students in your class.

more than 25 students	less than 25 students	more boys than girls
fewer boys than girls	ages range from 14 to 16	no students with red hair

When you conduct a survey, the entire group that you want information about is called the *population*. When a *population* is too large to survey, you may survey a part of it to find characteristics of the whole. The part that is surveyed is called a *sample*.

2. Cross out the model below that does NOT show the correct relationship between a *sample* and its *population*.

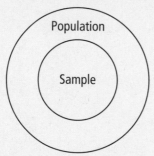

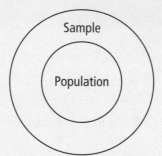

● Vocabulary Builder

bias (noun) **BY us**

Definition: A **bias** is a preference or an inclination that inhibits fair judgment.

Math Usage: A survey question can have **bias** if it makes assumptions that may or may not be true. A sample of people can be **biased** if the sample does not accurately represent the population.

● Use Your Vocabulary

3. Circle the words that have a similar meaning to *bias*.

impartial	influence	unfair	not representative
favoring	equal	favoritism	balanced

Quantitative data measure quantities and can be described numerically, such as test scores and ages. Quantitative data also have units. **Qualitative** data name qualities and can be words or numbers, such as hair color or ZIP codes.

 **Problem 1** Classifying Data

Got It? Is each data set *qualitative* or *quantitative*? Explain.

costs of CDs   eye colors

4. Complete each sentence with the words *qualitative* or *quantitative*.

Data that are words or numbers that do not have a value are __?__ data.

Data that can be described using numbers that have value are __?__ data.

5. Underline the correct word to complete each sentence.

The costs of CDs are data that can / cannot be described numerically.

So, data about the costs of CDs is qualitative / quantitative .

A person's eye color can be described using measurements / categories .

So, eye color is qualitative / quantitative.

A set of data that uses only one variable is **univariate.** A set of data that uses two variables is **bivariate.**

 Problem 2 Identifying Types of Data

Got It? Is a data set that gives the heights and weights of mammals *univariate* or *bivariate*? Explain.

6. Underline the correct words to complete the sentence.

You need one / two variable(s) to represent heights and weights,

so the data set is univariate / bivariate .

The table below shows three methods for choosing a sample to survey from a population.

Name	Sampling Method	Example
Random	Survey a population at random.	Survey people whose names are drawn out of a hat.
Systematic	Select a number *n* at random. Then survey every *n*th person.	Select the number 5 at random. Survey every fifth person.
Stratified	Separate a population into smaller groups, each with a certain characteristic. Then survey at random within each group.	Separate a high school into four groups by grade level. Survey a random sample of students from each grade.

Lesson 12-5

Problem 3 Choosing a Sample

Got It? You want to find out how many DVDs students at your school rent in a month. You interview all students leaving a school assembly who are wearing the school colors. Will this plan give a good sample? Explain.

7. Complete each sentence with the appropriate word from the list.

appropriately   goals   population

A sample is a portion of the __?__ surveyed to determine characteristics of the whole.

A good sample is one that __?__ represents the population.

If a sample is not good, the survey will not meet its __?__ .

8. Circle the population you are trying to collect information about.

| teenagers in your town | students in your school | staff at your school |

9. Will the plan give a good sample? Explain.

Problem 4 Determining Bias in a Survey Question

Got It? *Reasoning* A reporter wants to find out what kinds of movies are most popular with local residents. He asks the biased question, "Do you prefer exciting action movies or boring documentaries?" What unbiased question could the reporter ask instead?

10. Circle the words of the reporter's question that make the question biased.

Do you prefer exciting action movies or boring documentaries?

11. Underline the correct words to complete the sentence.

The words circled in Exercise 10 make certain types of movies

seem more appealing / the same.

12. Cross out the biased questions.

| Do you prefer exciting action movies or documentaries? | Do you prefer action movies or boring documentaries? | Do you prefer action movies or documentaries? |

Got It? You want to know how many of your classmates have cell phones. To determine this, you send every classmate an e-mail asking, "Do you own a cell phone?" How might this method of gathering data affect the results of your survey?

13. Suppose the samples described in Column A were surveyed. Draw a line from each sample in Column A to the reason the sample may be biased in Column B.

Column A	Column B
people using pay phones	These people may be more likely to own a cell phone since that may be their method of communication.
people who do not have a land line phone at home	These people may be more likely to not own a cell phone because they are using a type of phone that is less convenient.
people at a cell phone store	These people may be more likely to own a cell phone since they are in the store to purchase or replace a phone.

14. Look back at the original method of gathering data. How might this method affect the results of the survey?

_____

_____

_____

 Lesson Check • **Do you know HOW?**

15. State whether each sampling method is *random, systematic,* or *stratified.*

You survey every tenth student who enters the cafeteria.	You draw student ID numbers out of a hat and survey those students.	You survey two students at random from each classroom.
_____	_____	_____

 Math Success

Check off the vocabulary words that you understand.

☐ quantitative   ☐ qualitative   ☐ univariate   ☐ bivariate

☐ population   ☐ sample   ☐ bias

Rate how well you can *classify data and determine bias.*

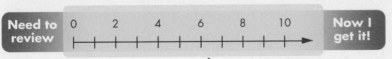

Lesson 12-5

12-6 Permutations and Combinations

Vocabulary

● Review

1. *Combine* the two sentences below to form one sentence.

I will order a hamburger.   I will pay for it with a $1 bill.

_____

2. *Combine* the bowling scores below to find the total for the three games.

103   149   97   Total: _____

Combine like terms in each expression.

3. $3x + 5x =$ _____

4. $4a^2 + 3a - 5 - 6a^2 - 2a =$ _____

5. $8x + 2y - x =$ _____

6. $2c^2 + 5cd - d^2 + 3d =$ _____

● Vocabulary Builder

permute (verb) **pur MYOOT**

Related Words: order (verb, noun), permutation (noun)

Definition: To **permute** a list of numbers means to rearrange the order or sequence of the numbers.

Math Usage: Sometimes you want to know how many ways you can **permute** a set of objects. Each ordered arrangement of the objects is called a *permutation*.

● Use Your Vocabulary

7. Underline the correct word to complete each sentence.

You can permute / permutation the digits in the number 394 to create different numbers.

The number 934 is a permute / permutation of the digits 3, 9, and 4.

8. *Permute* these race results to show another possible ordered arrangement.

first place: Rita   second place: David   third place: Beth

first place: _____   second place: _____   third place: _____

Key Concept Multiplication Counting Principle

If there are *m* ways to make a first selection and *n* ways to make a second selection, then there are *m* · *n* ways to make the two selections.

9. There are 4 types of bread and 5 types of sandwich meat. You choose one type of bread and one type of sandwich meat for your sandwich. How many different sandwiches are possible?

4 · ☐ = ☐ , so ☐ different sandwiches are possible.

10. You have 9 shirts and 4 pairs of pants. How many different outfits can you make?

☐ · ☐ = ☐ , so you can make ☐ different outfits.

A **permutation** is an arrangement of objects in a specific order. Here are the possible permutations of the letters A, B, and C without repeating any letters.

ABC   ACB   BAC   BCA   CAB   CBA

Problem 2 Finding Permutations

Got It? A swimming pool has 8 lanes. In how many ways can 8 swimmers be assigned lanes for a race?

11. Working from left to right, write how many choices there are for a swimmer to be assigned to each lane. (*Hint:* When you determine the number of choices for a lane, assume that a swimmer has been chosen for each lane to the left.)

Lane 1   Lane 2   Lane 3   Lane 4   Lane 5   Lane 6   Lane 7   Lane 8

☐   ☐   ☐   ☐   ☐   ☐   ☐   ☐

12. Write the missing factors below to show how many ways 8 swimmers can be assigned lanes for a race.

8 · ☐ · ☐ · ☐ · ☐ · ☐ · ☐ · ☐

13. There are ☐ ways 8 swimmers can be assigned lanes.

A shorter way to write the product in Problem 2 is 8!, read "eight factorial." For any positive integer *n*, the expression **n factorial** is written as *n*! and is the product of the integers from *n* down to 1. The value of 0! is defined to be 1.

You can use factorials to write a formula for the number of permutations of *n* objects arranged *r* at a time.

Key Concept Permutation Notation

The expression $_nP_r$ represents the number of permutations of *n* objects arranged *r* at a time.

$$_nP_r = \frac{n!}{(n-r)!}$$

Example $_8P_2 = \frac{8!}{(8-2)!} = \frac{8!}{6!} = \frac{8 \cdot 7 \cdot 6 \cdot 5 \cdot 4 \cdot 3 \cdot 2 \cdot 1}{6 \cdot 5 \cdot 4 \cdot 3 \cdot 2 \cdot 1} = 56$$

Lesson 12-6

14. Find the number of permutations of 5 objects arranged 3 at a time.

$$_5P_3 = \frac{\boxed{}!}{(\boxed{} - \boxed{})!} = \frac{\boxed{}!}{\boxed{}!} = \frac{\boxed{} \cdot \boxed{} \cdot \boxed{} \cdot \boxed{}}{\boxed{}} = \boxed{}$$

 Problem 3 **Using Permutation Notation**

Got It? There are 6 students in a classroom with 8 desks. How many possible seating arrangements are there?

15. Circle the expression that will help you solve the problem.

$$_6P_8 \qquad\qquad _8P_6 \qquad\qquad _8P_2 \qquad\qquad _2P_8$$

16. Circle the graphing calculator screen that shows the problem.

6 nPr 8

8 nPr 6

8 nPr 2

2 nPr 8

17. The number of possible seating arrangements is ⬚.

A **combination** is a selection of objects without regard to order. For example, if you are selecting two side dishes from a list of five, the order in which you choose the side dishes does not matter.

take note

Key Concept Combination Notation

The expression $_nC_r$ represents the number of combinations of n objects chosen r at a time.

$$_nC_r = \frac{n!}{r!(n-r)!}$$

Example $_8C_2 = \frac{8!}{2!(8-2)!} = \frac{8!}{2!6!} = \frac{8 \cdot 7 \cdot 6 \cdot 5 \cdot 4 \cdot 3 \cdot 2 \cdot 1}{(2 \cdot 1)(6 \cdot 5 \cdot 4 \cdot 3 \cdot 2 \cdot 1)} = 28$

18. Find the number of combinations of 4 objects chosen 3 at a time.

$$_4C_3 = \frac{\boxed{}!}{\boxed{}!(\boxed{} - \boxed{})!} = \frac{\boxed{}!}{\boxed{}!\,\boxed{}!} = \frac{\boxed{} \cdot \boxed{} \cdot \boxed{}}{(\boxed{} \cdot \boxed{})(\boxed{})} = \boxed{}$$

Problem 4 **Using Combination Notation**

Got It? In how many different ways can you choose 3 types of flowers for a bouquet from a selection of 15 types of flowers?

19. Does it matter in which order you choose the three types of flowers? Yes / No

20. Circle the expression that will help you solve the problem.

$_{15}P_3$ $_{15}C_3$ $_3C_{15}$ $_3P_{15}$

21. Find the number of possible ways to choose the three types of flowers.

22. There are _____ possible ways to choose the three types of flowers.

 Lesson Check • **Do you UNDERSTAND?**

Vocabulary Would you use *permutations* or *combinations* to find the number of possible arrangements of 10 students in a line? Why?

23. Underline the correct word(s) to complete the sentence.

If the first two students in line switch positions, the order of the 10 students

is / is not changed.

24. Would you use permutations or combinations to find the number of possible arrangements of 10 students in a line? Explain.

_____

_____

_____

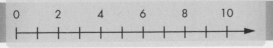 **Math Success**

Check off the vocabulary words that you understand.

☐ Multiplication Counting Principle ☐ permutation ☐ *n* factorial ☐ combination

Rate how well you can *find permutations and combinations.*

Need to review 0   2   4   6   8   10 Now I get it!

Lesson 12-6

Vocabulary

● Review

An *outcome* is the result of a single trial of an experiment. An *event* is a group of possible outcomes. When you roll a number cube once, the possible outcomes are 1, 2, 3, 4, 5, or 6. Write all of the possible *outcomes* for each *event* described below.

1. rolling an odd number

2. rolling a number greater than 4

3. rolling a number less than 6

4. rolling a number that is divisible by 3

● Vocabulary Builder

probability (noun) **prah buh BIL uh tee**

Definition: **Probability** is the likelihood that a certain outcome will occur.

Related Words: chance (noun), likely (adjective), trials (noun)

Main Idea: The **probability** of an event ranges from 0 to 1. You can write a probability as a fraction, a decimal, or a percent.

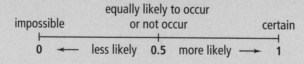

● Use Your Vocabulary

5. Draw a line from each *event* in Column A to the correct description of its *probability* in Column B.

Column A	Column B
randomly choosing a state that begins with the letter A from all 50 states	impossible
randomly choosing a year that is not a leap year from the past 100 years	unlikely
randomly choosing a value for x such that $x \cdot 1 = x$	likely
rolling a 7 on a number cube that is marked 1, 2, 3, 4, 5, 6	certain

When all possible outcomes are equally likely, you can find the **theoretical probability** of an event using the following formula.

$$P(\text{event}) = \frac{\text{number of favorable outcomes}}{\text{number of possible outcomes}}$$

 Problem 1 Finding Theoretical Probability

Got It? Our solar system's 8 planets, in order of least to greatest distance from the sun, are Mercury, Venus, Earth, Mars, Jupiter, Saturn, Uranus, and Neptune. You will randomly draw one of the names of the planets and write a report on that planet. What is the theoretical probability that you will select a planet farther from the sun than Earth?

6. Write the probability for a name from each of the indicated groups to be drawn.

Sun

not to scale

7. So, the theoretical probability that you will select a planet that is farther from the sun than Earth is ☐ .

The **complement of an event** consists of all outcomes in the sample space that are NOT in the event. The sum of the probabilities of an event and its complement is 1.

$$P(\text{event}) + P(\text{not event}) = 1 \qquad \text{or} \qquad P(\text{not event}) = 1 - P(\text{event})$$

 Problem 2 Finding the Probability of the Complement of an Event

Got It? In a taste test, 50 participants are randomly given a beverage to sample. There are 20 samples of Drink A, 10 samples of Drink B, 10 samples of Drink C, and 10 samples of Drink D. Suppose the number of samples of Drinks B, C, and D increases. What happens to $P(\text{not Drink A})$?

Suppose there are 50 drink samples, of which 20 are Drink A.

8. Write the probability of 1 participant sampling Drink A as a decimal.

9. Write the probability of 1 participant *not* sampling Drink A as a decimal.

$$1 - \boxed{} = \boxed{}$$

Suppose there are 1000 drink samples, of which 20 are Drink A.

10. Write the probability of 1 participant sampling Drink A as a decimal.

11. Write the probability of 1 participant *not* sampling Drink A as a decimal.

$$1 - \boxed{} = \boxed{}$$

12. As the number of samples of other drinks increases, $P(\text{not Drink A})$ increases / decreases .

Lesson 12-7

Odds describe the likelihood of an event as a ratio comparing the number of favorable and unfavorable outcomes.

$$\text{odds in } favor \text{ of an event } = \frac{\text{number of favorable outcomes}}{\text{number of unfavorable outcomes}}$$

$$\text{odds } against \text{ an event } = \frac{\text{number of unfavorable outcomes}}{\text{number of favorable outcomes}}$$

 Problem 3 Finding Odds

Got It? What are the odds against the spinner landing on a number less than 3?

In Exercises 13 and 14, circle the correct answer.

13. How many sections of the spinner show numbers less than 3? Circle your answer.

| 2 | 5 | 6 | 8 |

14. How many other sections does that leave? Circle your answer.

| 2 | 3 | 6 | 8 |

15. Write the odds against the spinner landing on a number less than 3.

$\dfrac{6}{}$ or   6 : ▢

16. Write the odds in Exercise 15 in simplest form.

$\dfrac{}{}$ or   ▢ : ▢

Experimental probability is based on data collected from repeated trials.

$$P(\text{event}) = \frac{\text{number of times the event occurs}}{\text{number of times the experiment is done}}$$

 Problem 4 Finding Experimental Probability

Suppose a manufacturer inspects 2500 skateboards and observes that 2450 skateboards have no defects. What is the probability that a skateboard selected at random has no defects? Write the probability as a percent.

17. Complete the steps to find the experimental probability.

$$P(\text{event}) = \frac{\text{number of skateboards with no defect}}{\text{number of skateboards examined}}$$

$P(\text{event}) = \dfrac{}{}$ Substitute.

$= \boxed{}$ Write as a decimal.

$= \boxed{}$ Change to a percent.

18. So, the probability that a skateboard has no defects is ▢ .

19. Does an experimental probability of 100% for an event mean that the event is certain to occur? Explain.

_____

Got It? A manufacturer inspects 700 light bulbs and finds that 692 of the light bulbs work. There are about 35,400 light bulbs in the manufacturer's warehouse. About how many of the light bulbs in the warehouse are likely to work?

20. Circle the experimental probability for a light bulb to work.

$$\frac{692}{700} \qquad \frac{700}{692} \qquad \frac{8}{700} \qquad \frac{692}{35,400}$$

21. Complete to find how many light bulbs are likely to work.

Number of light bulbs expected to work = P(a bulb works) $\cdot$ (number of bulbs in warehouse)

$$= \underline{\hspace{1cm}} \cdot \underline{\hspace{2cm}}$$

22. To the nearest thousand, about $\underline{\hspace{2cm}}$ bulbs are likely to work.

Lesson Check • Do you UNDERSTAND?

Error Analysis Eric calculated the probability of getting a number less than 3 when randomly choosing an integer from 1 to 10. Describe and correct his error.

$$\frac{\text{favorable outcomes}}{\text{total outcomes}} = \frac{3}{10}$$

23. Circle the numbers that are less than 3.

1 2 3 4 5 6 7 8 9 10

24. Describe Eric's error and give the correct probability.

_____

_____

Math Success

Check off the vocabulary words that you understand.

☐ theoretical probability   ☐ event   ☐ odds

☐ experimental probability   ☐ outcome   ☐ complement of an event

Rate how well you can *find theoretical and experimental probability.*

| Need to review | 0 | 2 | 4 | 6 | 8 | 10 | Now I get it! |

Vocabulary

● Review

Write whether the word *compound* is used as a *noun*, a *verb*, or an *adjective*.

1. This bank account pays *compound* interest.

_____

2. If he does not do his homework, he will *compound* his problems.

_____

3. The army *compound* has barracks and a general store.

_____

● Vocabulary Builder

independent (adjective) **in dee PEN dunt**

Related Words: dependent (adjective)

Definition: Events are **independent** if they do not influence each other. Events are *dependent* if one influences the other.

Examples: Rolling a number cube and spinning a spinner are **independent** events because the result of the cube toss does not affect the outcome of the spin. Drawing a second marble from a bag after drawing and keeping one marble is a *dependent* event because the first draw changes the possible outcomes for the second draw.

● Use Your Vocabulary

Write *independent* or *dependent* to describe each pair of events.

4. flipping a coin and rolling a number cube

_____

5. randomly picking a number from 1–100 and then randomly picking another number from the remaining numbers 1–100

_____

6. drawing a marble from a bag without looking, returning it to the bag, and then drawing another marble from the bag without looking

_____

7. drawing a marble from a bag without looking, keeping the marble, and then drawing another marble from the remaining marbles without looking

_____

A **compound event** consists of two or more events linked by the word *and* or the word *or*.

When two events have no outcomes in common, the events are **mutually exclusive events.** If A and B are mutually exclusive events, then $P(A \text{ and } B) = 0$. When events have at least one outcome in common, they are **overlapping events.**

Key Concept   Probability of A or B

Probability of Mutually Exclusive Events

If A and B are mutually exclusive events,
$P(A \text{ or } B) = P(A) + P(B)$.

Probability of Overlapping Events

If A and B are overlapping events,
$P(A \text{ or } B) = P(A) + P(B) - P(A \text{ and } B)$.

Problem 1 Mutually Exclusive and Overlapping Events

Got It? Suppose you roll a standard number cube once. What is the probability that you roll an even number or a number less than 4?

8. Underline the correct word to complete each sentence.

A number can / cannot be both even and less than 4.

So, the events *an even number* and *a number less than 4* are

mutually exclusive / overlapping events.

9. Circle the formula you will use to solve the problem.

$P(A \text{ or } B) - P(A) \mid P(B)$ $P(A \text{ or } B) = P(A) + P(B) - P(A \text{ and } B)$

10. Complete each ratio.

$P(\text{even number})$ $P(\text{number less than 4})$ $P(\text{number is even and less than 4})$

$\dfrac{}{6}$ $\dfrac{}{6}$ $\dfrac{}{}$

11. Find the probability that you roll an even number or a number less than 4.

Key Concept   Probability of Two Independent Events

If A and B are independent events, $P(A \text{ and } B) = P(A) \cdot P(B)$.

Problem 2 Finding the Probability of Independent Events

Got It? You roll a red number cube and a blue number cube. What is the probability that you roll a 5 on the red cube and a 1 or 2 on the blue cube?

Lesson 12-8

12. The probability of rolling a 5 on the red number cube is _____.

13. The probability of rolling a 1 or 2 on the blue number cube is _____.

14. Find the probability of rolling a 5 on the red cube and a 1 or 2 on the blue cube.

 Problem 3 Selecting With Replacement

Got It? You choose a tile at random from the game tiles shown. What is the probability that you choose a bird and then, after replacing the first tile, a flower?

15. Are the events "choosing a bird and then a flower" independent or dependent? Explain.

_____

_____

_____

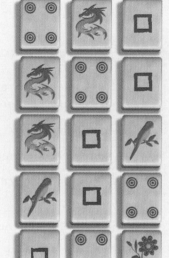

16. The probability of choosing a bird is _____.

17. The probability of then choosing a flower is _____.

18. Find the probability of choosing a bird and a flower with replacement.

take note

Key Concept Probability of Two Dependent Events

If A and B are dependent events, $P(A \text{ then } B) = P(A) \cdot P(B \text{ after } A)$.

19. Consider the tiles in Exercises 15-18. What is the probability that you will randomly choose a bird and then, *without* replacing the first tile, a square?

$$\frac{2}{15} \cdot \frac{5}{} = \frac{}{} = \frac{}{}$$

 Problem 5 Finding the Probability of a Compound Event

Got It? One freshman, 2 sophomores, 4 juniors, and 5 seniors receive top scores in a school essay contest. To choose which 2 students will read their essays at the town fair, 2 names are chosen at random from a hat. What is the probability that a senior and then a junior are chosen?

Chapter 12

368

20. Are the events of choosing a senior and then a junior independent or dependent? Explain your reasoning.

_____

_____

21. The probability that a senior is chosen first is ____.

22. The probability that a junior is chosen after a senior is chosen is ____.

23. What is the probability of choosing a senior and then a junior without replacement?

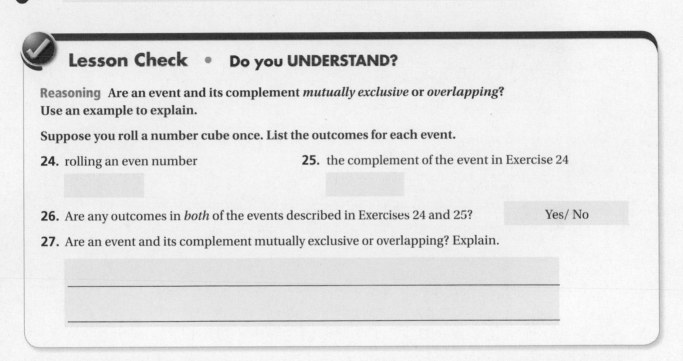

Lesson Check • Do you UNDERSTAND?

Reasoning Are an event and its complement *mutually exclusive* or *overlapping*? Use an example to explain.

Suppose you roll a number cube once. List the outcomes for each event.

24. rolling an even number

25. the complement of the event in Exercise 24

26. Are any outcomes in *both* of the events described in Exercises 24 and 25?   Yes/ No

27. Are an event and its complement mutually exclusive or overlapping? Explain.

_____

_____

Math Success

Check off the vocabulary words that you understand.

☐ compound events   ☐ mutually exclusive events   ☐ overlapping events

☐ independent events   ☐ dependent events

Rate how well you can *find probabilities*.

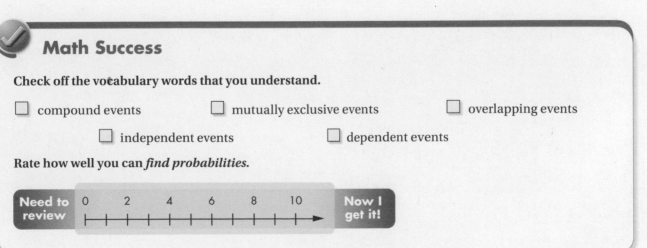

Need to review   0   2   4   6   8   10   Now I get it!

Lesson 12-8